Kabul Carnival

THE ETHNOGRAPHY OF POLITICAL VIOLENCE

Tobias Kelly, Series Editor

A complete list of books in the series
is available from the publisher.

KABUL CARNIVAL

Gender Politics in Postwar Afghanistan

Julie Billaud

PENN

UNIVERSITY OF PENNSYLVANIA PRESS

PHILADELPHIA

Published by
University of Pennsylvania Press
Philadelphia, Pennsylvania 19104-4112
www.upenn.edu/pennpress

Printed in the United States of America
on acid-free paper

1 3 5 7 9 10 8 6 4 2

Library of Congress Cataloging-in-Publication Data
Billaud, Julie, author.
Kabul carnival : gender politics in postwar Afghanistan / Julie Billaud.
pages cm — (The ethnography of political violence)
Includes bibliographical references and index.
ISBN 978-0-8122-4696-4 (alk. paper)
1. Women—Afghanistan—Social conditions—History—21st century.   2. Nationalism and
feminism—Religious aspects—Islam—History—21st century.   3. Postwar reconstruction—
Afghanistan.   4. Public spaces—Afghanistan—History—21st century.   5. Violence against
women—Afghanistan—History—21st century.   I. Title.   II. Series: Ethnography of political
violence.
HQ1735.6.B55 2015
305.409581—dc23

2014040354

Carnival is not a spectacle seen by the people; they live in it, and everyone participates because its very idea embraces all the people. While carnival lasts, there is no other life outside it. During carnival time life is subject only to its laws, that is, the laws of its own freedom. It has a universal spirit; it is a special condition of the entire world, of the world's revival and renewal, in which all take part. Such is the essence of carnival, vividly felt by all its participants.

—Mikhail Bakhtin, *Rabelais and His World*

CONTENTS

====

"If Only You Were Born a Boy"

"As I grew up, my mother constantly repeated to me: 'if only you were born a boy.' So I eventually became one." This is the pragmatic way in which eighteen-year-old Zahra explains how she became Zia. Zahra rents a small room in a family house located next to Kabul Polytechnic University. When, a couple of years ago, her parents divorced and remarried, none of them wanted her around anymore. Mistreated by her stepfather, neglected by her mother, and with no relatives to take care of her, she set out to take her future into her own hands and not to rely on anyone. Because of the fact that as a girl she could not enjoy this level of autonomy, she cut her hair short, purchased boys' clothes, changed her gender identity, and found herself a job in a small cultural organization. With her big hazel eyes, her confident appearance, and her direct way of staring at people, Zahra—who becomes Zia as soon as she steps outside the house—easily passes herself off as a handsome young man.

I met Zahra through my friend Fawzia who boards at the National Women's Dormitory. Fawzia befriended Zahra at the self-defense class they both attend once a week at Bagh-e Zanana, the women's park. The walls of Zahra's bedroom are covered with posters of Jackie Chan and Bollywood movie stars. As she casually lights up a cigarette, tipping her head back to blow away large clouds of blue smoke, she comments: "Now, I can do whatever I want. I can ride a bike, do the shopping, go to work. I can even be *mahram* [an unmarriageable kinsman; a woman must be accompanied by such an escort outside her house] for my girlfriends! I will never go back!"

"You see, Julie, she is a *bacha posh* [girl dressed like a boy]! She even thinks like a boy! Deep inside, she is a boy and a beautiful one!" says Fawzia, and then she leans forward to whisper in my ear: "I love Zahra! Zahra is my boyfriend!" and she bursts into laughter.

Figure 1. Man showing his muscles in a body-building club in Kabul.
Photo by Mélanie De Segundo.

Before I met Zahra, Fawzia had told me about her new friendship with
great excitement, recounting in a highly colorful manner how Zahra sometimes engaged in fights with boys and the respect with which her colleagues
at work treated her. Since they had met, Fawzia and Zahra had started to call
and send text messages to each other several times a day, exchanging sweet
words and pieces of poetry like lovers sometimes do. On that day, Fawzia had
brought Zahra a *nazarband* (lucky charm), a necklace meant to protect her
against *cheshme bad* (the evil eye).

Zahra immediately captured my attention. I wondered if *bacha posh* in
Afghanistan enjoyed some kind of social recognition as do the "third gender" *hijras* of India and Pakistan. It was apparently not the case and Zahra
took great risks masquerading as a boy in the streets of Kabul. If she was discovered she could be beaten up or even arrested by the police. Raised as a
girl, she had had to train herself hard to adopt the manners of a boy. "Now, I
cannot be shy anymore! I have to be tough, tough like a boy!" she said, roll-
ing up her sleeves to show me her muscular but rather thin arm. "I am lucky,
I don't have much here," she said pointing at her flat breasts.

When I asked friends around me if they knew some *bacha posh*, I was surprised to discover that many of them knew families who had turned one of their daughters into a boy. The cross-dressing of little girls is an option sometimes chosen by parents to cope with the social pressure to have a boy and the economic need to have a child able to work outside of the house. Parents who fail to produce a son sometimes decide to make one up, usually by cutting the hair of a daughter and dressing her in typical Afghan men's clothing. There is no law, religious or otherwise, prohibiting the practice even though it remains a taboo and families tend to keep their secret well hidden. In most cases, young women return to womanhood once they reach puberty.

Some prominent Afghan women politicians have once been *bacha posh*. This is, for instance, the case of Azita Rafaat, a member of the Afghan parliament, who returned to her original gender when she reached the age of marriage and was compelled to become the second wife of her cousin. After several failed attempts at producing boys, which provoked constant disputes between her and her in-laws, she decided to turn one of her daughters, Mehran, into a boy too. She considered her own experience as a *bacha posh* a positive one: it had increased her self-confidence and made her able to better understand the situation of women in the country. She is now a fervent advocate for women's rights at the Afghan National Assembly. Another famous case is Bibi Hakmeena, a councillor from Khost Province who dresses only like a man. Unlike other women, she wears a loose *peran tomban* (knee-length shirt and large trousers) and a black turban. Dressed in such a manner she is barely distinguishable from the men with whom she mixes. Bibi Hakmeena became a man at the age of ten when the Red Army invaded Afghanistan. With her one brother sent to study in Kabul and her younger brother too young to take up arms, the family lacked masculine protection. To get around the problem her father dressed her up as a boy and made her responsible for protecting her mother and younger siblings. He also took her to political meetings and made her participate in the armed struggle against the Russians. Now in her forties, she never returned to womanhood when she reached puberty. Bibi Hakmeena, who never goes out without a Kalashnikov, explains that she never "felt like a woman." A highly respected figure within her constituency, she is nicknamed "king of the women" because of her sensitivity to women's conditions (Hasrat-Nazimi 2011).

In contrast to these stories, Zahra had not been made a boy by her parents but had decided by herself to become one. When most *bacha posh* of her age would switch to womanhood and would consequently struggle to relearn the attitudes, manners, skills, and duties of a girl, disciplining their bodies to close down and express shyness, Zahra was tutoring hers in the opposite direction. From the confined feminine space of the home, Zahra's horizons had opened in unexpected new ways, allowing her to be drawn to the allures of the outside world, reserved for males. In a corner of her room, a battery of weights was on display. These were the instruments she used to develop a more muscular and therefore more masculine body. I asked her if she was not scared of getting caught like Osama, the little girl dressed as a boy to get around the interdictions imposed on women by the Taliban, in the movie *Osama*, written and directed by Siddiq Barmak. I wondered how she envisaged the future and if she sometimes hoped she could be accepted as a woman with the type of life she led. But Zahra had no intention to return to her previous life as a woman and seemed rather happy with her newly gained freedom. If she continuously feared being discovered, she insisted: "There is nothing that compares with a man's life!"

Zahra's story is of course revealing of the powerful gender ideology around which Afghan society is organized. But it also illustrates the formidable coping strategies Afghans in general, and Afghan women in particular, have developed in order to deal with norms that decades of war, destitution, and displacement have made more rigid with every passing year. Zahra bears witness to the double-edged dynamics of gender ideologies, reinforcing norms while simultaneously pushing the creativity of individuals to devise ways to get around them. This book pays homage to the extreme resourcefulness of Afghan women whose lives have been marked by unmet promises of "liberation" and continuous war. It is my humble attempt to share what I have learned from them, what I have understood and what I have not. This book does not intend to draw a complete picture or to produce a metanarrative about the condition of women in Afghanistan. Plenty of such books have been published in recent years with more or less convincing results. The "true" picture that I hope will come out of it will flit by "as an image that flashes up at the instant when it can be recognized and is never seen again" (Benjamin 1969, 255).

Carnival of (Post)War

In September 2001, a few weeks before the first bombs were dropped on Kabul, I was sitting in a small nongovernmental organization (NGO) office in Paris, watching on my computer screen news releases announcing the formation of a coalition of Western nations preparing to launch a war against a country that few people had paid much attention to before. For many Westerners, Afghanistan kindled fantasies of deserted landscapes, bearded tribal warriors, and burkas. The NGO for which I worked was born with the Soviet-Afghan conflict and had remained in Afghanistan since 1979 when the first French doctors were sent to the Panjshir Valley to care for war-wounded "freedom fighters." It was with a mixture of anxiety and sadness boosted by the adrenaline so characteristic of humanitarian work that the NGO's emergency unit was now organizing the repatriation of the expatriate volunteers who worked in Afghanistan. But to my astonishment the Afghan staff would have to stay in the country and "endure freedom," as the name of the U.S. military operations ironically phrased it. A page of history was being turned before my eyes, and I struggled to make sense of the flow of images and information I received. How to reconcile bombardments of already impoverished people and the war against terrorism? What was the rationale in the discourses that defended the war in the name of women and human rights? How could women be liberated through bombs and mass killings?

When the United States began bombing Afghanistan on October 7, 2001, the oppression of Afghan women was the moral grammar mobilized to rally popular support for the military invasion of the country. This rhetoric, far from initiating a new trope, echoed the words of Georges Marchais—the leader of the French Communist Party—who, twenty years earlier, had justified the Soviet invasion of Afghanistan using similar arguments: "It is necessary to put an end to *droit du seigneur* and feudalism that prevails in the land of the Khans," he argued in an interview for French television as the Red Army entered Kabul to come to the rescue of the *Saur* revolution. This classic form of colonial feminism was reactivated in a speech of American first lady Laura Bush, who triumphantly announced after five weeks of intense bombings: "Because of our recent military gains in much of Afghanistan, women are no longer imprisoned in their homes. The fight against terrorism is also a fight for the rights and dignity of women" (Bush 2001). She was soon followed by Cherie Blair, wife of British prime minister Tony Blair, who launched a campaign using similar arguments to support her husband's decision to go to war, despite massive demonstrations in the streets of London. This level of attention to the plight of Afghan women was in sharp contrast to the silence that had marked the years of civil war after the withdrawal of the Soviet Union in 1989, reminding us of the opportunistic alliances imperial powers are sometimes able to forge with feminism.

Cultural Battleground

This book is an attempt to capture the nature of the "reconstruction" project in Afghanistan, using the category "woman" as an entry point into broader questions around sovereignty, state building, and democratization. Playing with the metaphor of the "carnival of (post)war"—on which I will elaborate later in this introduction—I reflect on its implications for theorizations of military-humanitarian interventions as well as for the comprehension of subjectivities forged out of these global encounters. I put "women" at the center of my analysis because of an arresting conjuncture: the fact that the international community's interference into states' affairs, especially in Third World countries, has historically coalesced around a state's treatment of the "other" half of its population, namely women.

The literature documenting the consecutive wars in Afghanistan has generally focused on the transformations of ethnic, tribal, and religious allegiances from the jihad against the Russian occupying forces until the emergence of the Taliban. Its main objective has been to explore the limitations and potentials of the state, the tribe, and Islam for nation building and the formation of political ideologies (Roy 1985; Dorronsoro 2005; Barfield 2010). This literature has been particularly resourceful in identifying the various actors involved in the conflict, their source of authority and moral inspiration, as well as the transformations of Islam and interethnic relations through external interference. Tracing the life trajectories of three prominent characters from Afghanistan's recent history, David Edwards (1996) has attempted to capture the deeper structures of the conflict. In his view, Afghanistan's troubles have less to do with divisions between groups than with the moral incoherence of the country itself—an incoherence exacerbated by the imposition of a nation-state framework upon an unstable social fabric and a non-unified territory.[1]

This book builds on this important literature in its endeavor to understand nation/state building and conflict in the region, but also slightly departs from it. Indeed, the scholarship dealing with the Afghan wars has been mostly concerned with documenting formal political parties, tribal and sectarian groups, as well as broader geopolitical dynamics that have exacerbated the conflict. Its primary objective has been to trace the political, cultural, and religious roots of prominent political actors' engagement and the modalities of their transformation through colonial and imperial encounters. Apart from a few anthropologists who have looked at the effects of wars on the everyday life of ordinary Afghans, either through the prism of religion (Marsden 2005), migration (Centlivres and Centlivres-Demont 2007; Monsutti 2005), or access to justice (De Lauri 2012a; Barfield 2008), representations that come out of this scholarship remain rooted in the Orientalist tradition, presenting Afghan "culture" as a "fact" with an essence that can be grasped. Afghans tend to be depicted as proud, heroic, and fearless fighters and Afghanistan as a chaotic and ungovernable country: "the land of the unconquerable" (Heath and Zahedi 2011), the "graveyard of empires" (Isby 2011), or "the kingdom of insolence" (Barry 2002). Analyzed from the perspective of those directly involved in the conflict, women are often absent from these descriptions, or when they are present, they are portrayed either as powerless victims (Mann 2010) or as rooted in tradition and rural life (Lindisfarne-Tapper 1991).

One of my central arguments is that the political category "woman" is largely the product of unequal interactions between institutions of transnational governance and local power entities, a category that carries specific cultural meanings and assumptions regarding the responsibilities of the state or the community toward its "second sex." As much as I believe culture may inform structures of feeling and ways of inhabiting the world, I also want to pinpoint its primary relational, contextual, and contested nature. Indeed, the conflict in Afghanistan is not solely about warring factions competing for the control over a territory. It is also a symbolic battle in which the "woman question" acquires a specific salience and "culture" is articulated in specific gendered terms.

This book walks in the footsteps of postcolonial and subaltern scholars (L. Ahmed 1992; Yegenoglu 1998; Abu-Lughod 1986; Talpade-Mohanty 2003; Chatterjee 1993; Das 1988) by showing how "culture talks" are often enmeshed within broader power relations and reflect anxieties around national identity. It aims to contextualize both politically and historically the "woman question" in Afghanistan in order to identify the colonial continuities that persist in the current reconstruction effort. I choose to focus on urban women because their bodies, either covered or exposed, represent central sites of cultural struggles over identity and because urbanity offers a greater spectrum of possibilities and constraints. Indeed, because of the incapacity of the state to assert control outside the main urban centers, reconstruction efforts with their myriad of "women empowerment" projects have mostly focused on major cities, especially Kabul.

"Modernization" is not a new word in Afghan political culture. It refers to particular moments of the Afghan history when modernization theory exercised a powerful influence on the Afghan intelligentsia and political elite. As early as the 1920s, the presence of Afghan intellectual Mahmood Tarzi—whose family was exiled in Turkey during the reign of Abdur Rahman—in the close entourage of King Amanullah Khan (the leader of Afghanistan's independence) was critical in initiating major reforms that would conduct Afghanistan on its long journey toward modernization (Gregorian 1967). However, unlike in Europe where modernization was the result of endogenous processes of industrialization, production, and class conflict, Afghan modernization was the result of exogenous influences exercised on the elite. As Nancy and Louis Dupree have well documented (L. Dupree 1973; N. H. Dupree 1984), for these early modernizers social engineering through women's emancipation from the traditional Islamic way of life was pivotal in making Afghanistan catch up with more modern and developed countries. However, social reforms initiated by Amanullah Khan on his return from his trip around Europe in 1928 in a country still not united as a nation were received with great resistance in rural areas where tribal leaders felt challenged in their authority. For these segments of society "modernization" was synonymous with the corruption of the values, principles, and morals that were constitutive of *Afghaniyat* (Afghanness).

Despite the more careful manner with which King Zahir Shah continued the agenda of reforms initiated by Amanullah, the model chosen remained similar. Institutions, ideas, and manners that the king promoted were the reflection of his overt admiration for Europe (Cullather 2002a, 521). Kabul and, to a lesser extent, other cities became isolated islands in a society that remained predominantly rural. In the countryside, the government and Kabul inhabitants who received the greatest benefits from the reforms and the modest industrialization were seen as morally corrupt (Emadi 1991, 229).

The Red Army's invasion of Afghanistan in 1981 was understood as the concrete evidence of the corrupt nature of the ruling class (N. H. Dupree 2001). Here, as in other countries under imperial domination, the Soviets used the argument of the necessity to civilize and modernize a tribal society to justify their military intervention. Afghanistan's violent encounter with foreign occupiers revealed that its relationship to the "developed" world had never been based on equality and mutual recognition. Reforms conducted by the Communist government, such as secularization and women's emancipation, placed the West as a reference point of modernity.[2] The revolution's objectives had to do with extracting the country from the inherent backwardness in which it had been kept by tradition and religion. Individual men and women's forced enrollment in literacy programs and defense committees of the revolution while regime opponents were tracked, arrested, and tortured turned the experience of modernization into a painful experience of humiliation (Barfield 2010; Barry 2002; Roy 1985).

The resistance that emerged in the Afghan refugee camps in Pakistan and in Afghanistan's rural areas, and which was articulated in essentialized cultural terms, is to be understood in the light of these developments. Mujahideen groups were not simple "freedom fighters" supported by the United States in the context of the Cold War. Far from the romantic caricature of mystical holy warriors untouched by modernity that Western journalists made of them, the mujahideen were products of complex translocal assemblages. To get a greater sense of the insidious exchanges that existed between the resistant groups in Peshawar and the rest of the world, the work of earlier anthropologists such as Pierre and Micheline Centlivres (2007), Nancy and Louis Dupree, or David Edwards is worth rereading. In an article published in *Cultural Anthropology* in 1994, Edwards gives an interesting account of his first encounter with the mujahideen from the "interior":

It is cool in the mountains, cool enough that the few people I pass wear their shawls wrapped tightly around their shoulders. Climbing a short hill on the outskirts of the village, I see a mullah with a billowy white turban seated in the chair of a two-barrel Dashika antiaircraft gun. The Dashika is a Soviet design, but markings on the gun indicate that it is of Chinese manufacture. These guns are shiny and new and only recently arrived by camel caravan across the Pakistani frontier. The mullah is young—late-twenties—and he scans the sky for signs of Soviet MiGs. Only a few weeks before, mujahidin gunners had brought down a MiG-23 not too far from here, and there is fighting going on not too far away; so the mullah is keeping careful watch. As he does so, he listens to a cassette on his Japanese tape recorder of an Egyptian muezzin chanting verses from the Qur'an. . . .

Later in the day, I meet another ex-soldier, a Persian-speaking Tajik from the Kohistan region just north of Kabul. . . . Unlike most of the other mujahidin I have met, he has little time for Islam and openly admits to me that he had been a follower of a famous leftist guerrilla leader named Majid Kalakani who had been captured and killed by the government some years before. He talks proudly of his time with Kalakani and tells me of the American sniper rifle that he used to own. It had a scope on it, and once he killed four Soviet tankists as they drove in a convoy down the main road toward Kabul. The beauty of the American rifle, he says, is its small bullets and its silent action. (Edwards 1994, 347–48)

The Egyptian muezzin singing on a Japanese tape recorder, the Dashika antiaircraft gun designed in the Soviet Union and manufactured in China, the American sniper rifle—the material details Edwards provides in his description are revealing of the intricate translocal dynamics in which the resistance movement was entangled. Descriptions like these demonstrate that the mujahideen stood at the crossroads of modernity, technological innovation, and global conflicts.

The policies some of the most radical mujahideen groups implemented in the refugee camps they ruled were a direct reflection of the global interconnections that provided the background upon which an "authentic Afghan culture and tradition" were reinvented. Constraints imposed on women's movements and public appearances in the camps directly answered state-sponsored women's emancipation programs taking place in the country. In this sense their policies were performative, reinscribing in a dramatic manner a naturalized tradition in the social fabric in order to assert its difference with the Soviet project. As Homi Bhabha argues in *The*

Locations of Culture (1994, 2): "Terms of cultural engagement, whether antagonistic or affiliative, are produced performatively. The representation of difference must not be hastily read as the reflection of *pre-given* ethnic or cultural traits set in the fixed tablet of tradition. The social articulation of difference, from the minority perspective, is a complex, on-going negotiation that seeks to authorize cultural hybridities that emerge in moments of historical transformation."

The current "reconstruction" project presents similar trends with "modernization" efforts conducted under the Communist regime: a focus on centralized instances of governance to carry out important social reforms with the military support of foreign troops. In this project, like in the Communist one, women's public visibility is the benchmark upon which "progress" is measured. Despite the fact that the political jargon used to foster "modernization" is apparently less ideologically connoted, the neoliberal agenda associated with it is far from being value free.

In the Afghan postcolony, women are obliged to subscribe to norms and ideologies whose social effects further diminish their dignity and exacerbate their inequality. Women cannot make choices that do not show—at least partly—their adhesion to these norms without fearing the social sanction reserved for those who are considered as traitors. These norms take a variety of forms: some have to do with family honor and feminine modesty; others have to do with the glorification of motherhood and feminine virtue indexed on women's capacity to endure. Reading in these norms the expression of a fixed "Afghan culture" is misleading simply because the terms of participation are constantly negotiated in everyday practice. It is through the ambivalent work of "cultural intimacy" (Herzfeld 2005)—whereby aspects of Afghan cultural identity that are considered a source of international criticism for the state are nevertheless used to provide insiders with a sense of national comfort and ontological security—that women creatively transgress (and to a certain extent, reproduce) nationalist ideologies.

Women, far from being the powerless victims of identity politics, mobilize Afghan cultural imagination in order to render audible claims pertaining to their position in the family, the community, or society at large. They are neither simple dupes nor secret revolutionaries. What they often seek tactically (even without a theory to dress it up) is to optimize the terms of recognition in their immediate, local lives. As Gloria Goodwin Raheja and Ann Grodzins Gold demonstrate in their work on women's oral performances in North India, if women frequently speak from within the dominant discourse, it is important to "begin to recognize the discontinuity, the interpenetration between the hegemonic and the subversive, and their varied deployments, from moment to moment, in everyday life" (1994, 16). In their quest for a "voice," women have to express themselves in terms of actions and performances, which have local cultural resonance. Women's "capacity to aspire" (Appadurai 2004) is therefore not disconnected from the cultural regime within which their lives are entangled. And by taking part in the complex dynamics of identity politics—in often ambiguous and ambivalent ways—they also transform the dominant norms that frame the terms of culture.

Carnival of War

Let me now return to the metaphor of the "carnival." Shortly after the bombings over Afghanistan abated, a humanitarian theater was added to the military one. The use of the term "theater" to describe such interventions needs to be further examined. In general, theaters are premises that host plays, which can be played and replayed in various locations. The theater provides a stage for the recitation of a scenario that has been written somewhere else. The theatrical dimension of the humanitarian intervention in Afghanistan is perhaps best exemplified by a project called "We Believe in Balloons," an initiative aimed at promoting peace, which was carried out in May 2013. The U.S.-based artist Yazmany Arboleda, with the support of a half dozen internationally financed aid groups, set out to distribute pink balloons filled with helium and peace messages all over the capital city. His intention, as he explained to a reporter at the *New York Times*, was to "create a stream of shared instances of unexpected happiness" (Nordland 2013). This example together with a myriad of other projects conducted since 2001 (such as the Kabul Kids Circus, Skatistan, the Beauty Academy of Kabul, and others) demonstrate that the stage of the Afghan theater hosts a carnivalesque act in the sense that it provides a space where a world of utopian freedom can be imagined.

Here I am referring to the "carnivalesque" as defined in Mikhail Bakhtin's literary work *Rabelais and His World* (1984b). Bakhtin describes the carnival as a moment when rules are turned upside down and everything is permitted. It is shaped according to a pattern of play. It is a type of performance that is communal, without boundaries between performers and audience. The "Pink Balloons" project with its objective to bring happiness and peace to the war-torn country illustrates the inherent utopia that lies within the promise of postwar reconstruction.

The transition toward democracy in Afghanistan has triggered many apparent reversals that to a certain extent remind one of medieval Europe's "carnival" as described by Bakhtin (1984b). During the carnival, ordinary life, rules, and hierarchies are temporarily suspended and overturned. Slaves may be "crowned" as kings just as kings are "decrowned" as slaves. The suspended moment and upside-down world of the carnival presents some commonalities with the transition period in Afghanistan where "masked games" hide the continuity of injustice. Even though the current context is immune from and devoid of the carnival's liberating laughter, a number of inversions that work as leverages to reinforce the status quo can be identified in the same manner as the carnival offers a safety valve that ultimately sustains the dominant order.

First, in contrast with the religious edicts enforced by the Taliban, a new vision of "law and order" is being promoted, based on constitutional populism and a fetishized "rule of law" agenda destined to bring Afghanistan into the fold of "civilized nations." But the blinding screen of the law poorly hides the endemic disorder that constitutes its twin and inseparable side. Second, "democratization" has meant the return to power of "military commanders"—alternatively labeled "warlords" or "mujahideen"—that had been ousted from the political arena by the previous regime. The "democratic" election of alleged war criminals, some of whom still own private militias and are involved in the narco-economy, has reversed the taken-for-granted telos of modernity, making the line between the licit and organized crime difficult to tell apart (Comaroff and Comaroff 2006, 40). Finally, women have been encouraged to become visible and access the public realm when the Taliban's gender policies forbade them to do so. However, this visibility has become synonymous with danger and has obliged women to camouflage themselves in new ways.

This sudden inversion of the "old order" for a new one based on Western models of (neo)liberal democracies is marked by a schizophrenic state of uncertainty that has forced many Afghans to adapt and play roles in order to fit the dominant narrative of national reconstruction. For Mikhail Bakhtin, images of reversal twist through the folklore tradition of premodern Europe, celebrating the poor fool who becomes king and condemning the powerful to ruin. In his view, such reversals express the creative energy of "a carnival sense of the world" (Bakhtin 1984a, 107). "Postwar" (which, in the case of Afghanistan, would be better described as "ongoing war") is, of course, a moment that is in many ways deprived of the festive atmosphere of the carnival. However, the ambivalence of moral and social meanings produced by the "transition" limbo bears the disorienting and liminal characteristics of the "carnival." The superposition and competition between various moral orders—Islam, international law, human rights, customary law—and the displacement of sovereignty into more concentrated forms of power and accumulation such as NATO troops, militiamen and commanders, and international organizations and NGOs as well as private contractors can be compared to the outrageous and contradictory images that make up carnival ambivalence.

(Post)war situations are often described as dramatic moments that involve violence, abuses, and a general state of lawlessness that necessitates prompt international support, especially in the legal field, to reestablish order. If this anarchic state of affairs is to a large extent a reality, the everyday experience of (post)war/reconstruction is also one that is marked by ambivalence, contradictions, and ironies that carry both constraining and enabling potentialities. The daily encounters between international humanitarian workers and Afghan aid recipients, reconstruction experts and Afghan civil servants, and Western feminists and ordinary Afghan women are often full of misunderstandings and divergent expectations that translate into a "dialogue of the deaf." The necessity to master the dominant jargon of the "rule of law," "human rights," "democracy," and "development" in order to access resources often creates ironic situations whereby Afghans are pushed to play roles and discipline themselves in certain ways. The story of Zahra, who decides to "become a man" in order to facilitate her access to the "public" illustrates the gender ironies of the reconstruction carnival. That transnational governance has opened new spaces for women contradicts the fact that many remain socially inaccessible to them.

Of course, it would be a gross exaggeration to detect in the current situation of Afghanistan the same utopian freedom that is enacted during carnival time. The daily NATO bombings made legitimate under international law and the state of destitution in which the vast majority of Afghans must live are concrete reminders of the violence that accompanies the "democratization" masquerade. What I want to emphasize here, using Bakhtin's concept of the "carnivalesque," is the new moral imagination born out of this violent encounter whereby the lines between the "good" and the "bad," the "legal" and the "lethal," to use Walter Benjamin's terms in his "Critique of Violence" (1969), are blurred and displaced.

The "carnival of the (post)war" brings together actors with various subject positions, agendas, knowledge claims, and values and sometimes offers opportunities for subversion of the same kind as the ones deployed during the medieval carnival, absorbing its authoritarian other in a way that does not totally destroy but rather contains the threat it poses. Because Afghans have a long experience of foreign interference that has complicated their relationship to the state, they have developed a political consciousness and an instinctive sense of the "masquerade" that has allowed them to preserve a sense of continuity and personal autonomy. From this long history of resistance has emerged the reputation of Afghanistan as "Yâghestan" (the land of the rebellious). Historian Michael Barry (2002) has well illustrated the creative strategies of dissimulation Afghans have developed over the centuries to resist imperial domination, something he defines as the "yâghestan reflex."

Because "democratization" efforts are accompanied by a sharp rise in crime and violence, with a more or less elected and representative regime that has brought with it a rising tide of lawlessness, Afghans' mode of engagement with the "public sphere" has been marked by a general feeling of suspicion, mistrust, and resentment that defies dominant liberal conceptualizations of the "public" as a space for rational-critical dialogue. Indeed, in Jurgen Habermas's view (1989), the "public sphere" is the locus of "communicative action," that is, a site where cooperative action is undertaken by individuals based upon mutual deliberation and argumentation. Individuals engaged in such dialogic transactions are making full use of reason in order to reach a consensus, which in turn guarantees the protection and defense of "the common good." The formation of (inclusive and rational) public spheres in Western societies has been instrumental in establishing democracies and in producing citizens. Western classical liberalism has presumed the universal necessity of differentiated public and private spheres for the development of citizenship, civil society, and democratic statehood.

This idealized vision of the "public sphere" is in sharp contradiction with the social reality not only of those who have been excluded from the public in both the developed and the developing world (women, minorities) but also of the countries that must bear the burden of neocolonial/neoliberal domination. In the context of Afghanistan, the "public" domain, far from being a site of dialogical negotiations, is better understood as a stage for performance (Göle 2002), "poetic world making" (Warner 2002, 114), and carnivalesque expression. Commenting on the experience of voluntary "modernization" policies in Turkey, Nilüfer Göle emphasizes the performative dimension of non-Western public spheres, especially in countries where the process of state formation has been shaped by unequal interactions with the West. She writes: "Because the public sphere provides a stage for performance rather than an abstract frame for textual and discursive practices, the ocular aspect in the creation of significations and the making of social imaginaries becomes of utmost importance" (Göle 2002, 177). I would add to her analysis that the notion of the carnivalesque further highlights the regenerative potential of performances in the public life of occupied countries like Afghanistan. This is not to reiterate the common stereotype according to which Third World subjects would be stuck in irrationality. On the contrary, envisioning non-Western public spheres as "carnivalesque" underscores the creative, energetic, ambiguous (and often horrifying) forms of subversion and resistance that have emerged as a result of neoliberal or military occupation. Because the carnivalesque creates a sense of togetherness, a lived collective body that is constantly renewed, non-Western public life challenges the moral assumptions that underpin the liberal public, especially in the domain of gender relations where "emancipation" is often thought of in terms of a public "coming out" and a breakup with "tradition."

Furthermore, the notion of the carnivalesque can help us rethink women's agency, especially in contexts where women are confronted with the double burden of nationalism and imperialism. In this book, I attempt to explain how women from different walks of life, generations, and ethnic and social backgrounds use carnivalesque performances and repertoires to get around or accommodate norms and prescriptions that regiment their lives. I focus on women's everyday practices and in particular women's body work, emotional performances, and expressive genres because resistance to systems of domination is often taking place at the margins of these systems, in the interstices left uncontrolled or in spaces opened up at a specific historical moment (Cowan 1990). A study of women's everyday practices demonstrates that "agency" is not only shaped by cultural systems of values that the occupation has radicalized but is also made more complex by motives and social imaginaries that inhabit a specific moral universe and in which women's bodies have come to occupy a central symbolic role.

The feminine performances I analyze in this book allow the eruption of a feminine experience that is silenced in language but that receives validation through the mobilization of broader social imaginaries pertaining to the potentially threatening nature of women's bodies. I push this idea to its limits by examining how the public visibility of women's suicide, through self-immolation or poisoning, acts as a transgressive symbol of femininity excluded, rejected from existing fields of discourse, thus forcing an opening in representation. The nature of power relations in Afghanistan today is such that women cannot speak in many political contexts, which is precisely why women come to recognize that they must, as Veena Das puts it, "learn to communicate by non-verbal gestures, intonations of speech, and reading meta-messages in ordinary language" (1988, 198).

The study of Afghan women's poetry and the cultural imaginaries that constitute their world helps us to better understand how an individual woman's ability to access public life is dependent on her capacity to mobilize socially appropriate cultural expressions. I show how public women play with the polysemic nature of hegemonic political/religious repertoires (notions of jihad and martyrdom, for example) in order to assert their presence in male-dominated arenas. These covert reinterpretations, in spite of their inherent ambivalence, bring nuances to and marginally challenge traditional gender discourses. In the same way, women's emotional performances, even under their most dramatic forms like suicide attempts, carry with them communicative potential in the same way as the grotesque and the exuberant in carnivalesque performances. These highly dramatic gestures that follow gendered forms of emotional expression strengthen realities of identity while bringing some legal validity to women's demands. By creatively engaging with these well-known cultural repertoires, women do not only confirm their allegiance to the gender order but they also demonstrate its intrinsic fragility. These "polyphonic discursive formations within the tradition itself" (Raheja and Gold 1994, 25) do not function in my view as mere "rituals of rebellion" (Gluckman 1963), ensuring the continuity of the political and moral order of society. Their repetition, while reinforcing the "reality" of gender difference (Butler 1990), also allows for the shifting of meaning according to contexts and situations.

Fictional State Building

"Democratic transition" in Afghanistan has to be studied from the perspective of women because women represent a central catalyst of disputes and controversies. Indeed, as in other colonial encounters, women have become central subjects of public debates and political attention over the past ten years. The vitality with which the visibility of women in public life is discussed in contemporary Afghanistan by the international community, Afghan politicians and power holders, as well as ordinary people, underscores the centrality of women in symbolically shaping the future of the country. An analysis of reactions to and effects of their presence in public can help us unpack the political reconfiguration of public life in the "post-Taliban" period. Indeed, polemics that have emerged around women's roles signal the broader moral anxieties around culture that have emerged as a result of the occupation. In a society torn by violence and war, women's bodies have become the field through which statehood enacts its power (Aretxaga 1997; Das 1996).

With other academics who have attempted to theorize the state as a fantasy (Navaro-Yashin 2002), as a fetish (Taussig 1992a), as an idea (Mitchell 1991), or as a fiction (Aretxaga 2003), I want to underline the elusive, porous, and mobile boundaries of the state in a context where the "state" is considered as "failed." In the context at stake a myriad of actors such as NGOs, UN agencies, the World Bank, private companies, and local militias and narco-traffickers assume a large part of the traditional Weberian functions of the state to the extent that the state mostly materializes itself through the use of violence, symbolic or real. In order to understand what "state building" may mean when the state is no more in charge or able to regulate many areas of social life, one needs to rethink the state beyond traditional categories of "structures" and "apparatus" (Navaro-Yashin 2002).

The reconstruction process has mostly focused on rebuilding state infrastructures: ministries, hospitals, schools, and courts, most of which have remained dysfunctional—and sometimes, even empty—for lack of security, personnel, and resources to pay civil servants' salaries. Once the stage for the performance of statehood has been set, the state has largely remained a ghostly figure, a powerful fiction fueling popular anxieties and discourses of corruption, secrecy, and arbitrary violence. The "virtual reality" (Aretxaga 2003) of the state, its phantomatic presence, is nevertheless enacted in the relation of simultaneous attraction and repulsion that holds together its sovereign power. The state, therefore, is perhaps better captured in its margins (Das and Poole 2004) than in its supposedly transparent and rational bureaucratic forms. Veena Das and Deborah Poole argue that "the forms of illegibility, partial belonging, and disorder that seem to inhabit the margins of the state constitute its necessary condition as a theoretical and political object" (2004, 4).

But there is a more general point to be made. The uncertainty that surrounds the state is not specific to the Afghan context. Indeed, everywhere the state, as any institution endowed with the power to produce "the real in the world" (Boltanski 2008), is a semantic reality, a "being without a body" that can only speak through spokespersons. Ambivalence toward the state is inherent to social life since spokespersons who are supposed to translate the will of the state may in fact impose their own judgment. This tension between the need to have institutions in order to preserve a sense of stability and the impossibility to fully rely on them because of their fictional nature is what Luc Boltanski calls a "hermeneutical contradiction" (Boltanski 2008, 28).

In the case of Afghanistan, this fundamental state of suspicion is heightened by the fact that state representatives are less easily identifiable. They are to be found within a myriad of more or less formal organizations, with diverse and sometimes even contradictory political agendas, what Jane Cowan (2007) has identified as a "spectrum of sovereignties" in the context of the "supervised state." Meanwhile, as much as the state is feared, nationalist discourses feed social imaginaries with expectations toward the state that often contradict the actual experience of disempowerment, violence, and marginalization (Comaroff and Comaroff 2006). It is precisely in this tension that I want to think of the subjective and affective reality of the state as it unfolds in the everyday events of public life through desires, fantasies, rumors, and moral panics.

Following Yael Navaro-Yashin's work on the psychic life of the state (2002), this book highlights the dialectic relationship between various social and political actors (Afghan civil servants and politicians, international forces, and citizens) that produces and refashions the political in the context of statebuilding efforts conducted under international supervision. My definition of the political is therefore informed by Michel Foucault's definition of power as pervasive, relational, and productive and as a force that permeates bodies, shaping affects and subjectivities. Because political representation in contemporary Afghanistan remains highly contentious, an approach of the political that remains focused on formal institutions and political discourses is limited. A broader definition of the political is necessary to understand the psychic dimensions of state power and public life (Butler 1997b; Kafka 2012), especially in contexts where state institutions are emptied of their meaning. Because, as Navaro-Yashin (2002, 3) argues, "power is everywhere," the political should not be "sited" solely in rationalized institutions but should rather be traced under its most "fleeting and intangible" forms. Metaphors of "no man's land" (Navaro-Yashin 2003) and "ruins" (Navaro-Yashin 2009) powerfully illuminate the modern condition of confusion and estrangement embedded within transnational conceptions of the state, especially in contexts where, like in Afghanistan, international narratives of "liberation" and "justice" produce the actual experience of entrapment and immobility (Sanford 2003; Englund 2006; Mattei and Nader 2008; Castillejo-Cuéllar 2005).

The dominant narrative of the reconstruction is one of a "return to order" ("normalization") that clashes with the actual state of emergency that continues to affect the everyday life of men and especially women, who have to bear the burden of a double occupation: one of international military troops and another of the state, enacted through military performances of masculinity attempting to assert themselves through the control of their bodies. Discourses of "freedom" and "liberation" reiterated by international actors have had the unintended effect of reinforcing a sense of urgency in maintaining communal boundaries along stereotypical gender lines with the nation imagined as an idealized desexualized maternal figure in need of "protection." In the process of rendering the state legible, the "law" has been the main instrument for the enforcement of this ideal vision of the national community.

"Because my husband's beating became so bad, I ran away from home and turned myself in to the police. The police sent me to prison. Nobody helps me! There is no government here to help! For the one who is poor, there is only God!" Bibi Gul's story of repetitive abuse, by her in-laws and then by state laws at the very moment when her need for a caring state was the most urgent is sadly common among the inmates of the women's prison in Kabul, recently rehabilitated with the financial support of the international community. Most of these women have been sentenced to jail for "moral crimes" such as *zina* (illegal sex) or elopement, both punishable by a twenty-year jail sentence. In reality, many of them simply tried to escape domestic violence, forced marriage, or forced prostitution. Some have made the unforgivable mistake of dishonoring their family by falling in love with the man of their choice. Others have been raped and have been accused of adultery. Since marriage is the only way to avoid prolonged jail time, much pretrial time is spent negotiating terms of marriage between their otherwise reluctant families. Paradoxically, since the downfall of the Taliban regime, the women's prison population had risen to 600 in 2011, up from 380 in 2010 (Farmer 2011). The director of the prison observes disdainfully that the prison is full "because these days women are given too much freedom."

The sexual violence so pervasive in "postwar" Afghanistan is the lethal labor that provides the state—and the people it is supposed to embody—with a semblance of sovereignty and legibility in the face of an occupation experienced as a source of moral pollution. To counter the hegemonic discourse of human rights that has accompanied the military occupation, "lawfare"— which John Comaroff (2001) defines as the judicialization of politics and the resort to legal instruments to commit acts of political coercion—has been the symbolic terrain upon which national sovereignty has attempted to affirm itself. It is through the language of the law that "brute power has been laundered in a wash of legitimacy, ethics, propriety" (Comaroff and Comaroff 2006, 31), subjecting women to various forms of abuses ranging from virginity tests to sexual harassment and domestic violence.

The Anthropologist and the "Reconstruction" Business

What legitimacy does a white European anthropologist have to represent Afghan women? In her famous essay "Can the Subaltern Speak?" (1988), Gayatri Spivak urges Western anthropologists to question their motives in studying non-Western peoples. She remains doubtful of their attempt, no matter how well intentioned, to "speak for others" unless they engage in serious self-critique and incorporate analysis of their positionality in the power/ knowledge nexus that underpins their research.

Spivak's distrust is all the more justified in that anthropology as a discipline is historically entrenched within the legacy of European colonialism. Talal Asad reminds us that anthropological knowledge may not have been that significant in the expansion of colonial domination; it remained too esoteric to be of practical use for the colonial establishment (1991, 315). However, the fact that anthropologists' discourses and practices were part of particular imperial times and colonial places is precisely what renders anthropological knowledge worthy of investigation for anyone concerned with the practical workings of domination.

The fieldwork on which this book is based is not removed from the imperial dynamics that led to the occupation of Afghanistan. There is little chance that this country would have come under my consideration before 9/11 and the subsequent military intervention that made the resources of NGOs, international organizations, and other "Aidland" subcontractors multiply in a matter of a few weeks—hence providing career opportunities for young (and often naive) graduates who want to change the world, much like the one I was when I was first sent to Afghanistan. However, the objective of this book is neither to speak for Afghan women nor to represent the culture to which they are supposed to belong. Rather, this book endeavors to tell the multifaceted story of an occupation. While seeking to define the nature of the encounters occurring in one of the world's most important humanitarian theaters, this book illustrates the intended and unintended effects of international supervision in the everyday lives of women and its impact on their capacity to speak.

Like any research conducted in highly unstable environments, this study has been accompanied by many constraints, which have deeply influenced the design and methodology of my work. Unable to settle in one single site location in the manner classic ethnographers traditionally work, I was forced to adapt and navigate in different circles according to the opportunities that arose out of my encounters. I became a "mobile ethnographer" (Marcus 1995, 96), pushed and pulled according to circumstances over which I had little control—an experience I share with other anthropologists who have worked under similar circumstances and whose texts bear witness to life's inherent precariousness (Nordstrom 2004; Green 1994; Taussig 2003; Aretxaga 1997; Scheper-Hughes 1992).

This research was for me a sort of embodied discovery of what living in a climate of fear exactly meant. The existential shock I experienced when I discovered the other side of the invisible border that separates expatriates from Afghans was a necessary step to start envisioning the dark side of humanitarianism. It is through the working of my "nervous system"—these "applied embodied thoughts" as Michael Taussig (1992b, 7) puts it—that I began to grasp the moral tensions in which the people around me were caught. I understood that the purpose of my work was less about finding the most efficient way of interpreting the deeds and thoughts of my informants than about having to face the existential problem of living in a constant state of emergency with no possibility to envision what tomorrow would entail (Hoffman 2003; Nordstrom and Robben 1995). Although there were many differences in our respective experiences—due to the simple fact that I could decide to leave and take the next flight back to Europe—I gradually started to share some of my informants' anxieties as well as some of their coping mechanisms, in particular humor and irony, arts in which Afghans have an excellent reputation.

Research in an insecure context corrodes the founding myths of ethnography as a method that privileges social stability, bounded and coherent communities, and the possibility of engaging in significant human relationships. The fragmented nature of my fieldwork and the fragile relationships I managed to develop were somehow a reflection of the fragmented relationships the social landscape was made of. But more generally, the mobile dispo-sition I had to adopt in order to follow the "pulse" of the field—or its "rhythm" to use Henri Lefebvre's (2004) terminology—demonstrates that movement instead of stability is perhaps best apt to capture the changing and dynamic nature of modern human life. Like most Afghans who have become "exiles in their own homelands" (Stewart 1988, 235), I was there as an uprooted wit-ness, manipulated, influenced by my emotions, always confused by rumors that circulated around me. This experience was crucial, however, to get an understanding of the nature of "postwar reconstruction" and to incorporate into my "witnessing" knowledge of causes and implications unavailable to observers who were not so immersed in the daily life of Afghans.

Most of my fieldwork was conducted in Kabul even though I traveled to other regions on several occasions. The city has often been the setting where changes in gender relations first occur. As much as the city also creates new hierarchies of power and domination, it also remains the locale from which women may experience new forms of mobility. My focus on Kabul as the center of power was informed by the fact that it represented a site of political pos-sibilities for women, a site where modern citizen making was being processed while simultaneously notions of corruption and pollution remained deeply associated with that space in the collective imagination.

Because of the difficulties of conducting independent research in a coun-try still at war, I had found myself a position in a communication agency spe-cializing in social marketing and public information. I worked there as a project manager/researcher for a few months until I had managed to develop enough contacts in the women's groups I was interested in studying to con-tinue the fieldwork on my own. My position within the company allowed me to gain access to various institutions where my presence as a simple researcher may have otherwise looked suspicious. It also gave me direct insight into the "reconstruction" business and access to key development "brokers and trans-lators" (Lewis and Mosse 2006).

At the same time, I had recruited a translator/Dari teacher, Lutfia, who supported me in conducting interviews, translations, and in building con-tacts among women MPs, students, and activists. Lutfia was a twenty-two-year-old university student originally from Kapisa Province where her family still lived. She boarded at the National Women's Dormitory on Kabul Univer-sity campus. Thanks to her intercession with the dormitory's director, I was offered a room among female students in return for English and French les-sons. I lived there for four months, sharing girls' daily activities, improving my Dari while gaining insight into what made up their everyday lives: worries, dreams, gossip, Indian soap operas, poetry, music, makeup, and, of course, studies. My relationship to Lutfia gradually moved toward friendship. I did not only benefit from her linguistic skills but also from her patience and kindness in explaining to me the complex rules of Afghan etiquette.

I also volunteered for a few months at the Afghan Women's Network (AWN), a local network of women's NGOs, assisting them with proposals, reports, and fund-raising. I taught English to the staff and in return for my services I was introduced to the women's organizations working under the umbrella of AWN. Thanks to this new connection, I gained access to other women activists in Kabul and Herat where AWN had recently opened an office. I also followed for a few weeks two renowned women's rights advocates who ran programs in Nangahar and Hazarajat.

Fieldwork in an environment where public figures in general and public women in particular were the targets of political assassinations necessitated a high degree of flexibility. My navigation in different circles was dependent upon the willingness of the women I met to open up and on the quality of the relationship I managed to develop with them. There was no guarantee that the doors that were opened one day would still be opened the next. I shadowed a woman activist in her activities for a few days here, conducted participant observation in a women's organization for another few days there, eagerly jumping on each opportunity that presented itself. Planning was a useless exercise. I ended up following a metaphor, an idea, instead of the specific informants I had initially thought of. It is through my navigation among various circles of women enjoying different degrees of public visibility that I could start sensing the erratic nature of public life at a time of rapid and intense political change.

In spite of all my efforts to get some kind of insight into the spaces I was interested in, it is undeniable that my particular position within that space profoundly affected the nature of the work I could do. My informants had some valid reasons for showing suspicion toward my ultimate intentions: there were very few independent researchers in Kabul; I was not representing any particular institution and I was an unaccompanied French woman. As a result, it was not rare for me to be taken for either a spy or a journalist. The only solution I found to make my presence less awkward was to offer concrete services whenever possible, to follow women's projects and support them the best I could.

In order to preserve the anonymity of my informants, I have sometimes changed their names and used pseudonyms. I have anonymized some of the women I interviewed at the National Assembly when they explicitly asked me to do so. When it is the case, I only mention whether they come from rural or urban areas since it is a significant distinction that involves a radically different position. I have coded their interviews and removed biographical elements that may make them too easily identifiable. I kept the original names of the women activists and politicians who were willing to gain some public visibility through my writing. All the women who have shared with me some intimate stories that I have used to support and inform my argument have been given pseudonyms.

Researching Women's Political Expression

This book is structured around two main parts. The first part focuses on the state and the various manifestations of its power over women's bodies. I locate the current project of "state building" in a continuum of modernization attempts conducted in the early 1930s, in the 1960s–1970s, and during the Soviet occupation of Afghanistan. In the course of a history marked by forced modernization and Islamic fundamentalism, I show how the state has remained a phantom figure that haunts Afghans' collective imagination in powerful ways. In the second part, I show how Afghan women routinely respond, through embodiment and performance, to the various sources of pressure pertaining to their visibility in public life.

The first chapter is a historical overview of the fashioning of the Afghan nation and of its articulation along gender lines. I show how the modern history of Afghanistan is marked by a constant focus on women's bodies as either sites upon which the state strove to apply the stamp of modernization or, on the contrary, the stamp of an imagined tradition. I place the contemporary moment in the continuity of these numerous attempts at remaking women.

Chapter 2 uses the example of a "gender empowerment" training program carried out by the Ministry of Women's Affairs as part of its broader "gender mainstreaming" mandate to illustrate how ideas associated with modern state building and citizenship are being infused into Afghan society. I show how "reconstruction" does not simply consist in the formation of a bureaucratic apparatus based on Western models of liberal democracies but primarily involves cultural and symbolic production.

Chapter 3 focuses on the justice sector as a major site of attention of current state-building efforts. Through interviews and observations conducted in Family Response Units (FRUs), Kabul Family Court, women's shelters, and defense attorneys associations, I unpack some of the contradictions, ambivalences, and ironies of justice sector support programs conducted under a fuzzy "rule of law" agenda. The inaccessibility and impotency of formal justice institutions has led women to take justice into their own hands and turn to community-based forms of mediation. Using observations conducted during Koran classes taught by an Afghan women's rights activist, I underline the centrality of Islam and kinship in legitimizing claims for rights, especially in the highly sensitive arena of family law.

Chapter 4 is an ethnographic account of young women's responses to moral panics that have emerged in the national and local press as a result of the appearance of some commodities and cultural products such as cosmetics, fashion, and Indian soap operas on the local market. These panics flagged the threat of moral dilution and cultural pollution and urged policy makers to react in order to reestablish social order. While unpacking the multiple meanings of these moral anxieties, I explore how female students boarding at the National Women's Dormitory in Kabul struggled to position themselves in a new life environment away from their families. I argue that these young women's bodily practices revealed a constant tension between the necessary fulfilment of different roles as dutiful and modest daughters and as young urban educated women aspiring to present themselves as "modern" and Muslim. The fact that Islam remained a central element of their self-justification should not be understood as a reflection of the conservative nature of Afghan society but rather as a form of resistance to foreign domination.

Chapter 5 aims to characterize new meanings attached to women's veiling in the new Islamic republic. While the *chadari* (burka) has become the ultimate symbol of women's oppression for Western audiences, it is necessary to take a closer look at its multiple and often contradictory uses and to contextualize the reasons for its maintenance, despite the downfall of the Taliban regime. The ethnographic data I collected among women's rights activists and women MPs demonstrate that women who are attempting to access public spaces have developed creative strategies of dissimulation to get public recognition. They have become visible under the veil and have sometimes been able to challenge gender hierarchies behind the appearance of compliance and conformity. These findings challenge liberal ideas according to which women's visibility in public spaces is a necessary guarantee for their emancipation and their agency.

Chapter 6 investigates women's emotional performances and discourses of suffering, jihad, and martyrdom. I show how these ambiguous communicative tools serve to make commentaries on social relations and gender hierarchies without totally disrupting the honor code and the ideal of female modesty. I also analyze more dramatic gestures, such as suicides, and suggest conceiving of them not as mere signs of despair but rather as nondiscursive communicative acts that are part of women's broad repertoire of emotional performances. I highlight the ambiguous symbolic power of suicide and its anchorage in the subversive imaginary universe of women's poetic expression.

PART I

Phantom State Building

CHAPTER 1

Queen Soraya's Portrait

In December 2001, a few days after the Afghan interim government was officially appointed, the Ministry of Information and Culture opened on its ground floor a hall for press conferences. On the large walls of the conference room, paintings of the different kings of Afghanistan—Timur Shah, Abdur Khaman, Habibullah, Amanullah, Nadir Shah, and Zahir Shah—were displayed in chronological order. Only in one painting did the king appear with his wife. The painting was a replica of a famous photograph of King Amanullah and Queen Soraya Tarzi. However, the Afghan authorities had modified the original picture of the royal couple. A very large veil had been painted over Soraya in the manner of traditional wedding veils, which hung down to the floor, a veil that did not appear on the original photograph.

The addition of such a garment to the portrait of a queen is more than a simple anecdote. By adding it the authorities had deliberately rewritten one of the most symbolically significant pages of Afghan history. In her wedding veil, Soraya's status as the Muslim wife of the king was reemphasized while her eminent political role in the modernization effort undertaken during his rule in the 1920s became a secondary historical fact. Her solitary feminine presence in a portrait gallery dominated by men was nevertheless a powerful reminder that women had once played their part in Afghan politics.

In George Orwell's novel *Nineteen Eighty-Four* (1949), the ruling party has a slogan: "Who controls the past, controls the future. Who controls the present, controls the past." The way history is written, transmitted, and told influences the way we envision the future. Historical distortions always serve political purposes. In the aftermath of September 11 and the nation-building process that soon thereafter followed, the veiling of Soraya symbolically inscribed on her body the continuity of shared religious values and the contested position women would come to occupy in the new Islamic republic.

RIVALLING QUEEN ELIZABETH IN THE SPLENDOURS OF HER WARDROBE: QUEEN SURYIA OF AFGHANISTAN, THE CHARMING CONSORT OF KING AMANULLAH.

Figure 2. Official portrait of Queen Soraya Tarzi published in the *Illustrated London News*, March 17, 1928. Source: http://www.phototheca-afghanica.ch.

This constant reinvention of gender norms through the rewriting and re-interpretation of Afghan history "hints both at the precariousness of cultural homogeneity within the national community and at the centrality of gender in articulating and perpetuating a sense of national belonging. Somebody has to invoke and perform the rituals that reinforce these norms and to inculcate them into the next generation in order to ensure historical continuity. This 'somebody' is woman-as-mother-of-the-nation" (Peterson 1994, cited in Einhorn 2006, 197). Her body is a site of political struggle over collective identity.

In the portrait gallery of the Ministry of Information and Culture, history pays homage to the great Afghan leaders who have led soldiers to the battlefield against foreign invaders or carried out national development projects to modernize their country. However, little is said about their fellow women and the ways in which they have experienced the various social transformations initiated by the political regimes that have succeeded one another. Yet, "to speak about the 'situation of Afghan women' is to generalize unconstructively. Women's roles and status in society and the division of productive activity between men and women vary according to region and ethnic group" (Centlivres-Demont 1994, 334). With 80 percent of the population living in rural areas, and limited development outside major cities, changes in gender relations initiated in Kabul have continuously been perceived with suspicion, as threats to Islam and tradition or as proof of the elite's moral corruption.

In this chapter, I explore four key periods of Afghan history when the issue of "women" emerged in the political agenda: the modern monarchies (1920–73), the Communist regime (1979–92), the civil war (1992–96), and the Taliban regime (1996–2001). I look at these periods from the standpoint of the political category "women" in order to underline the ways in which the different political regimes have used women's issues in order to articulate ideas about national identity and develop a vision for their respective societies. Gender politics, expressed in political discourses around the necessity of "remaking women" (Abu-Lughod 1998), were at the center of each of these respective historical moments.

I also relate the "woman question" to the geopolitical context of the wider region, to the process of nation building, and to the complex relationships between tribal, religious, and central institutions of power. I argue that political interest in the condition of women was triggered by the intensification throughout the twentieth century of Afghanistan's relationships with the rest of the world, in particular with Turkey, Iran, Great Britain, the Soviet Union, and the United States. Far from creating consensus, the status of women has been (and continues to be) a highly contested issue that opposed conservatives and reformists. Hence, debates over the future of the country are never only debates about the model of economic development to follow. The model of gender relations to promote remains a core feature of such disputes because interventions in this domain always indicate a civilizational shift with changes in lifestyles, clothing habits, and ways of being in public (Göle 1996).

Since women's emancipation has been from the outset enmeshed within unequal power relations between Afghanistan and the various powers trying to assert their dominance over the region, attempts at reforming the status of women have traditionally been perceived as alien to Afghan culture. Now as before, orthodox readings of women's role in Islam should not be read as reflections of an essentially traditionalist culture but rather as symbolic attempts at preserving sovereignty in a context where imperial domination triggers moral panics over national identity.

Starting with the controversial portrait of Queen Soraya, the chapter builds on archive images of women collected in various official documents. These images bear witness to the centrality of "women" in promoting narratives of progress for the outside world. Their disappearance from the public domain during the civil war and the Taliban regime can be interpreted as a direct reaction to foreign-sponsored emancipation programs. It is because this "swing of the pendulum" (Zulfacar 2006) has shaped Afghan women's memories and subjectivities in powerful ways that this history needs to be recounted. The present moment, far from representing a radical rupture with the past, is rooted in a long history of imperial interventions justified by feminist arguments anchored in the colonial tradition: what Gayatri Spivak (1988, 296) has identified as the white man's burden of "saving brown women from brown men."

Brief Background

The creation of a modern state in Afghanistan is largely the product of competing imperial influences in the region, providing financial subsidies and arms to the ruling elite in Kabul in an attempt at asserting their own control over the country while providing the state with the means to impose its will on the tribes (Dorronsoro 2005). It is unlikely that a centralized state governing a unified territory would have been able to impose itself without external financial and military aid. However, the state always remained rather peripheral in the political life of the country: threatened by frequent tribal uprisings and the growing influence of the ulema, its survival depended on external aid for the financing of its administration, heavy policing techniques to contain rebellions, and the co-optation of the tribes and the religious class to ensure its legitimacy.

During the nineteenth century, Afghanistan was under the influence of two imperial powers: Russia to the north and England in the Indian subcontinent. It was the threat of the expanding Russian Empire beginning to push for an advantage in the Afghan region that placed pressure on British India in what became known as the "Great Game." The Great Game set in motion the confrontation of the British and Russian empires whose spheres of influence moved steadily closer to one another until they met in Afghanistan. It also involved Britain's repeated attempts to impose puppet governments in Kabul. Afghanistan gradually fell under British control (1880) and was eventually used as a buffer state to prevent the expansion of Russia until the country obtained its independence in 1919. King Amanullah, whose political legitimacy was strengthened by his victory in the struggle for national liberation, engaged the country in a vast program of reforms aiming at modernizing the country.

Modern Monarchies, 1920–73

Described by historians as the "Atatürk of Afghanistan," King Amanullah's entourage was composed of liberal and nationalist intellectuals whose political views were influenced by modernization reforms conducted in neighboring countries such as Iran and Turkey. Amanullah's modernization program was undeniably inspired by the liberal ideas of Mahmud Beg Tarzi, father of Queen Soraya, Amanullah's wife. Educated in Syria and Turkey, son of the famous poet Gulham Mohammad Tarzi, Mahmud Beg Tarzi is one of the most influential intellectual and nationalist figures of his time. The Tarzi family was forced into exile by Amir Abdur Khaman Khan after Gulham Mohammad broke with the amir over his strictness and brutality toward his enemies (L. Dupree 1973, 437). The Tarzi family only returned to Afghanistan in 1903. In 1911, Mahmud Tarzi began publishing a modernist-nationalist newspaper, the *Siraj-ul-akhbar-i Afghan* (Lamp of the News of Afghanistan). His writings, influenced by modern interpretations of Islamic jurisprudence, advocated for modern education while denouncing Western imperialism (L. Dupree 1973, 440).

Exposed to the new gender policies implemented in other Middle Eastern countries where he had traveled during his years of exile, Tarzi became a strong supporter of women's rights in his own country. He believed in women's ability to participate in public life, claimed that fully "educated women were an asset for future generations and concluded that Islam did not deny them equal rights" and that women should be therefore entitled to become full citizens. One section of his newspaper, entitled "Celebrating Women of the World," was dedicated to women's issues and was edited by his wife, Asma Tarzi (Ahmed-Ghosh 2003a, 3–4). But in spite of his liberal approach toward the position of women in society, Tarzi believed in authoritarian modernism to maintain the monarchy and the creation of a centralized state responsible for the development of the country.

The Reign of Amanullah, 1919–29

As soon as independence was achieved, Amanullah recruited Tarzi, his influential father-in-law, as his minister of foreign affairs. Soraya Tarzi was King Amanullah Khan's only wife. The decision of the king to present himself to the world in a monogamous relationship and in the company of the queen was intensively commented on by the international press. In an article of the *Illustrated London News* published March 17, 1928, which displayed a photo documentary of the royal couple's European tour, the journalist commented:

> Queen Suryia [Soraya], who arrived in England with King Amanullah on March 13, is the first Consort of an Oriental monarch to visit Europe with her husband. She is a daughter of the Afghan Foreign Minister, Tarzi Khan, and is the only wife of the King, who firmly upholds the ideal of monogamy. Already she has made an immense impression in Rome, Berlin, and Paris by her personal beauty and her

adaptability to Western ways. "It is difficult to realise," writes Sir Per-
cival Philipps [sic], who accompanied the Afghan royal party from India to Europe, "that this charming lady has, according to our standards,
been virtually a prisoner all her life. She lived in the strictest seclusion at Kabul. . . . The Queen is deeply interested in every aspect of life
in Europe, particularly the position of women." In Paris she was hailed
as a queen of fashion, and had some fifty dresses made there. "She bids
fair," it has been said, "to rival Queen Elizabeth in the number of her
gowns."

The photo documentary and the journalist's report are classic examples
of "Orientalism" (Said 1979). As in other representations of the Middle East
produced in the West, the photographers' and reporters' interest in the foreign "other" was shaped by a number of stereotypical certainties about the
Orient: its inherent backwardess, its rootedness in tradition, its treatment of
women. The narrative that emerges out of the documentary is marked by a
fascination for the queen's exotic beauty and a feeling of compassion for her
status as "an Oriental woman living in seclusion in her country." Between
the lines, and in spite of her presence by the side of her husband in this important diplomatic mission, Soraya's status remains rooted in the imaginary
of the "harem." She is presented as the domesticated and subjugated "other"
as opposed to the liberated, independent, and enlightened Western self
(L. Ahmed 1992). The standard for measuring women's emancipation (and
the standards of "civilization" more generally) are those set by Europe, not
only in the ways Oriental subjects are to dress but also in the manners they
are to adopt.

However, it remains undeniable that Soraya played a central role in redefining the position of women in Afghan society at a major moment of social
change and nation building. As in Iran and Turkey, the issue of women was
a central concern of the ruling class who predominantly adopted a secularist, rationalist, and universalist Western model of social transformation (Göle
1996, 29). By having his wife take part in all national events, Amanullah strove
to present an image of Afghanistan in the path of "catching up" with Western civilization. Hence Soraya participated with him in hunting parties, riding on horseback, and attending some cabinet meetings. She appeared in the
king's lodge during military parades. It was with her support that King
Amanullah was able to campaign against the veil and polygamy. "At a public

THE ILLUSTRATED LONDON NEWS

REGISTERED AS A NEWSPAPER FOR TRANSMISSION IN THE UNITED KINGDOM AND TO CANADA AND NEWFOUNDLAND BY MAGAZINE POST.

SATURDAY, MARCH 24, 1928.

The Copyright of all the Editorial Matter, both Engravings and Letterpress, is Strictly Reserved in Great Britain, the Colonies, Europe, and the United States of America.

THE BRITISH GOVERNMENT'S ROYAL GUESTS FROM AFGHANISTAN: KING AMANULLAH AND QUEEN SURAYYA.

The King and Queen of Afghanistan took leave of their Majesties at Buckingham Palace, on the termination of their State visit, on March 15. They then drove to Claridge's Hotel, where the above photograph was taken, to stay there as guests of the British Government. Since their arrival in England King Amanullah and Queen Surayya, besides attending a number of official functions, have already seen many aspects of our national life, and will doubtless have seen many more before their departure on April 5. They are keenly interested in everything, and have made themselves very popular wherever they go. Some of their activities are illustrated on a double page in this number. Among their engagements was a flight over London in an aeroplane on March 21. They have also arranged to visit Windsor, Oxford, Manchester, and Liverpool, and to attend the Grand National and the Boat Race.

Figure 3. King Amanullah and Queen Soraya during their stay in England. Photograph published in the *Illustrated London News*, March 24, 1928. Source: http://www.phototheca-afghanica.ch.

THE DISTAFF SIDE OF THE WESTERNISATION OF AFGHANISTAN : AFGHAN
LADIES IN EUROPEAN DRESS—A PHOTOGRAPH JUST RECEIVED FROM
KABUL.

The Europeanisation of Afghanistan proceeds apace, thanks to the recent tour of King
Amanullah and his Consort. Her Majesty is at least as modern as her husband, and is
keenly interested in the welfare and freedom of her country-women. A photograph of
her pigeon-shooting is reproduced on our front page.

Figure 4. Afghan ladies in European dress. Photograph published in the *Illustrated London News*, November 3, 1928. Source: http://www.phototheca-afghanica.ch.

function, Amanullah said that Islam does not require women to cover their bodies or wear any special kind of veil. At the conclusion of the speech, Queen Soraya tore off her veil in public and the wives of other officials present at the meeting followed [her] example" (Ahmed-Ghosh 2003a, 4).

That the king put so much emphasis on banning the veil is not surprising: the modernizing elite hastening to show images of women throwing off their veil is a common leitmotif of Orientalist discourses. As Meyda Yegenoglu (1998) argues, the figure of the woman who cannot be seen yet who troublingly can hold the Westerner in her own unseen gaze operates as the ultimate trope of the Orient that the West desires to penetrate. The desire to unveil her reveals "the unique articulation of the sexual within cultural difference in Orientalist discourse" (Yegenoglu 1998, 47). As the caption of a photograph published in November 1928 in the *Illustrated London News* (Figure 4) demonstrates, the level of progress achieved in Afghanistan was primarily measured by women's unveiled appearance, the veil symbolizing the traditional, sub-servient domestic roles of Muslim women. However, in practice, women did not literally embrace European norms but creatively interpreted them by combining Western hats with face veils.

This exhibition of modern feminine fashion largely inspired by Europe became part of national rituals aiming to symbolically bolster the idea of "modernization," especially for the rest of the world. For instance, the queen's visit to Turkey in 1929 made the headlines of *Cumburiyet,* an Istanbul daily paper sympathetic to the goals of the new republic's modernizing regime in which photographs of her wearing a sleeveless summer dress with hair, face, and shoulders uncovered were displayed (Shissler 2004, 113). The circulation of images of upper-class women dressed in European clothes and their pub-lic visibility at official ceremonies represented a radical step in a society where most women had historically been segregated from men and protected from the gaze of outsiders.

However, the introduction of women into public life was undertaken to serve other ends than the development of women's autonomy. This public per-formance of European lifestyles through clothing "played a symbolic role in the determination of the definition of the regime, beyond its significance from the point of view of women" (Göle 1996, 64). These new clothing habits served to exalt a new civilization, a new way of life, and new behavior patterns. As in Turkey where Atatürk banned the Ottoman fez and replaced it by the hat, Amanullah made it compulsory for men to wear European suits when en-tering the capital city and for women to remove their *chadari* in specific areas of Kabul. These laws were significant in conveying Afghanistan's aspira-tion to be part of the union of contemporary nations. Hence, Kabul was used as the shop window of reforms, which were mostly cosmetic and in reality had limited impact outside of the city. Corruption and governmental injus-tices practiced in rural parts of the country rendered these public ceremoni-als outrageous to villagers (Zulfacar 2006, 31).

In Amanullah's view, women could only be emancipated through West-ernization led by the upper class, the queen, and her sisters (Centlivres-Demont 1994, 336). Many women from Amanullah's family publicly participated in women's organizations and went on to become government officials later in life. For instance, the Anjuman-i Himayat-i-Niswan (Association for the Pro-tection of Women) was established in 1928 by Seraj al-Banat and Queen Soraya to encourage women to demand the rights provided by King Amanullah's reforms of marriage customs and restrictive social practices (L. Dupree 1973). With the support of Queen Soraya, women were encouraged to get an education and, as an initiative to that end, fifteen young women were sent to Turkey for higher education in 1928.

These societal reforms were further accelerated following a six-month trip around Europe that Soraya and Amanullah took in 1927–28. On their return the royal couple initiated a program of new reforms, including the creation of a constitutional monarchy, an elected assembly, a secular judiciary, and, most significantly, compulsory education for both sexes and plans for co-educational schools. However, the European tour of the royal couple was received with hostility in their own country (Majrooh 1989, 94). While Soraya and Amanullah were touring Europe, conservative forces at home began a campaign condemning their personal life and their modernization programs as anti-Islamic. Images of the queen unveiled and wearing Western clothes, presumably distributed by the British eager to destabilize a regime that had defeated them during the third Anglo-Afghan war, circulated in the tribal regions of Afghanistan (Ahmed-Ghosh 2003a, 5). According to Louis Dupree (1973, 452), "Amanullah struck at the roots of conservative Islam by removing the veil from the women, by opening co-educational schools, and by attempting to force all Afghans in Kabul to wear Western clothing."

As the reform increased in momentum, resentment grew among conservative religious leaders. The revolt quickly spread and a tribal army moved on Kabul, recruiting supporters on its way. The king's neglect for the creation of a national army to support his programs at a moment when Afghanistan was barely united as a nation left him disarmed with no choice but flight (L. Dupree 1973, 450). Despite his last minute attempts to negotiate with tribal leaders and his efforts to tackle public discontent by withdrawing some of his reforms, Amanullah was finally overthrown and replaced by a new generation of kings who avoided pushing the women's agenda to the detriment of tribal rules.

After his eviction in 1929, his successor Habibullah Ghazi insisted upon a return to conservative customs regarding women. "He demanded that women remain behind the veil under strict male control and that girls' schools, together with all other vestiges of the women's movement, be suspended" (N. H. Dupree 1984, 319). Zahir Shah, his successor, introduced limited reforms that remained nonbinding in order to avoid the opposition of the mullahs. The institutional model deployed to promote women's rights remained rooted in royal initiatives, with upper-class educated urban women gradually join-ing as the country started to develop its economy.

The Reign of Zahir Shah and the Decades of Daud, 1953–73

By the midcentury, massive foreign and technical assistance from the Soviet Union pushed Afghanistan forward on its journey toward modernization. Women were encouraged to participate in the economic effort in order to support the country's development goals. The 1940s and 1950s saw the first women nurses, teachers, and doctors (Ahmed-Ghosh 2003a, 6). In 1950–51, university faculties reserved for women were created in medicine, the sciences, and the humanities—parallel to those exclusively for men—in the newly founded Kabul University (Centlivres-Demont 1994, 338).

A number of women's associations with members recruited in the liberal upper and middle classes were created. The Muassasa-i Khayriyya-i Zanan (Women's Welfare Association, WWA) was established by Zaynab Inayat Siraj and Bibi Jan, both members of the royal family. Although it tried to promote unveiling, the emphasis of WWA was to encourage income-generating ac-tivities and to modernize women by providing literacy, family planning, and vocational classes. In 1953 it established the journal *Mirman*. In 1975 WWA became institutionally independent and changed its name to the Women's Institute (WI). The WI had branch offices in ten provincial cities and grew to eight thousand members. However, despite its attempts at reaching out to rural women by opening offices in the provinces, the organization failed to take steps outside elite social classes (Majrooh 1989, 95). Kubra Noorzai, the institute's director, was nevertheless elected to the National Assembly under President Daud and the organization began to promote gender equality through the state's modernization policies (Emadi 2002, 91–92).

In 1959, the government of King Zahir Shah formally announced the vol-untary end of female seclusion and the removal of the veil. However, it was left to individual families to decide how to respond to these greater freedoms and, outside the major urban centers, life for most women remained largely unchanged (Zulfacar 2006, 33). Nevertheless, in the following years the gov-ernment introduced girls' schools and medical facilities for women where they could receive training in both nursing and administration. The Constitution of 1964 granted significant rights to women, including the right to vote. How-ever, the overall participation of women in politics remained extremely low.

Figure 5. "Rural nurse from village clinic near Kabul." From *Afghanistan: Ancient Land with Modern Ways* (Afghanistan Ministry of Planning, 1969), 56.

As a result of the slow process of modernization initiated in the 1960s and 1970s, especially in the capital city, deeper changes began to take shape in urban areas. With new education and employment opportunities available, the urban population became more stratified. This period saw the emergence of an educated middle class in the major cities of Afghanistan. Women who found employment in the public administration began to develop new viewpoints and expectations. In the 1970s the stratum of urban elite women began to grow. These women had very different lifestyles from those of rural women, working alongside men in professional, technical, and support functions in government services and the private sector (Moghadam 1994, 863). The visibility of women in offices, in the streets, and at parties indicated a new habitus with gender mixing becoming the distinctive sign of the urban upper class.

In 1965, the People's Democratic Party of Afghanistan (PDPA), a Soviet-backed socialist organization, was formed. That same year the women's section of the party, the Democratic Organization of Afghan Women (DOAW), was created. Its main objectives were to eliminate illiteracy and ban bride-price as well as forced marriage. A few years after the republic was declared in 1973 a penal code (1976) and a civil law (1977) were introduced, "both of which followed the constitutional injunction that 'there can be no law repugnant to the sacred religion of Islam'" (N. H. Dupree 1984, 310). These laws however maintained the ideal of patriarchal control, and women were kept in positions that did not challenge their "honor" as well as that of their family. By contrast, during the Communist regime, the more aggressive approach to women's empowerment and the overtly secularist rhetoric that accompanied these reforms were decisive factors in the resistance that emerged all over the country.

Violent demonstrations took place in the country's major cities, especially in universities where some unveiled women wearing short skirts became the target of acid attacks. Conservative religious reactions to women's education and emancipation were a key feature of the antigovernment protests of the 1970s, which finally resulted in the leftist coup d'état of April 1978.

Cultural and Artistic Life

For urban upper- and middle-class women, the reign of Zahir Shah was a period of openness and freedom. Afghanistan was at peace. Located on the hippie trail, Kabul attracted tourists from Europe and North America, search-

Figure 6. Record store, Kabul. From *Afghanistan: Ancient Land with Modern Ways* (Afghanistan Ministry of Planning, 1969), 145.

ing for spirituality, adventure, and cheap drugs. In Kabul, Chicken and Flower Streets had shops, cafés, guesthouses, and restaurants where Afghans and foreigners met, intermingled, and sometimes made friends.

Radio Television Afghanistan broadcast foreign movies in which new lifestyles were promoted. With the creation of the first national film production company, Afghan Film, in 1965, the Afghan film industry blossomed. It produced documentaries and news films highlighting the official meetings and conferences of the government before it started to produce its first feature films in the 1970s. Radio Kabul, later on renamed Radio Afghanistan, the state-owned radio, hosted a whole generation of modern Afghan artists such as Ustad Mohammad Hussain Sarahang, Ustad Farida Mahwash,[1] and Ustad Mohammad Hashem Cheshti. These master musicians were revered not only in Afghanistan but also in India, Pakistan, and the entire Middle East. King Zahir Shah promoted dramatic art by creating the National Theatre Company

Figure 7. "Radio Kabul announcer during one of the station's many daily news programmes." From *Afghanistan: Ancient Land with Modern Ways* (Afghanistan Ministry of Planning, 1969), 110.

and building Kabul National Theatre, and with its construction the first generation of female actresses were recruited.

This version of "modernity" that the different governments, from Amanullah to Zahir Shah and later on Daud and the Communists, tried to impose remained largely alien to the majority of the Afghan population. Outward looking, the agenda of reforms and foreign tastes kept the poorer classes alienated from the process. This reconfiguration of Afghan identity along values and lifestyles considered as "foreign" indicated a move away from a traditional Islamic lifestyle that did not help unite the Afghan population and in fact achieved the opposite. Ideals of equality conveyed by the new media challenged patriarchal authority and created intense public distress. The visibility of women in public life disturbed the norm of private family life, turning women and sexuality into contested political matters. Modernists envisioned the veiling of women as the main obstacle to Westernization, while the Islamists saw it as the leading symbolic force against the degeneration of society (Göle 1996, 52). The absence of communication between the ruling class and the rural majority was largely caused by the secular criteria for modernization. This meant cultural alienation for those who felt threatened by these new norms, a situation that became acute when a Marxist modernizing elite started to exert its influence within the government from the mid 1960s onward.

The Communist Regime, 1979–92

In 1965 the People's Democratic Party of Afghanistan (PDPA) was formed, a pro-Communist group that may have helped Mohammad Daud to seize power from his cousin King Zahir Shah and declare Afghanistan a republic in 1973. He was toppled in turn by his former PDPA allies in April 1978 during what is known as the Saur Revolution.

The Communist period was marked by a proactive approach toward the implementation of gender policies. Decrees were introduced as part of a program of social and political reforms intended to effect the rapid transformation of a patriarchal society (Moghadam 2004, 454). For instance, a decree limited the payment of bride-price and gave greater freedom of choice to women with respect to marriage. Another one raised the marriagable age for girls to sixteen years. In addition, the government launched an aggressive literacy program aimed at educating women and removing them from seclusion (Majrooh 1989, 90). However, in the city each family accommodated aspects of modernity compatible with their general lifestyle, which generally meant a certain degree of compliance with patriarchal demands and norms when it came to important decisions regarding female mobility and, above all, marriage. Such intimate family matters belonged then as now to personal space (*mahrem*) and still suffer no interference in urban and rural families alike.

During this period, women were present in all major government departments as well as in the police force, the army, business, and industry. Women taught, studied, and acted as judges in the Family Court, dealing with issues

related to divorce, custody of children, and other family matters. They composed over 75 percent of teachers, 40 percent of medical doctors, and almost
50 percent of civil servants, all of them city based (Emadi 2002).

Women were also present in the different ranks of the party and the government with the exception of the Council of Ministers. The Loya Jirga (parliament) counted seven female members in 1989. The Central Committee of
the PDPA included Jamila Palwasha and Ruhafza (alternate member), "a
working-class grandmother and 'model worker' at the Kabul Construction
Plant, where she did electrical wiring" (Moghadam 2002, 24). Women were
working in security, in intelligence, and on the police force. They were
employed as logisticians in the Defense Ministry. In 1989, all female members of the PDPA received military training and weapons.

The true innovation of the People's Democratic Party of Afghanistan was
the women's branch of the party, the Democratic Organization of Afghan
Women, also founded in 1965, which set about to address specifically every
aspect of women's conditions, not only limited to issues of marriage, with the
aim of turning women into citizens and partners in an egalitarian secular
society (Moghadam 1994).

The program of the DOAW was very much based on strategies of public
visibility, which involved women's enrollment in grand marches organized
by the party to foster ideas of women's emancipation. Nancy Hatch Dupree
writes: "Frequently, these grand marches ended in 'volunteer clean-up' sessions, and the people of Kabul were treated for the first time to the sight of
girls wielding brooms, sweeping the streets in public in the company of men"
(1984, 318).

Nevertheless, the distance between reforms on paper and actual practice
was considerable. The DOAW and its supporters were generally sophisticated
cosmopolitan middle- to upper-class women with a foreign education—just
like the progressive circles around Kings Habibullah and Amanullah with
equally limited connections to the rural majority. According to Nancy Hatch
Dupree (1984, 317), women activists under the Communist regime were totally co-opted to "the purposeful manipulation of the women's movement as
an appendage to national politics." As a result, no strong and well-organized
women's movement emerged from this period.

In the countryside, the imposition of compulsory education for both boys
and girls, forced enrollment of men and women in "detachments for the Defence of the Revolution,"[2] and coercive secularization attempts provoked
strong resentment and resistance. In general, gender policies implemented

Figure 8. General Khotul Mohammadzai, 1970s. Collection of Julie Billaud.

under the Soviet occupation were imposed with little sensitivity for local codes and practices, often using heavy-handed tactics to implement programs. The PDPA coup of 1978 met with violent opposition not so much because of its progressive ideology but because of its brutal implementation, which cost the lives of thousands of Afghan citizens. The reforms, instead of being presented in a pragmatic, technical manner, were given a Marxist packaging that

Figure 9. "Women at a demonstration in Kabul" (original caption). From
The Revolution Continues, ed. Makhmud Baryalai, Abdullo Spantghar, and
Vladimir Grib (Moscow: Planeta, 1984), 58.

alienated the vast majority of the population. Compulsory education, especially for women, was largely perceived as an encroachment of the state in
families' private affairs. The secular narrative that accompanied the reforms
was seen as going against tradition, as antireligious, and as a challenge to
male authority. This lack of regard for religious and societal sensibilities
resulted in massive backlash, especially in rural areas.

The war against the Soviet occupation had a devastating impact on Afghanistan's economy. An estimated five million people fled to Pakistan,
Iran, and further afield. As a result of the war, social services provided by

Figure 10. "Volunteer detachments for the Defence of the Revolution include urban and rural workers, men and women, middle aged people and young patriots of the Democratic Republic of Afghanistan. Their country has given them arms to fight the enemies of the Revolution and they are defending it without thought of their own life" (original caption). From *The Revolution Continues*, ed. Makhmud Baryalai, Abdullo Spantghar, and Vladimir Grib (Moscow: Planeta, 1984), 193.

the government became largely limited to the urban centers. Both the human and economic costs and losses of the war were enormous.

Jihad

Armed by the United States, the different mujahideen factions organized resistance from the refugee camps in Pakistan to their villages of origin. Village women participated in the movement in various ways: by transporting weapons under their *chadari*, installing landmines around their village, looking after the wounded, and cooking for the combatants (N. H. Dupree 1984).

Women did not only support the jihad but they also encouraged their husbands to go to war. Of the time of resistance against the Soviets, cultural historian Nancy Dupree writes: "During the *jihad* one would often see men coming home from the war to rest with their families in the Pakistani camps. If they were a little slow about going back to the battlefield, the women would push and shame them into doing their duty for the *jihad*. The women therefore played a vital part in the war, for it was their strength that motivated men to keep fighting" (1986, 10). From their participation in the resistance movement, women developed a sense of pride and usefulness. In recognition for their participation in the war effort some of them were given political positions once the mujahideen government took over Kabul.

Pul-i-Charkhi

Conducting clandestine activities was not without risk. Repression was severe, systematic, and merciless. Political opponents were tracked by the secret services, arrested, tortured, and executed. Located just east of Kabul, the prison of Pul-i-Charkhi became one of the darkest holes in the last quarter century of Afghanistan's war-torn history. During the years of Soviet and Communist control, hundreds of thousands of prisoners were kept behind the solid stone walls in dark concrete cells with unknown thousands never coming out alive, victims of nightly executions on the military range beyond the prison walls (Barry 2002).

What happened behind the stone walls of Pul-i-Charkhi reflects the dark side of the PDPA's political agenda. Modernization projects conducted under the Communist government were meant to convey an ideology, a particular vision of social organization that tolerated no opposition. The immense enterprise of social engineering was conducted by the regime under the guise of development aimed at gaining people's consent for the Red Army's occupation of the country. But the remolding of the Afghan nation along secular lines triggered fierce resistance to social changes that were perceived as threats to Afghan culture and tradition. In obedience to the Islamic principle of leaving lands occupied by infidels, millions of Afghans sought refuge in Iran and Pakistan.

Life in the Refugee Camps

During this period Afghanistan became the battlefield upon which the United States conducted a proxy war against the Soviet Union. The Afghan resistance movement was organized around U.S.-sponsored conservative

Islamist groups under the rubric of the mujahideen. The very first refugee camps were probably extensions of military training camps that the Pakistani government built for the opponents of the left-wing and pro-Soviet elements of the Afghan government. Since 1973 (nearly six years before the Soviet intervention) Gulbudin Hekmatyar, Ahmad Shah Masood, and Burnan-uddin Rabbani—the leaders of resistance—had fled to Peshawar to build up support with the help of the Pakistani government. A number of camps, military in origin, may have been conceived as rallying points around specific military commanders with strong fundamentalist leanings, not just as neutral gathering places for refugees (Mackenzie 2001).

As in Chile, Guatemala, Indonesia, and the Congo, the United States supported opponents to the pro-Soviet regime, without any regard for their violations of human rights or their reactionary social goals. Warlords such as Gulbuddin Hekmatyar, who later became a fervent supporter of the Taliban and who received substantial financial support from the United States, were considered by the United States as "freedom fighters" and were trained in military camps in Afghanistan and in Pakistan.

Unlike other liberation movements elsewhere, the Afghan mujahideen never encouraged the active participation of women in jihad. Women in Peshawar who criticized the politics of the mujahideen were threatened and sometimes killed. This is what happened to Meena Keshwar Kamal - almost universally known by just her first name - founder of the Revolutionary Association of the Women of Afghanistan (RAWA), who denounced the gender discriminatory policies of the fundamentalist groups together with the Soviet occupation of Afghanistan (Moghadam 1994).

Attacks against women did not begin with the Taliban. In the mujahideen-ruled refugee camps in Pakistan, women had to face constant restrictions of movement and threats to their lives. In 1989, a fatwa (religious decree) was promulgated against women who worked for humanitarian organizations. Women were also requested to wear the *hijab* (head covering) and to strictly respect the rules of purdah. According to the fatwa, "women were not to wear perfume, noisy bangles or Western clothes. Veils had to cover the body at all times and clothes were not to be made of material which was soft or which rustled. Women were not to walk in the middle of the street or swing their hips, they were not to talk, laugh, or joke with strangers or foreigners" (Moghadam 2002, 25). A year later, girls were forbidden to attend school. The United States never reacted to these decrees and simply abandoned the Afghans once their proxy war with the Soviet Union was over.

Under mujahideen control, the camps provided laboratory conditions to experiment with modern forms of gendered repression. The rigorous separation of the sexes was reinforced through the mobilization of men to the cause of jihad and military operations. Separated from their male relatives, women were rooted in the camps, under the control of religious and fundamentalist leaders (Olesen 1996). Therefore, the fundamentalist attitude to women could be summarized as a vindictive application of sharia within the context of a political program aimed at the establishment of a complete Islamic state, justified by what they considered to be a literal interpretation of the Koran. Traditional appeals to modesty and self-effacement were turned into systematic interdiction of any visible form of feminine expression that was interpreted as anti-Islamic. These policies were implemented by the mujahideen when they took control of Kabul in 1992 and further reinforced when the Taliban came to power.

The Civil War, 1992–96

During the years of Soviet occupation, Kabul had been perceived as the origin of all the country's misfortunes. For the conservative rural-based mujahideen opposition, which had been supported by the United States during the Cold War, Kabul and other cities were perceived to be the centers of "sin" and "vice" precisely because of the high visibility of educated, emancipated urban women. There was a widespread perception that the population of Kabul had collaborated with and had been therefore corrupted by the Soviet regime. Many mujahideen groups shared the idea that the people of Kabul should be punished for their "immoral values" (Kandiyoti 2005). As Tamin Ansary (2001) puts it: "When the Mujahedin finally toppled the last Communist ruler out of Afghanistan and marched into Kabul, it was not just the triumph of the Afghan people against the foreign invaders but the conquest, finally, of Kabul (and its culture) by the countryside."

One of the first orders of the new mujahideen government was that women should be veiled in public. In August 1993, the government's Office of Research and Decrees of the Supreme Court went a step further by issuing an order to dismiss all female civil servants from their posts. The decree stated that "women need not leave their homes at all, unless absolutely necessary, in which case, they are to cover themselves completely; are not to wear attractive clothing and decorative accessories; do not wear perfume; their jewelery must not make any noise; they are not to walk gracefully or with pride and in the middle of the sidewalk" (Emadi 2002, 124).

The decrees promulgated under the Taliban regime presented the same recommendations. The Taliban did not introduce a radically new political agenda but officialized dress codes and social conduct for both men and women, which were in any case followed by the majority of the population under the different mujahideen governments for fear of repression.

The high hopes that greeted the arrival of the new mujahideen government were quickly dashed as conflict erupted between the different factions in the coalition. Most of Kabul was reduced to rubble as ceasefires were agreed to and then quickly broken. As alliances changed, the front lines of conflict shifted within the city. There were widespread reports of women being raped as different factions wrested control of opposing neighborhoods of the city. Women, who represented the majority of trained teachers and nurses, lost their employment due to the closing and destruction of most of the city's infrastructure.

The mujahideen rule was therefore the blueprint upon which the Taliban phenomenon could rise. Instead of a breach in policies, the Taliban regime radicalized the mujahideen legacy. Their success in getting control over the country was not the result of their fundamentalist ideology, which was generally perceived as excessive and unacceptable among the majority of the population, but rather the outcome of a well-trained and properly equipped military contingent gradually gaining strength as the country grappled with war and destruction.

The Taliban Rule, 1996–2001

The Taliban emerged in a political vacuum created by the civil war and people's longing for security and the end of conflict between the different mujahideen factions. The movement was created in the Afghan refugee camps in Pakistan where its major figures received religious and military education. Indeed in 1977, Pakistan's dictator, General Zia-ul-Haq, enforced an Islamic constitution, ostensibly to bring legal, social, economic, and political institutions of the country in conformity with the Koran. He unsurprisingly backed the Afghan militants in Peshawar and financed the building of thousands of madrassas in the vicinity of refugee camps with help from Saudi Arabia. Impoverished Afghan widows reassured by the promise of regular meals and a minimum education eagerly entrusted their sons to the care of the madrassas that became the training grounds for the Taliban and Al-Qaeda supporters. Herded in decrepit boardinghouses, cut off from contact with mothers and sisters, they were fed an extremely simplified messianic Islam, which was to become the Taliban creed. Three years after their emergence on the Afghan military scene, the Taliban had taken control of over 80 percent of Afghanistan. As they gradually consolidated their power, security improved in the cities, facilitating exchanges and circulation of goods and therefore reviving the economy.

According to Nancy Dupree (2001, 151), the Taliban's decision to impose the strict curtailment of women together with their compulsory veiling under *chadari* in public was a means for the regime to "send a message of its intent to subordinate the personal autonomy of every individual, thereby strengthening the impression that it was capable of exercising control over all aspects of social behaviour, male and female." When the international community reacted against these measures and denounced what became labeled as "gender apartheid," the Taliban high authorities argued that their aim was to ensure their sisters' security in a period when the priority was the establishment of law and order. Whether or not the limitations imposed on women would have progressively disappeared had the Taliban totally eliminated their opponents and had been recognized by the international community remains a difficult question to answer. However, the Taliban policies were marked by many contradictions and inconsistencies that left much room for interpretation and accommodation at the local level.

The Taliban central government was far from functioning effectively. Its base of power lay primarily in a very young militia nurtured in the isolation of ultraconservative madrassas where they imbibed ideas by rote without the encouragement of open inquiry. Most of them had never been exposed to urban living. The weakness of the central government allowed decisions to be made to a great extent at the local level. Women's condition therefore varied from one region to another according to the degree of flexibility of the local Taliban authorities (N. H. Dupree 2001).

The management of local affairs was deeply reliant on local Taliban leaders, some of whom allowed a certain level of negotiation on their policies. It is in the cities where women had traditionally enjoyed a greater degree of personal autonomy that the rules imposed by the new regime appeared the harshest. As the Taliban captured Kabul in 1996, they closed schools and Kabul University to female students and teachers. These policies had a devastating impact on both boys' and girls' education as women represented an important proportion of teachers and university professors. Women's seclusion was announced on Radio Sharia on the day Kabul fell into Taliban's hands. During the entire length of the Taliban rule, the regime would inform the population about new rules and regulations through this same station: "Women, you should not step outside of your residence. If you go outside the house you should not be like women who used to go with fashionable clothes wearing cosmetics and appearing in front of every man before the coming of Islam. . . . Women should not create such opportunity to attract the attention of useless people who will not look at them with a good eye. Women have the responsibility as a teacher and coordinator for her family. Husband, brother, father have the responsibility for providing the family with the necessary life requirements (food, clothes, etc.)" (Rostami-Povey 2007, 24).

But men were not protected from the regime's hold on their lives. The length of their beard and the appropriateness of their clothes were under the constant scrutiny of the religious police. The regime focused upon punishing them for infractions committed by their female relatives, reflecting the acceptance of male responsibility for controlling women (N. H. Dupree 2001).

In a matter of a few decades, Afghanistan had moved from a regime that in the 1920s, under the reign of King Amanullah, had imposed the wearing of European clothes in Kabul to a regime that wanted to break away from any form of Western influence and return to what it perceived as "authentic tradition." In both cases, ideas about modernity and tradition were translated in regulations targeting individuals' physical appearance in public spaces. This disciplining of bodies and the specific emphasis on regulating and controlling women's appearance in public are symptomatic of the broader struggle between Kabul and its peripheries, on one hand, and the irreconcilable viewpoints of the reformist elite and the Islamists, on the other hand. Women's bodies stood at the front line of this ideological battle. The failure of the successive governments to carry out positive development projects in the peripheries together with foreign interference in internal affairs had produced a unique form of countermodernity.

As a social, ideological, and political phenomenon the Taliban are indeed utterly modern. The origin of the Taliban movement, its military development, and its political project highlight characteristic features of globalized warfare. Their emergence on the Afghan political scene is not to be interpreted as a simple return to an authentic Afghan tradition. On the contrary, the global assemblages in which the movement was enmeshed provided the fertile ground from which tradition could be imagined and reinvented. These assemblages are partially the products of the influence of external Islamic sources on their political ideology. Educated in madrassas, the Taliban were introduced to the Deobandi school of thoughts by semi-literate Pakistani mullahs associated with Pakistan's Jami'at-e Ulema-e Islam (JUI) political party (Rashid 2002). A lack of appreciation on the part of the mullahs of the reformist Deobandi agenda brought the schools and their curricula closer to ultraconservative Wahhabism (founded in Saudi Arabia), which claims to teach strict adherence to the practices of the Prophet Muhammad and the Four "rightly guided" Caliphs (Rashid 1999, 26). This interpretation of Islam provided the ideological framework from which the Taliban formulated their opposition first to the Communist government and later on to the mujahideen in cultural terms that were relatively efficient to rally the rural masses, especially in the Pashtun southern part of the country. Deobandi Islam had no roots in Afghanistan; however, it provided a template for reinterpreting the Pashtun code of honor, codifying it through decrees and finally unevenly implementing it at the national level when they came to power. Second, the Taliban political project is quintessentially cosmopolitan. Armed by Pakistan, supported by the United States and Saudi Arabia, and trained by transnational Islamic mercenaries, the Taliban were well equipped to win on the military front. Their political agenda aimed at creating a pure Islamic state based on sharia law, a state that would protect people from the polluting West. Ironically, the ones who called themselves "Taliban" (literally, "students in religion") were often illiterate and therefore unable to read a line of the Koran.

Most of them had had little contact with women prior to entering the capital city. Like the young mujahideen who came to Kabul in 1992, they shared "similar ideas about upright female behaviour: 'good' women stay home, 'bad' women expose their faces" (N. H. Dupree 2001, 150). However, the policies that they implemented regarding women provoked adaptations that were far from their initial intent. As Nancy Dupree points out (2001, 160), women creatively adjusted to this political change by making their own fashion statements. Reporting on the forced veiling of women under *chadari*, she writes: "Burnt orange and forest green are fashionable in Jalalabad; various clear shades of blue accented by occasional canary yellow flit about Kabul; black was never usual, except among some groups in Herat. Made mostly of soft artificial silk, the veils shimmer and billow with a certain mysterious seductiveness."

The Taliban enforced the total curtailment of women's freedom to move, to work, and to be educated. Discrimination was officially sanctioned and pervaded every aspect of women's lives. Girls were forbidden to attend school, even when provided at home. Women faced draconian punishment for adultery. Women were denied the freedom to work and were forbidden to leave their homes unless completely veiled under *chadari* and accompanied by a male relative (*mahram*). Such restrictions were particularly alien to women in Kabul and many were slow to comply. Confrontations between women and the religious police supervised by the Ministry for Prevention of Vice and Promotion of Virtue, the most powerful arm of the regime, occurred daily until, paralyzed by fear, women finally complied. Women were beaten up in the streets for wearing nail polish, white socks (the color of the Taliban flag), shiny shoes, or a *chadari* that was not long enough (N. H. Dupree 2001, 152).

These recent and traumatic events are strongly engrained in the psyche of urban women. In spite of their fear, many women, often with the support of male family members, started to organize underground activities and support networks. These activities helped them cope with the stress of their secluded life. By morally supporting each other and providing services for their community, women regained a sense of worth and usefulness.

Most women who conducted such activities did not view their involvement as a political act but as a survival strategy, deeply embedded in the material conditions of their everyday lives. To be able to run such activities and keep a minimum of mobility, women had to develop creative strategies. Some of them recruited and employed fake *mahrams* when male relatives were not available. Others mobilized other women from public spaces where women's presence was not suspicious such as mosques and *ziharat* (sites of pilgrimage). During this period, the *chadari* became a protective device, a "mobile home" that allowed women to circulate in public spaces without being questioned or threatened. Women used their *chadari* to smuggle books and stationery for their schools, the same way they had smuggled weapons during the jihad.

Thanks to these informal courses secretly attended, many young women managed to continue their education and to escape from total isolation. Women demonstrated a real sense of creativity and ingenuity in the face of particularly difficult economic and social conditions. For most women, belonging to a network was a means to escape from boredom and to find moral support. By attending or running courses, women opened for themselves spaces where they could share their sorrows and exchange small services. If these everyday small acts of resistance empowered women and enhanced their self-confidence, they led them to sternly challenge broader gender hierarchies, especially in a context where maintaining social relations was and is still perceived as vital.

The Taliban regime affected different women in different ways. The relative peace the Taliban brought in rural areas provided women with a sense of safety they had not been able to enjoy during the civil war. The stability they recovered during this period allowed them to participate in the local economy. In cities, however, the brutality with which the Taliban implemented their policies remains a traumatic experience for most women.

Conclusion

The addition of a veil over Queen Soraya in the portrait gallery of the Ministry of Information and Culture just after the collapse of the Taliban while at the same moment images of women lifting their veils in the streets of Kabul were broadcast on Western TV channels as symbols of "women's liberation" underlines the complex and contested position of women in the reconstruction period. Their bodies, at times veiled and hidden, at others displayed and unveiled, are sites of political struggles over national identity. From the 1920s onward, the "woman question" has been manipulated to serve political purposes and to assert opposite views of civilization. The archive pictures that illustrate this chapter should not be taken at face value: their purpose was less to document everyday life in Afghanistan than to promote an image of progress and development for external audiences. The display of images of women taking part in public life, wearing Western clothes, and working side by side with men was meant to portray Afghanistan as contemporary to "modern and civilized" nations.

A closer look at the history of women in Afghanistan demonstrates how, in addition to gender, other sets of variables such as class and the urban/rural divide have to be taken into account in order to understand the variety of women's experiences. Women in the countryside benefited neither from the expanding public services nor from the dynamic cultural and intellectual movements and events that made the period prior to the Soviet occupation exhilarating for urban women. The revolutionary changes and relatively liberal social values and norms experienced by educated middle- and upper-class women in the 1960s and 1970s stood in stark contrast to the tribal and traditional values shaping the life of the majority of Afghan women at the time.

The plight of Afghan women under the Taliban rule was widely publicized in the aftermath of the September 11, 2001, attacks on the United States as one of the humanitarian issues justifying intervention. However, the political context in which the Taliban movement emerged was hardly mentioned. Their gender discriminatory policies, which resulted in the social exclusion of women, were mostly explained by misidentified expressions of local "culture." But the Taliban did not arise out of thin air. The emergence of religious fundamentalism in the region has been the result of broader geopolitical developments that involved the interference of foreign countries such as the United States, Pakistan, and Saudi Arabia during the Cold War period.

Finally, the history of Afghanistan shows that reforms aimed at changing the status of women raised hopes and fears, expectations and resistance in the social arena. From the reign of Amanullah to the Taliban regime, the contested rights of women became a primary symbol of the new order. All efforts by reformist kings from the early twentieth century onward were doomed due to their incapacity to incorporate the rural peripheries into their programs and to envision indigenous paths for social transformation. When the Communist government attempted to introduce an egalitarian society and implement women's rights under a secular framework and through coercion, acute civil strife ensued.

The Islamist movements that have regained power in the region since the 1980s have focused on the disciplining of women's bodies because they represent a political site of difference and resistance to the homogenizing and egalitarian forces of Western modernity (Göle 1996). By promoting the return to strict Islamic clothing, these movements attempt to reassert a collective identity. Far from being a return to greater religiosity and ritual practice, these movements have focused, like the modernists before them, on lifestyles and attitudes in public because they signal shared societal values and moral norms.

CHAPTER 2

National Women's Machinery: Coaching Lives in the Ministry of Women's Affairs

Four years after my first journey, in winter 2007, I landed in Kabul for the second time. Renovations had somewhat improved the appearance of the small airport trapped between snowy mountaintops. Customs officers in uniforms were equipped with computers, the moving walkways were running, and passengers were directed toward waiting lines. A semblance of organization prevailed. But what surprised me the most was to discover that even though the city's infrastructure still remained in disarray, billboards and commercials had anarchically invaded the streets of Kabul. "Roshan, Nazdik shodan!" (Roshan, close to you!), a new mobile phone company advertised. "Urdu y melli Afghan ba shoma zaroorat darad!" (The Afghan National Army wants you!) stated a military officer pointing a finger at an imaginary observer on a poster that copied the famous World War I military recruitment campaign in the United States. "Hafteh se parvaz ba Dubai baa Kam Air" (Fly three times a week to Dubai with Kam'air) announced the new airline company owned by the powerful commander Rashid Dostum. The advertisement boom signaled a radical shift not only because under the Taliban images had totally disappeared from public spaces—a decree had declared visual representations of human beings un-Islamic and banned TV sets and cameras—but also because of the sharp contrast between these consumerist messages and the increased visibility of public poverty resulting from internal displacements and massive returns of refugees.

Sayara Media and Communication, the firm for which I worked for a while at the beginning of my fieldwork, was one of the many advertising and communication companies that had opened offices in Kabul in the first days of the "reconstruction." Equipped with brand new Macintosh computers, a re-

Figure 11. Woman's face erased on an advertisement billboard, Herat, 2007.
Photo by Julie Billaud.

cording studio, and a video department, Sayara resembled any other communication agency that could be found elsewhere except for the invasive dust
and the deafening sound of the generator that produced electricity. Here too,
employees were trendy young people, badly shaved and wearing blue jeans
under the local *kameez* (long shirt or tunic) in a self-conscious modern reinterpretation of traditional Afghan clothing. Saraya's employees had been recruited locally and internationally by a team of three European managers,
who had initially come to Afghanistan as development workers. From behind
their computer screens, graphic designers, video producers, and project managers were designing the new face of Afghanistan.

This new visual culture is not only shaping the aspirations of the Afghan
population but is also a powerful instrument in the hands of the government
and the international community to promote new lifestyles and ideas about
modernity and development. The emergence of the advertising industry and
its overwhelming presence on television and radio is also symptomatic of the
broader shift that Afghan society under NATO occupation is witnessing. In
a country where electricity and roads are seriously lacking, a third of the population is living below the poverty line (World Bank 2011),[1] and access to

health services(WHO 2014)[2] and education (UNICEF 2013)[3] remain quasi-nonexistent, advertisement is the symbol of a pending reconstruction, a reconstruction taking place mostly on paper, television screens, and radio waves. The messages delivered through these different media outlets associated modernity with Western lifestyles and modes of consumption. However, the erasure of the unveiled woman's face on an advertisement billboard (see Figure 11) shows that this version of modernity remains highly contested and is a source of deep social anxieties. Indeed, with the arrival of international development experts, diplomats, NGO workers and NATO troops, Western ideas and "modernization" policies are being imposed through economic and cultural programs in tandem with a new urban conception, shaping new social imaginaries regarding the appearance of men and women in public.

It is ironic that while images of women have reappeared on media interfaces, flesh and blood women have gradually disappeared from the streets of Kabul as the security situation continues to deteriorate. Women's faces show up in stylized color on the laminated covers of magazines. In the third season of *Afghan Star*—the local equivalent of the famous television show *American Idol*—broadcast on Tolo TV, the first commercial television station in Afghanistan, a young Kandahari woman called Lima Sahar sang her way to the top three finalists. To the external observer, Afghanistan seems to have set its time on the global clock.

Since the invasion of Afghanistan, the reappearance of women in the public sphere has been the benchmark upon which the success of the democratization process has been measured. In the same way as the Communist regime appropriated the rights and visibility of women as the central symbol of modernity, the current government has been encouraged by the international community to increase women's participation in public life. Among the different legal and institutional instruments put in place to increase women's participation in public life, a Ministry of Women's Affairs (MoWA) was created shortly after the Bonn conference in December 2001. Based on the Women's High Association, a welfare-oriented women's institute hailing from the pre-Communist era, this national women's machinery had as its main objectives the improvement of the situation of women and mainstream gender issues. As in earlier modernization attempts conducted under King Amanullah in the 1920s, King Zahir Shah in the 1960s and 1970s, and the Communist regime in the 1980s, this institution was grounded on a top-down approach to women's emancipation. Detached from any strong indigenous women's movement, staffed with an urban middle-class elite, and deprived of significant financial means to carry out its vaguely defined mandate, the MoWA represented the "window dressing" of the new Islamic republic.

The current efforts to include women in politics and to promote women's rights are integral parts of the reconstruction process. However, despite attempts at presenting these reforms in technical terms, their content is not value free and contains the seeds of important social changes. In the absence of concrete material improvements in most Afghan people's lives, these reforms have created anxieties and tensions related to a form of social engineering broadly perceived as foreign to Afghan culture and tradition. This chapter illustrates how liberal ideas of freedom, progress, and rationality usually associated with modern state building are being introduced into Afghan society not merely through the use of coercive force but through positive technologies of power enshrined in bureaucratic practice. Building on a case study of a "gender empowerment" training program run by the Ministry of Women's Affairs and supported by an international organization, I underline and analyze the cultural dimension of the current agenda of reforms. I show how the adoption of the development jargons (and in particular the ones related to gender) and the reproduction of specific bureaucratic practices have become the means for Afghan elites and development actors to maintain relationships and to preserve a rank and position, even when such discourses are in sharp contrast with the social reality and material needs of ordinary people. I unpack the ideological framework through which "reconstruction" is implemented and show its historical continuity with earlier modernization attempts. I argue that the construction of the modern Afghan state does not simply consist in setting up a bureaucratic apparatus based on the Western model of liberal democracies but primarily involves cultural and symbolic production by means of rituals such as workshops, training, meetings, and the fabrication of information.

"Live Your Best Life! It Is Liberating!"

"I came to the United States with fifty words of English and fifty dollars in my pocket." This is how fifty-two-year-old Sonila Danaj, an American of Albanian origin employed as a women's empowerment trainer at the Ministry of Women's Affairs in Kabul, likes to introduce herself on her blog.[4] Sonila is officially a life empowerment coach and gender adviser in the United States. Her employer is a firm that specializes in identifying public speakers and entertainers for corporate events. Sonila runs a gender empowerment training program tailored for Afghan civil servants and political leaders. She is also one of the many advisers working beside the Minister of Women's Affairs under a broader gender program funded by GTZ, the German agency for cooperation and development.

I met Sonila at the Ministry of Women's Affairs during one of her training programs. On the business card she gave me she had written: "Inside every person there are strengths that can help you achieve an amazing success and fulfilment in your life. LIVE YOUR BEST LIFE. Empower yourself and change the world. It is liberating." In the meeting room, about twenty-five participants gathered. These men and women were representatives of provincial councils from Baghlan, Samangan, and Jozgan.[5] Some of them were *rish safed* (white beards) who proudly wore the turban and the *chapan*, a long-sleeved silk coat worn on the shoulders, the traditional uniform of authority figures in Afghanistan.

Sonila did not speak a word of Dari but she wore a full covering Arabic-style black *abaya*, a garment rarely worn in Afghanistan. Her training was simultaneously translated by two Afghan interpreters who seemed to struggle to find Dari equivalents for some of the concepts Sonila used. My friend Haroon, a medical doctor and part-time civil servant at the Ministry of Health, was one of the two interpreters. I asked him for his assessment, thinking that I could rely on his opinion since he had worked with Sonila on several occasions. He answered, smiling: "The Master is an unmarried woman. She is living with her cats in America and she has no children. In Afghanistan, we are polite with our guests. We have to make her feel at home." Unconvinced by his answer, I joined the group and took a seat in a corner of the room.

The first part of the training was conducted by a local staff member of Women's Campaign International, an NGO promoting women's political participation in developing countries. She explained the concept of "gender," its historical origin and why it is a relevant category to use in order to explain women's problems in Afghanistan. As the trainer was lecturing the audience, a man looked at his watch. Another one played with his mobile phone. A participant eventually interrupted her. He explained that currently neither men nor women can complete higher education because of the different problems facing the country. "Women who live in the West can study for twenty years," he said pointing at Sonila, "but here, women are just starting to study." Another male participant added: "In Afghanistan, women have more freedom than anywhere else in the world. They don't need to wear the full *hijab*, like in Iran. Why is the facilitator wearing *hijab*? She does not need to. We would have accepted her if she had come with the clothes she is used to wearing in America." This last comment was not translated to Sonila but she could already feel that tension was growing in the room. In an attempt to restore calm, she interrupted the debate and started a relaxation exercise. "Stand up! Shake your hands! Let's get rid of our bad energies. Hands up! And now grab apples! Let's find the positive energies!"

While Sonila was already jumping in the middle of the room, embarrassed smiles appeared on people's faces. An old man wearing *chapan* (traditional coat with long sleeves worn by men over their clothes) threw an interrogative glance at one of his colleagues. Watching these women and men dressed up in their traditional clothes jumping together in a room and grabbing imaginary apples in the air created a surreal air to the scene. I wondered what people's thoughts were behind the veil of compliance and docility. How does it feel when, after a long journey from Samangan, you find yourself in a ministry in Kabul doing relaxation games with your colleagues? Were they truly enjoying themselves or were they just trying to be polite with their guest from America? With these questions in mind, I did strange moves with my body, mimicking the greatest harvest of imaginary apples I have ever had in my entire life. And while doing this I tried to forget that I was in Kabul, that it was winter, and that outside, in front of the ministry, children without proper shoes were selling matches to passersby to make a living.

Time for a tea break had eventually come. I found Sonila sorting out papers she would need for the second part of the training. I congratulated her for her energy and asked her what the training programs have been like up to now.

It is hard work, you know, but I think they are starting to get it. Look at the faces of the participants I had in my previous training. This is how they looked before the training [*she passes me a sheet of paper with identification photographs of people*]. Watch their faces! They are all closed, unhappy. They look sad and worried. Now look at their faces after the training [*she passes me another sheet of paper with pictures of the same people taken after the training was completed*]. Look at them carefully and compare! Their faces have opened up. They are smiling. They are happy! I think these photographs are very telling.

I had come across such methods of success measurement in women's magazines where pictures of women are sometimes displayed before and after a specific diet, a facial makeover, or a cosmetic surgery operation. I was surprised to discover that marketing strategies were now being applied to development programs. I looked at the photographs and I read the names attached to them, trying to find in people's eyes what Sonila called "happiness."

The second half of the training was dedicated to techniques of self-empowerment. A participant was asked to come to the center of the circle in order to talk about his problems to the rest of the audience. The man seemed embarrassed and not very much willing to be the guinea pig for this experiment. But pressed by his colleagues, already laughing with excitement, he finally surrendered.

> SONILA. So tell us, what is exactly your problem? What do you really want?
> PARTICIPANT. The problem is that lots of people come to me to explain their problems. And I cannot do anything for them.
> SONILA. When you want something, you need to envision what you want in your head first. If you want to get a house, you need to see it in your head. What does your house look like in your head? How many rooms? How many stories? [*Addressing the audience*] He only sees the obstacles!
> PARTICIPANT, *looking totally disoriented*. For instance, I have some people who come to see me. Some of them have a university degree, a very good education, and they cannot find any job. I want to help them. But I cannot do anything for them.
> SONILA. He does not get it! I want to know what you want. What is your house?
> PARTICIPANT, *losing patience*. Of course, with time we can achieve some things. But worries remain in our heads until the problem is solved!
> SONILA. So how do you feel when you face such problems?
> PARTICIPANT. I get upset, emotional . . . [*looking for more adjectives*] I worry, I get angry . . . and bored.
> [*Translator writes on the white board: "upset," "emotional," "worried," "angry," "bored."*]
> SONILA. Do you feel powerless?
> PARTICIPANT. [*Nods.*] Yes.
> [*Translator writes "powerless" on the white board.*]

SONILA. Do you feel helpless?

PARTICIPANT. Yes.

[*Translator writes "helpless" on the white board.*]

SONILA. Do you feel discouraged?

PARTICIPANT. Hmmm . . . yes . . . I have headaches.

[*Translator writes "discouraged," "headaches" on the white board. Participants start losing patience. Murmurs spread in the room.*]

SONILA. Be patient! This is actually the most important key of this training!

TRANSLATOR, *pointing at participant.* He thinks it's enough.

[*Participants laugh. Translator reads the words he wrote on the white board.*]

SONILA. How do you feel when you hear that?

PARTICIPANT. When I hear that, I feel sad.

SONILA. Read it!

PARTICIPANT, *reading.* "Hopeless, headaches, discouraged . . ."

SONILA. Are you still upset?

PARTICIPANT. [*Nods.*]

SONILA. Let's make him even more upset. Let's read it together!

PARTICIPANTS, *reading together* "Hopeless, headaches, discouraged, disempowered . . ."

SONILA. How do you feel?

PARTICIPANT. OK.

SONILA. Let's help him find a solution! What is the opposite of powerless?

PARTICIPANTS. Powerful!

Participants find the opposite of each feeling written on the white board.

SONILA. Now let's read these words and help him feel better!

PARTICIPANTS. *reading the words aloud altogether.* "Powerful, hopeful . . ."

SONILA. And now? How do you feel? Do you have hope now?

PARTICIPANT, *looking totally bored.* Yes.

SONILA, *to the translator.* So now, write on the white board: "In the name of Allah, I will make my dream come true." So that the problem just becomes small. [*To the man*] Please, read it!

PARTICIPANT, *reads.* "In the name of Allah, I will make my dream come true."

SONILA. You have to write this twice and repeat this sentence everyday so that it helps you.

Modern Governmentality

Training programs like these are regularly held not only in the Ministry of Women's Affairs but also in other ministries. They are part of the NGOs' package of standard solutions for building upon the capabilities of civil servants and for creating a "team spirit" within ministry departments. Their long-term objective is usually labeled under the broader term of "good governance." But training programs and workshops, like advertisement in the streets of Kabul, are not value free. They represent platforms from which ideas about progress, modernity, and development are spread. Inspired by corporate management culture, their message is based on the view that the individual is the main actor of social change, an individual detached from outside constraints and whose will is essential to bring about progress.

This vision of the "natural order of things" is generated by development discourses, transmitted through workshops, training programs, and conferences and reproduced by development actors from within both the developed and the developing world. This "culture of modernity," to use R. L. Stirrat's words, is marked by "a faith in 'rationality'" (Stirrat 2000, 35) and a belief in a world that can be described through fixed, universally valid categories ("individual," "community," "nation," "free will"). These are the guiding principles of the liberal project that inevitably reflect the specific culture from which these ideas emerged, that is, a vision of "progress" and "advancement" that can only be achieved through a radical break with a "medieval past." The political rationality that underpins this teleological approach of history is that notions of sovereign/despotic power need to be replaced by modern frameworks of governmentality (D. Scott 1995, 207). Among those is a systematic attempt to intervene at the level of society itself by altering its previous structures, a distinctive feature of what David Scott calls "colonial governmentality," that is, the setting up of new instrumentalities and technologies of power aiming at governing colonial conduct.

Obviously, Sonila had a hard time trying to convince participants of the benefits of "having a positive perspective on life." Discussing the session with people at its end, I found that most of them took it as an entertainment, a way to pass the time, an escape from the repetitive and conventional rural life. What else is one supposed to find in a capital city if not shows and entertainments? "Sonila is funny! I like her!" one woman told me. "She has a great personality," another one mentioned. Very few comments were made on the content of the training itself, which I believe remained quite obscure for most participants.

Several female participants mentioned the importance of maintaining contact with Kabul because it represents the center where most resources are concentrated. They viewed Sonila's training as a means to become part of national and transnational networks that could provide them with opportunities in the future, such as attending conferences, receiving fellowships, or getting positions in prestigious international organizations. "It is good to have friends in America. I like having friends everywhere in the world," one woman told me. "We want Afghan women to be able to do the same as Western women—to study, to work, to travel. Unfortunately, it is not possible now, but *inshallah* [God willing], in the future, it will be," another participant remarked.

Seen as a sort of private joke among civil servants, training sessions held in Kabul are part of the panel of activities offered by international experts to the new Afghan elite. And if what is discussed does not make much sense, at least participants get a chance to meet other people, have a nice meal, discover the capital city, and return home with a nice handbag and stationery for their children. Moreover, participating in a conference, a training, or a workshop, all the more when it takes place abroad or in Kabul, strengthens participants' sense of belonging to a cosmopolitan ruling class. This productive dimension of transnational governmentality (Ferguson and Gupta 2002, 994) indicates a modality of governance by which state actors under the influence of both local and global forces are individually empowered to mobilize specific knowledge practices, institutional codes, and norms that are part of a "modern" and "rational" state apparatus. In the meantime, actors' capability to use this new knowledge, and in particular "to point out the unreason in the old," becomes the condition sine qua non for their participation in public affairs (D. Scott 1995, 210). "If we stay in our provinces, we remain ignorant. We remain stuck in the Middle Ages. Women don't know anything about their rights there. They are the slaves of their husband and their family," a female participant told me.

Most of the women perceived the capital city as the setting where changes in gender relations could occur. As Martina Rieker and Kamran Asdar Ali

(2008, 1) put it in their study of urban spaces in the Third World, "the city emancipates women far more than rural life or suburban domesticity." While the city also creates new hierarchies of power and domination, it remains the location where some women may experience new forms of mobility and gain some visibility. For the few women who attended the training, Kabul was full of promises.

The underlying script of these training programs might not be very clear to the Afghan audience, but it is easily readable for the Western observer. Informed by her own life experience as a "successful" immigrant to the United States, Sonila wanted to convince her audience that positive change is merely a matter of individual will and self-confidence. The complaints participants made about the structural barriers they faced in their daily tasks were in her view signs of a general negative attitude and reluctance to assume responsibility. On her blog, she commented about a workshop she had run earlier.

> In the class they resist everything I say. They doubt, question, debate and refuse to accept. I had one of the worst groups ever because they would not cooperate and would not give it a chance. It took so much energy to convince them that governance and the government are two different concepts, or the difference between politics and policy. Even though they had no clue, they gave me such an argument like: "Our government does not listen to us, it is corrupt, we have no power." So when I tried to tell them that we should look at the Afghan constitution to understand the government policies, they skipped the constitution and started fighting about the President. This group did not like the meditation, did not like conflict resolution, did not like anything I did. What they liked is telling jokes and so they invented a ground rule if a phone rings the person whose phone rang had to tell a joke. So they would call each other and they wasted most of my sessions by telling jokes and giggling because they thought I did not get their games, while I patiently waited to connect with them. They loved money and their only complaint was that they did not receive the complete transportation reimbursement which they had spent to get to Kabul after traveling for days. They asked for $800 per person. When we told them that the Ministry of Transport has fixed rates for these provinces and it does not exceed $40, a big fight emerged. So they lied, had no receipts, argued, threatened and at the end said that nothing was good and this training was a waste of time.[6]

The frustrations Sonila expresses in her online diary echo the comments I often heard among expatriate circles during my fieldwork in Afghanistan. Experts and technical assistants placed in ministries came, like Sonila, with a whole set of ready-made solutions to reconstruct the state apparatus. But the jargon they used—"governance," "conflict resolution," "policies," to cite some of the concepts Sonila unsuccessfully tried to pass on to her trainees— did not match the political and social reality in which civil servants had to perform their work.

Civil servants themselves made great use of the development jargon, identified as the "language of power," without necessarily understanding its meaning or being very much convinced of its practical application. One can argue that this practice, often observed by anthropologists of development, is symptomatic of what Jean-Pierre Olivier de Sardan calls "graft" (2005, 106). In this process, actors of social change are aware of the potential benefits they can gain from using the language of development. These benefits are varied: credibility, inclusion, access to resources. However, the "graft" remains exogenous and mostly assumes a populist dimension: it serves to show the outside world that concerns are focused on people. When talking to civil servants in ministries, I often heard the word "gender" in unexpected situations. Discussing this with an Afghan female friend, I was told that the use of this jargon was a means of creating a bond with a Western woman interested in women's issues. "This is our culture," she said, "we try to find commonalties with our guests to make them feel at ease."

A similar concern for maintaining "order" and "stability" was observable during Sonila's training. Participants were very careful not to upset the consultant to the extent of putting aside the self-consciousness of their status as local authority figures in order to participate in stress-relief exercises with a grace that I found particularly stunning. Contrary to critical views that depict development as a means to achieve social regulation and expand bureaucratic control, David Mosse (2004, 654) describes development as a "relationship-maintaining system." Building on Foucault's notion of "governmentality" according to which social life is regulated through productive power, engendering subjectivities, and aspirations, Mosse suggests that relationships built in development encounters necessitate compromise and collaboration. The training was a good illustration of this dynamic. By showing respect to their "guest from America," participants were demonstrating their allegiance to the Ministry of Women's Affairs and to the central government as a whole. Of course, this does not mean that they were convinced by the

ideas conveyed during that particular moment, but this was the "public tran-
script" (J. Scott 1985; 1990) they had to express in order to maintain their
public persona.

On a broader scale, the training I have described here is symptomatic of
the weakness of the Ministry of Women's Affairs as an institution. A simple
walk in the corridors of the ministry conveys a sense of the inertia that par-
alyzes the system. Hidden behind their computer screens, civil servants im-
patiently wait for the end of the working day, sipping tea and chatting with
colleagues.[7] Nothing seems to happen here except endless cycles of meetings
during which no decisions are made. Boredom is the rule.

"We don't want pens! We don't want workshops! We want money to run
real projects!" the director of the Department of Provincial Relations at the
Ministry of Women's Affairs told me once in an outburst of anger.[8] Most
MoWA departments have indeed no other budget than the one allocated to
cover salaries. Offices have been equipped with computers and Internet access and civil servants receive regular training, but department directors run
very few projects of their own since funding is seriously lacking.

In the long corridors of the ministry, anonymous women sometimes turn
up, desperately seeking assistance. Many of them are war widows or victims
of violence in their families. Their appeal to the ministry often represents for
them the last option when they have exhausted all other alternatives provided
by informal community support networks. Unfortunately, the MoWA has
little to offer and most women are referred to other ministries supposedly
better equipped to answer their demands.

The ministry's vague mandate to mainstream gender and plan policies
prevents it from answering individual demands, a role it used to play under
the reign of King Zahir Shah. Indeed, in the early 1950s, the Women's Institute (MoWA's ancestor) was a state agency that implemented very practical
projects for women. It collected different women's embroideries from throughout Afghanistan, modernized them, and developed new techniques that were
taught to women. Empowered by these new skills, women were able to gen-
erate greater incomes for their family while supporting the cultural heritage
of Afghanistan. Girls who were married at an early age were able to attend
MoWA's schools and continue their education without suffering from the
stigma they might have faced had they attended regular state schools. Unlike the Ministry of Women's Affairs, the Women's Institute was a highly respected institution and was generally perceived as a socially appropriate place
for women to go.[9]

The scarcity of funding in the Ministry of Women's Affairs reveals the scant interest of the president's cabinet in advancing women's issues. Since its creation in 2002 until the period of my fieldwork in 2007, four different ministers had been appointed. Each new appointment had resulted in changes in the ministry's administrative structure, with new staff appointed in each department. In a 2007 interview, Masooda Jalal, the former minister of women's affairs, underlined the difficulties she faced when attempting to change the status quo. She associated her removal from the cabinet with the discontent she created when trying to implement initiatives favorable to women.

> At the beginning, they [conservative members of the cabinet] told me in a soft way that this much is enough for the women: one school or two schools and that's it. Women are now in the office. It's enough . . . enough! They were asking for cooperation. They were saying this way is the good Afghan approach. But I did not believe that. I was not the type of person to be convinced by politicians obsessed with their own interest. I am thinking about my own interest as well and my own interest is that women can reach equality and can live like men because I know the life of women inside families and outside families . . . even the educated ones, how it is in Afghanistan. We need to decrease their pain. So we opened offices in all the provinces. At the district level, we set up women's councils. We created a big network of women. When this was created, I heard from fundamentalist leaders: "Dr. Masooda, please stop these councils." But we went ahead and it's going on up to now. So finally, they decided altogether, all the fundamentalist leaders including the government's high authorities, the warlords, to remove people whose power would disadvantage them. They all joined hands together, they sent me home, and made a housewife out of me. Some of them are sending me messages sometimes. They send me their "little ones" to tell me: You're cooking now?[10]

Divested of their authority, those appointed as ministers of women's affairs have had limited opportunities to make a real difference for women. In some departments, directors have been appointed through political affiliations and neopatrimonial networks. Some of these directors were not very much committed to women's issues and therefore worked with the view of reinforcing the status quo. This was for instance the case of the director of the Training and Advocacy Department, a man in his midforties, who was in charge of developing training and public information material for the ministry. On March 8, 2006, for International Women's Day, he unilaterally changed the messages on the banners that were to be displayed all over the capital city, using his own slogan instead: "Bakeragi-ye yak dokhtar manand-e negin ast bar taj-e shawharesh" (A woman's virginity is a jewel on her husband's crown). Aware of the internal politics, other civil servants who might have had a more progressive approach to women's issues were discouraged from expressing themselves for fear of losing their jobs. Sonila's training itself did not address gender issues in great depth. The training rapidly turned into a self-empowerment session of the same kind as the ones run in the West for alcoholics or women victims of domestic violence.

In the Public Relations and Information Department, a great amount of time was spent negotiating the content of each message to be broadcast through media outlets. The validation process sometimes took months, with meetings being organized at each level of the hierarchical ladder until the message's content was eventually emptied of any transparent and readable meaning. The content of the produced documents faded away behind the "aesthetics of communication" itself (Riles 2004, 20). Designed in the newly opened advertisement companies of the capital city, leaflets, posters, TV and radio spots, brochures, and other institutional artifacts were developed under the guidance of local and international civil servants as part of a daily bureaucratic practice meant to consecrate the construction of a modern state. The practice of producing communication and information, as Annelise Riles (2004) has demonstrated in her ethnography of the 1995 UN Fourth World Conference on Women, became the ultimate end of such projects rather than a means to enact social change. Keeping up with the information age and modern media, almost all of the Afghan ministries had developed their own websites in English and Dari by 2006 (only four years after my first journey to Afghanistan)—a fact that could be understood as a symbolic marker of Afghanistan's entry into modernity.

In a booklet entitled *Violence Against Women*, developed by the MoWA as part of a public information campaign, one could read: "Jahad-e yak zan moraqebat-e dorost az shawharesh ast" (A woman's jihad is to take care of her husband). The American adviser employed to assist and train the staff of the Public Relations and Information Department often complained about the lack of opportunities for women to receive consideration outside of their traditional roles as mothers, daughters-in-law, and wives. However, these complaints received little attention from MoWA staff, most of whom considered those roles to be socially honorable and in conformity with Islam and Afghan culture. Feminist expatriates and advisers often drew amused comments from MoWA employees who looked upon these women—who had come "alone from abroad" to support them in their work—with an ambivalent mixture of suspicion and sympathy.

On the occasion of the International Day for the Elimination of Violence Against Women, the issue of rape was illustrated by a screaming woman having her veil pulled away by an angry man. Because the topic represented such a major social taboo but could not be ignored due to the international publicity it had gained since the 2001 intervention, the Ministry of Women's Affairs struggled to find a way to address the issue while avoiding controversy. When the visual was shown to random Afghans, interpretations varied widely, but the issue of rape was never mentioned. In spite of its ineffectiveness to illustrate the topic discussed, the Public Relations and Information Department approved the visual on the basis that it would not upset anyone. Pressured by the international community to increase its visibility by conducting public campaigns and quick impact projects on the one hand and constantly criticized by conservative political forces on the other, MoWA struggled to preserve its legitimacy. The quest for consensual validation and maintenance of relationships with the broader national political apparatus and the aid community ended up being a central activity of the ministry. At the same time, producing information, organizing meetings, conferences, and training, and drafting policy papers and writing reports were practices that maintained a semblance of professional managerialism for the institution.

Finally, MoWA's activities were hobbled by a hierarchical structure that impeded collaboration between its departments. This fragmented structure was partly due to the fact that various donors, with different agendas, supported different departments of the ministry, making them function as NGOs competing against each other. During the period of my fieldwork, the United Nations Development Programme (UNDP) was supporting the training and advocacy section, the United Nations Population Fund (UNFPA) was supporting the Health Department, the Asia Foundation was funding the Public Relations and Information Department, the Japan International Cooperation Agency (JICA) was supporting the Economic Empowerment Department, and the United Nations Fund for Women (UNIFEM) was supporting the Planning and Legal Department. The presence of these different actors, despite their efforts to coordinate, contributed to the already deeply fragmented structure of the MoWA.

As already noticed in other humanitarian scenes, the "marketization" of international organizations and NGOs has enhanced interorganization competition (Cooley and Ron 2002). This phenomenon is observable not only in Afghanistan as a whole, but also within ministries, preventing collaboration between organizations that have had to follow the different agendas set up by their respective donors. Driven by organizational imperatives of implementing programs and securing new contracts to remain solvent, NGOs have been driven by self-interested actions and consequently are weak at sharing information between themselves (Azarbaijani-Moghaddam 2006).

The political context in which the MoWA is operating explains in large part its inherent impotence. But on the expatriates' side, the malfunctioning of state institutions was generally explained in strictly cultural terms rather than political ones. The absence of a "public service culture," the nonexistence of a "culture of rights and responsibilities," or the predominance of the "*inshallah* culture" were common explanations for the ineffectiveness of the state bureaucracy. The same way Sonila complained about participants' greediness in her online diary ("they loved money"), allusions to a "culture of impunity" or a "culture of corruption" were frequently made in reports written by journalists, international organizations, and funding bodies.[11] Through these representations, the Afghan culture was used as a deterministic explanatory device, depicted as given, static, fixed. The general assumption was that culture was shared and collectively agreed upon rather than contested, negotiated, and constantly recreated. Arguments of these kinds simply ignored broader political and structural reasons for people's resentment and resistance.

As Olivier de Sardan (2005, 68) puts it, "those who intervene in development . . . when applying in the field . . . the technical methods acquired through training . . . are confronted with a shocking reality: the behaviours of the people with whom they enter into contact do not coincide with their expectations." The lack of consultation with Afghans concerning their needs has fed feelings of shame, despair, and dispossession. Putting the blame on culture for the poor results achieved in terms of reconstruction over the past ten years leaves the modes of engagement of the international community with Afghanistan simply unquestioned. It also participates in a neocolonial narrative according to which Afghanistan is stuck in a feudal mentality and needs enlightened guidance from modern and rational Western forces in order to set itself free from the conditions of its chronic "backwardness."

In order to understand the real nature of the reconstruction project in Afghanistan, one needs to reverse the gaze and consider how such a vast range of reforms can also be understood as a cultural exercise itself. In the Ministry of Women's Affairs, the contours of a "culture of modernity" (Stirrat 2000) inspired by Western models of liberal democracy are being shaped and molded through workshops, meetings, conferences, and information production. However, the absence of solid roots within the social context in which these new cultural forms appear makes these bureaucratic performances a sort of parody or mimicry of Western forms of governance. In addition, by participating in these rituals, civil servants have created significations and social imaginaries that assert their belonging to a class elite endowed with national and international responsibilities.

Reconstruction as "Modernization"

The description I have presented of the functioning of the MoWA underlines the complex relationships between development actors working under an international mandate for reconstruction, on the one hand, and local actors caught between divisive ideologies of development and nationalism on the other. Conflicting views on the role of women in the postwar period constitute one of the most controversial arenas among reconstruction actors. Indeed, an observation of everyday affairs taking place in governmental institutions reveals that the current model for social change remains highly inspired by modernization ideology. As a result, instead of providing concrete opportunities for negotiating gender policies in the new Islamic Republic of Afghanistan, the MoWA has become the symbol of hegemonic liberal Western views on gender.

This direction was given during the 2001 Bonn conference when the agenda for reconstruction was initially designed. The plan consisted of defining efficient structures that would eliminate terrorism, reconstruct the state, and kick-start the economy. But the plan for postwar reconstruction was more than a simple set of measures to deliver aid, ensure security, and allocate resources. This series of agreements was intended to reform the Afghan society as a whole and make it converge toward a Western model of democracy. The ultimate aim, therefore, had less to do with mere reconstruction than with an exhaustive and ambitious project for modernizing the Afghan society according to criteria defined by international donors and international financial institutions. Program implementation was indeed guaranteed by international funding and the presence of foreign troops. In addition, progress was to be monitored and evaluated according to indicators "collaboratively" agreed upon.

As in other postwar contexts, the model for reconstruction and development was derived from Western experiences in liberal political development and economic growth. In Astri Suhrke's words (2007, 1298), the "Bonn Agreement was basically a script for transition to a liberal, constitutional democracy, served by an effective state apparatus ('competence and integrity') and a single army, with a commitment to 'social justice,' respect for human rights, and 'sensitivity' to the rights of women." The economic framework for development was later designed through a series of additional documents.[12]

The current reconstruction programs conducted under foreign leadership in many ways resemble the modernization projects conducted in the 1960s and 1970s. In Chapter 1, I demonstrated how early modernization attempts undertaken by King Amanullah, King Zahir Shah, President Daoud, and, later on, the Communist regime presented similar aspirations to reshape the Afghan social landscape. Inspired by post–World War II development literature (the "Washington consensus"), the Afghan elite bought into the idea that social progress would occur as a result of large-scale social reforms intertwined with technological innovations (Cullather 2010, 261). Modernization projects were therefore designed as a package of integrated measures. This package included transfer of technologies and capital from more developed countries, the development of a rational and highly centralized state operating through an effective bureaucracy, and the transformation of social mores through secularization, legal reform, and state education. It was believed that social engineering was necessary to lift up the country and steer away from traditions perceived as major barriers to development. As the ruling elite failed to reach out to the peripheries, the link between attempts at modernization and social change for women became gradually perceived as a form of foreign interference.

Many critical thinkers have pointed out that this vision of progress remains the blueprint for contemporary development strategies (Gardner and Lewis 1996; Shanin 1997; Crewe and Harrison 1998). However, in comparison to modernization projects conducted under King Amanullah in the 1920s and King Zahir Shah in the 1950s, the foreign foothold on the current project is much stronger. The "post-Taliban" democratization process was from the outset more heavily internationalized than other reforms in Afghan history except under the Communists. Technical experts from Europe and the United States, such as Sonila whom I introduced earlier, were shipped in to implement the agenda for reforms. Placed in ministries as advisers on short-term contracts, they earned international salaries. Salary differentials between "internationals" and "locals" also enhanced tensions and fostered disillusionment as concrete reconstruction projects were slow to start.

Expatriate modernizers, informed by their previous experiences of postwar reconstruction in other countries, have tended to ignore local modes of knowledge and traditional practices in order to impose their own agendas. This tendency was highly noticeable in the gender empowerment training programs that were run in the MoWA, as well as in other governance workshops taking place in state institutions. Technical assistants dedicated little time and thought to analyzing indigenous forms of social organization or assessing local needs and learning lessons from previous modernization attempts. This lack of knowledge has had a direct impact on Afghan people's lives and subjectivities, forcing certain categories of the population—women in particular—to present themselves according to categories defined by aid agencies (widow, disabled, businesswoman) in order to access new economic opportunities (Daulatzai 2006).

This process of "internationalised state-building," dominated by contradictory political agendas, can find its parallel in earlier foreign funded development projects in Afghanistan, notably during the Cold War period (Rubin 2006, 178; Cullather 2002b).[13] Referring to the period following the Second World War, Barnett R. Rubin shows how the United States and the Soviet Union used their financial support to the Afghan government in order to maintain their influence in the region. "Afghanistan's rulers built a state with co-ordinated flows of foreign aid; the state exploded in civil war when the aid flows instead subsidised competing military forces; and the state collapsed when the aid flows ended. The post-2001 reconstruction project constitutes a new round of internationalised state-building, with the UN formally recognised as the co-ordinator of international assistance" (Rubin 2006, 178).

The first reforms undertaken by the interim government consisted of reintroducing women into politics through a quota system, creating a Ministry of Women's Affairs (the first in the history of Afghanistan), and, more largely, promoting women's visibility in the public sphere. These reforms were the easiest ones to introduce in order to meet international demands for gender equality and political plurality. However, the inclusion of gender in the political agenda is labeled by many as a purely cosmetic move, espoused by the power elite to maintain international aid flows.

Moreover, the heterogeneous and contested positions of the actors appointed to implement the reforms and to foster social change are another explanation for the limited legitimacy the reconstruction project received. On the Afghan side, the technocrats who were brought to the negotiation table in Bonn were selected among members of the Afghan diaspora in exile in Western countries, some of whom had occupied ministerial positions under previous regimes (Mustafa Kasimi, Younis Qanooni) or had worked with NGOs (Dr. Sima Samar) and international organizations during the war. Others were higher representatives and military commanders from the Northern Alliance (General Fahim) who, with the support of the coalition forces, had overthrown the Taliban regime in the weeks following September 11. If the former were well represented in the early cabinets, persons selected on purely ethnic and political criteria and not committed to the reconstruction agenda were also included.

This scenario is well illustrated by the case of Ismail Khan, a powerful Tajik commander from Herat who had fought beside Masood's troops in the last days of the war against the Taliban. Appointed governor of Herat Province after the fall of the regime, Khan maintained his private army and ruled his province like a private fiefdom. Refusing to pass on to Kabul the revenues gained from custom taxes on goods from Iran and Turkmenistan, Khan's autocratic rule was soon to increase discord with the Afghan interim administration. The United States has viewed Ismail Khan's ties with Iran with concern and advocated ousting him. In March 2004, the central government sent units of its newly trained Afghan National Army to assert its authority over Herat (North 2004). This led to clashes with Ismail Khan's men during which one hundred people were killed. Among these was Ismail Khan's son Mirwais Sadiq, then minister of civil aviation. Under constant pressure from both the government and local rivals, Ismail Khan was removed from his position in September 2004. As a conciliatory gesture, President Karzai appointed him minister of energy in his cabinet. Since Khan's replacement by a new governor of Herat Province, the security situation has continuously deteriorated. Rumors say that current unrest in the provincial capital is sustained by Khan's militiamen as a strategy to challenge the current governor's legitimacy and to maintain the amir's stronghold in his province. The case of Ismail Khan is far from being an isolated story. Several other commanders who received cabinet positions in the interim government remained unwilling to abandon their personal militias and to withdraw from their fiefdom of origin. The collusion of diverging interests within the central government, with political actors providing the commodity of violence and its counterpart, that is, security, is perhaps best described as "warlord democracy" (Pejcinova 2006, 35).

On the international side, the coalition in charge of the reconstruction was equally factious. International agencies and bilateral donors had different visions and competing interests. The United States, for instance, openly supported the recognition of private militias while the UN Assistance Mission for Afghanistan and other international agencies and bilateral donors strongly opposed this strategy to counter terrorism. In addition, since its creation, the NATO unit in charge of the International Security Assistance Force (ISAF) has faced difficulties in coordinating the activities of the thirty-five units under its command. Indeed, the different NATO countries are unevenly involved in the ISAF's mission with the United States, Britain, Canada, and the Netherlands bearing the burden of the most sensitive and risky operations.

From an initially peacekeeping mandate, NATO has been forced to engage in the "war on terror" as the insurgency gained in strength in many regions of Afghanistan. These unpopular military operations followed a strategy of collateral damage that cost the lives of many innocent civilians. These operations were counterbalanced by small humanitarian projects carried out by Provincial Reconstruction Teams, NATO soldiers involved in small reconstruction projects in order to "win the hearts and minds" of the local population. This dangerous mixture of military-humanitarian operations blurred the boundaries between the actors in charge of the reconstruction and the ones in charge of the security and reinforced the population's resentment toward the central government and its international supporters.

Conclusion

The gender empowerment training that I have described above reveals the symbolic dimension of the post-2001 reconstruction and the cultural project that is embedded within it. I argue that this training is a kind of governance ritual in the sense that it can be analyzed as an example of what Victor Turner (1967), in his study of the Ndembu ritual in Zambia, referred to as an event that sheds lights on "dominant symbols" by providing analytical keys to a cultural system and its underlying elements. Indeed, this dramaturgical perspective on the way governance functions helps us to understand how the ceremonial repetition of bureaucratic activities (training sessions, workshops, meetings, information production) allows individuals to design and reproduce symbolic implications that reassert their belonging to a dominant class. For civil servants and state actors, the ability to participate in rituals

of governance is a means to assert rank and status, to maintain relationships, and to assume national and international responsibilities, even if only
symbolically.

In contrast to the Taliban regime, which used the public sphere to demonstrate its absolute sovereignty, resorting to public punishments and disciplining people's appearance in public, the new Islamic republic is attempting
to transform the symbolic meanings of "the public" through bureaucratic policing activities. Instead of resorting to coercive force, the new state apparatus is using productive means of governance, creating narratives of progress
and shaping modern subjectivities. For civil servants, the inscription of the
reconstruction project within global discourses of modernity and the
"ideoscape" (Appadurai 1996) of liberal governance carries the promise of
social mobility and access to resources and transnational networks. Their willing participation in the training should therefore not be read as a mere act of
obedience to dominant power but rather as a performance.

Under such circumstances, addressing women's issues, far from being a
neutral act of good governance, has become part of a cultural project that
aims to break away from ignorance and tradition. Threatened by conservative political leaders and staffed through neopatrimonial networks, the MoWA
has become democracy's shop window—a space where cultural notions of
progress and modernity are processed and diffused through bureaucratic rituals such as workshops, conferences, training sessions, and information campaigns. Caught between indigenous nationalist agendas and transnational
neoliberal forces, the MoWA bears witness to the unmet promises and contradictions of foreign-driven democratization programs.

CHAPTER 3

Public and Private Faces of Gender (In)Justice

> The cloaked magician wanders like a beggar,
> Trying to find some more forces to kill me.
> The green parrots of the United Nations are mute;
> Those who talk of human rights have sealed their
> mouths shut.
>
> —Qari Yousuf Ahmadi, Taliban spokesman

In thirty-five years, Afghanistan has known a series of regime changes: a constitutional monarchy (under Zahir Shah), a republic (under Daud and the PDPA), an Islamic emirate (under the Taliban), and finally an Islamic republic (under President Karzai). Each of these regimes has defended contrasting—and contested—interpretations of sharia law and granted it a different position within the legal apparatus, especially in areas concerned with family law. Family law reforms have constituted—and still constitute—one of the most hotly contentious sites of reform in Afghanistan. This is because, as Nancy Tapper (1984, 296) phrases it, "In Afghanistan . . . the legal code relating to marriage and the family is based directly on the Shari'a or canon law of Islam, and reforms in this area have typically provoked extreme reactions, explicitly in defence of Islamic principles." As the poem of Taliban spokesman Qari Yousuf Ahmadi quoted above highlights (Strick van Linschoten and Kuehn 2012), the human rights framework that is now mobilized to establish justice adds another layer of complexity to these dynamics.

The new Afghan constitution approved by the Loya Jirga in January 2004 was broadly acclaimed in the worldwide press as a major step forward for the establishment of democracy[1] and for gender equality in Afghanistan. In this chapter, I examine this view and argue that constitutional engineering is of

Figure 12. Mahbouba Seraj teaching the Koran in Panjao, Hazarajat, 2007.
Photo by Julie Billaud.

little significance for gender justice unless issues of legitimacy are seriously
analyzed. In recent years, scholars of human rights (Hart and Irving 2005;
Chinkin 2003; Waylen 2006) have started to argue that processes of constitution making are key moments in peace building since they provide an opportunity for a national debate to take place and for citizens to collectively
decide about their future. In the case of Afghanistan, the tight schedule allocated to draft the new constitution, the absence of nationwide consultation,
and the poor representation of civil society in key debates demonstrate that
the international community's interest lay more in producing a text that would
bolster the idea of reconstruction in the West than in setting up the conditions for participatory citizenship. As a female MP from Farah Province told
me, "The constitution does not mean anything for women if we are not able
to put in place the adequate infrastructure that will enforce it."[2]

As this chapter will demonstrate, the approach chosen to establish the
"rule of law" has been inspired from Western legal tradition with little sensitivity to the historical foundations of the Afghan legal apparatus. Initially
perceived as obsolete and undemocratic, deemed to disappear as the Afghan
state would expand its power over the territory, the customary legal system

and practices have been largely ignored and even despised, only to be later repackaged in an opportunistic move to "win the hearts and minds" within the counterinsurgency strategy (Wimpelmann 2013). International legal experts, guided by a state-centric vision of social transformation, focused on modernizing the official legal apparatus with its structured system of provincial and district courts. As this approach rapidly appeared to be unsuccessful, later initiatives led by a *"governmental assemblage* . . . of institutional practices, political imageries, scholarly repertoires, and strategic considerations" (Wimpelmann 2013, 406) informed by Orientalist discourses about Afghanistan as defined by its inherent "non-stateness" and localized forms of governance, aimed to reinforce collaborations between the formal and the informal justice sectors. By delegitimizing as "inherently sexist," "violent," and "backward" existing customary practices used to settle disputes and make decisions to subsequently take a diametrically opposite view that only the informal sector could ensure the "local ownership" of justice, the international community has ignored the existing areas of collaboration and competition between the various normative orders that constitute the Afghan legal field. This opportunistic form of "lawfare" (J. L. Comaroff 2001) is similar to what Ratna Kapur recognizes in other postcolonial situations where the First World/ Third World divide is reinforced in order to justify Western domination:

> Law has been used not only as a site of empowerment, but also as a device for excluding the world's Others, or including them on terms that are quite problematic, both historically as well as in the contemporary context. These inclusions and exclusions have been produced in and through law, either by emphasising the difference of the subaltern subject as incapable of choosing and consenting, and thus incapable of exercising rights, or as backward and uncivilised, to be redeemed and incorporated into the liberal project through the process of assimilation. (Kapur 2004, 2)

The first section of this chapter analyzes the legal framework and institutional infrastructure that have been put in place in order to promote and protect women's rights in the "postwar" period. I show how the confluence of private security contractors, international legal experts, and a general climate of popular suspicion toward state institutions has created tensions and contradictions that impinge upon the real capacity of state actors in charge of justice delivery to actively protect women. Building on field observations and interviews conducted in Family Response Units (FRUs) established in Kabul's main police stations, in Kabul family court, and in women's rights and defense attorneys' organizations, I unpack the power dynamics that are activated when the implementation of gender justice is conducted under international supervision. In particular, the training of law enforcement officers is a critical area since the transmission of international standards of practices, instead of providing practical tools for tackling the complex issue of violence against women, tends to reinforce the multilayered forms of injustice, abuse, and violence that women face on an everyday basis.

In the second part of the chapter, I provide ethnographic examples that contradict the dominant narrative of opposition between "formal" and "informal" justice. I show how the promotion of women's rights at the grassroots level has had to follow the structures of the informal justice sector (family mediation, *shuras*,[3] and jirgas) or necessitated cooperation between shuras and official legal institutions in order to bring together favorable conditions for preserving public legitimacy. However, as Antonio De Lauri (2010; 2012b; 2013) has shown in his ethnographic work in Kabul district courts, the priority given to locally recognized forms of authority—with their normative insistence on the maintenance of the community's harmony, cohesion, and equilibrium over the necessity to protect victims—often leads to the silencing of the most vulnerable (women, children). In the ongoing struggle between different interpretations of women's rights entangled in broader nationalist discourses that call upon essentialist notions of "traditional values" (*rawaj*), I underline the centrality of Islam in legitimizing claims for rights, especially in the highly sensitive arena of family law. These findings invite us to evaluate the potentialities and limits of both human rights and normative pluralism as frameworks for advancing the rights of women, especially in situations where legal interventionism under the fuzzy label of "the rule of law" is used to justify military occupation.

(In)Justice from Above

On October 25, 2007, I interviewed Mustafa Kazemi, an eminent sayyid, Shia member of the Afghan parliament, and representative of Parwan Province. Kazemi, who had participated in and organized the resistance against the Soviet occupation with the mujahideen group Hizb-e-Wahdat Islami, had been appointed minister of commerce during the transition government put in place after the fall of the Taliban. He was now the spokesman of the United Afghan National Front, an opposition political party composed of Northern Alliance commanders, former Communist leaders, and various ethnic groups. For political analysts and foreign diplomats familiar with Afghan politics, Kazemi's role in the United Afghan National Front was seen as a tacit recognition of his consistent stance that Afghan politics must cross ethnic and regional boundaries. In the exasperating internecine tensions within the anti-Taliban Northern Alliance in the late 1990s, Kazemi had often played a key role, bridging ethnic and personal rivalries among various groups. In the office of a small journal for which he acted as editor in chief, Kazemi commented on current Afghan affairs in the following terms:

> I have a fear and I hope this will not become true. When the Communists invaded our country, we were young. They said that they wanted to bring democracy and they encouraged women to go to school and to go to work and to participate in meetings, study and wear beautiful clothes, and remove their *hijab* and wear short skirts. It was a pain in people's heart, people could not accept that, but they could not speak. And the people knew that something dangerous was happening and that it would destroy our religion. And suddenly it exploded like a bomb, everything was finished, and the Communists went away. I fear the same thing, the same democracy, will happen in Afghanistan. In the twentieth century, under Amanullah Khan, the same scenario happened. During the Communist regime and under Amanullah Khan, democracy was defeated and I fear the same will happen. At the moment, democracy is not a natural development in Afghanistan. When Westerners see images of Afghanistan with women wearing short dresses, they think democracy is established in Afghanistan. But if you want to establish democracy in this country, *you should start from the mosque.*[4]

A few days after this interview, Kazemi headed a delegation of the National Assembly's Economic Commission to visit a newly built sugar factory located in Baghlan, a northern province of Afghanistan. As the delegation stepped into the factory, a bomb exploded and the deputy, together with six others who had accompanied him, died on the spot. The Taliban officially denied their involvement in the attack. But since then, Kazemi's vision resonates with the bitter taste of a fulfilled prophecy.

Because of the centrality of the law to the legitimacy of the state, legal reform represented a top priority for Afghanistan's international supporters.
"A ten-year plan for reform worked out by the Ministry of Justice with substantial aid from the donors identified four main areas: (1) legal reform to
streamline existing laws and introduce new ones to support the development
of "a modern, rule of law democracy"; (2) institutional development, including reform of the Ministry of Justice, the court system, legal education, and
infrastructure; (3) extension work to provide legal aid, assistance to victims,
and monitoring of judicial assistance; and (4) consultations with institutions
of traditional justice" (Suhrke and Borchgrevink 2009). The project, which
explicitly recognized the necessity of involving customary institutions in the
negotiations, promised to "bridge modernity and tradition" by building on
the existing foundations of justice in the country, that is, Islamic law as well
as Afghan traditions, *islamiyat* and *afghaniyat*.

However, if these commitments were echoed in the various reports that
mapped out the road to justice reform (USAID 2005; Afghan Ministry of Justice 2005; Wardak, Saba, and Kazem 2007), little was concretely done in the
first years of the reconstruction to ensure that the new legal system would
reflect the complex social fabric of the country that years of war and political unrest had deeply transformed. As Thomas Barfield (2008, 365–66) has
demonstrated, the traditional system of justice and conflict resolution, together with orthodox readings of sharia law, became increasingly influential
as the state lost control over most rural regions during the Communist era
and, later on, the civil war. In the meantime, this system enjoyed a certain
degree of popular legitimacy because the religious leaders at its head were
able to protect civilians from the abusive authority of military commanders.
This legitimacy was gradually challenged as military commanders started to
assert their influence over the decisions of the shuras.

In addition to a lack of historical awareness, international actors involved
in the justice sector had rather clear-cut opinions toward the informal sector. Some were largely dismissive of the potentialities of legal hybridizations,
even though collaboration already existed in practice. They considered shuras and jirgas to be responsible for reproducing injustices and therefore as
incapable of promoting the modern vision of the rule of law that they had in
mind. During interviews with international actors involved in the promotion of women's rights in Afghanistan—International Development Law Organization (IDLO), United Nations Development Fund for Women (UNIFEM),
Justice Sector Support Program (JSSP)—the dominant narrative was that once

the state's legal personnel had received proper training and the population was sensitized to human rights, the relevance of the informal legal system would naturally diminish. In this teleological vision of legal modernization anchored within the liberal peace project—where democracy, free market, and the rule of law are seen as complementing each other (Richmond 2006)—the implementation of the rule of law meant the transplantation of a legal system having its roots in Western models of liberal democracies. The problem with such a vision is that the theory of the rule of law that had justified international interventionism in Afghanistan has hardly been able to disguise the enormous economic and strategic interests that motivated this intervention in the first place (De Lauri 2010).

From 2007, as the model of centralized justice largely appeared to have failed, a new group composed of international donors, experts, military diplomats, and scholars started to develop a different approach whereby the "local"—ironically, who was eligible to represent the "local" was decided from "above"—was this time acknowledged as the only legitimate stakeholder for justice delivery (Coburn and Dempsey 2010; Smith and Lamey 2009; Wardak, Saba, and Kazem 2007). Again, essentialist cultural arguments were used to justify this reversed strategy: in a country with a heroic tradition of resistance against central government institutions, only the tribes could ensure the kind of stability necessary to deliver justice.

The arguments that see culture either as an impediment or as leverage in the development of rights derive from debates that oppose universal human rights and rights claims based on culture. In international platforms (the United Nations, international NGOs), the term "culture" often refers to the customs and traditions that constitute the untouched rural way of life of the developing world. These conceptions are grounded in an essentialized understanding of cultures as bounded "wholes" that fails to recognize the continuous processes of contestation and transformation that world cultures have experienced as a result of globalization. As much as it would be a rather hazardous experiment to try to define what constitutes "Afghan culture," attempts at doing so should be questioned in regard to the type of projects they seek to support. In this sense, Lila Abu-Lughod (2002, 784) is right to highlight the imperialist logic in the discourses about "Afghan culture" that have accompanied the military intervention in Afghanistan:

The question is why knowing about the "culture" of the region, and particularly its religious beliefs and treatment of women, was more

urgent than exploring the history of the development of repressive regimes in the region and the U.S. role in this history. Such cultural
framing, it seemed to me, prevented the serious exploration of the roots
and nature of human suffering in this part of the world. Instead of
political and historical explanations, experts were being asked to give
religio-cultural ones. Instead of questions that might lead to the exploration of global interconnections, we were offered ones that worked
to artificially divide the world into separate spheres—recreating an
imaginative geography of West versus East, us versus Muslims, cultures in which First Ladies give speeches versus others where women
shuffle around silently in burqas.

In order to move away from the theoretical impasse produced by debates
that oppose universalism and cultural relativism, Jane Cowan, Marie-
Bénédicte Dembour, and Richard Wilson (2001, 3) invite us to "examine 'culture' as an object of rights discourses, as well as the local and global conditions
which compel and constrain such claims and the contexts in which they are
articulated." This definition of culture as contested and as a mode of legiti-
mating claims to power and authority allows us to detect the potentialities
for social change that local cultural practices may carry. "Culture in this sense
does not serve as a barrier to human rights mobilization but as a context that
defines relationship and meanings and constructs the possibilities of action"
(Merry 2005, 9).

The dichotomous opposition between "formal justice" and "informal justice" that dominates the discourse of legal pluralism in Afghanistan is often
represented by a rigid juxtaposition of central and local authorities competing against each other. If this is sometimes the case, the everyday practices
of judges and law enforcement officers reveal that far from being antagonistic to customary practices, these actors also refer to the normative order of
customary law in complex and contradictory ways (De Lauri 2013). Instead
of facilitating "bottom-up" avenues for the "vernacularization" of human
rights (Merry 2005), the international community has opted for experiments
whose logic follows the military imperatives of the moment. The assumption
behind this move, which is symptomatic of liberal legal interventions in Third
World countries, is that "culture" is something that needs to be governed and
disciplined. Ideally the legal system should be culture-free, autonomous, separate from society, technical, and non-political: "a cold technology for an efficient market" as Ugo Mattei and Laura Nader put it (2008, 5). Because

"traditional" countries like Afghanistan are so much "rooted in culture," the "civilized" world needs to supervise and decide who speaks for culture and which elements of culture are sufficiently acceptable to be preserved.

Since the Bonn Agreements, the task of reforming the judiciary has mostly remained in the hands of the international community. In this sense, justice reform in Afghanistan bears many resemblances to colonial projects carried out at other times, in other places, building relationships whereby law sanctions a pattern of subjugation. The ideology of the "rule of law" and the corollary rhetoric of "good governance" and "democracy building" have mostly been translated into a top-down "civilizing mission" exercise with no participation from Afghans on the ground. For example, the drafting of the new criminal code has been entirely realized by Italian jurists with the support of U.S. military lawyers with no input from the Afghans (F. Ahmed 2007). The final text, like the changes made to the constitution,[5] was adopted under strong foreign political pressure. Behind the rush of the international community to produce a new criminal code were beliefs in the necessity to develop standardized juridical practices in a country where wars had created a myriad of different jurisdictions over the territory.

The present judiciary structure of state-run courts in Afghanistan includes a Kabul-based Supreme Court, provincial high courts of appeal, and local district courts dispersed in some of the major cities of the country, including Kabul, Herat, Kandahar, Nangahar, and Balkh. Since the downfall of the Taliban regime, the international community has concentrated its efforts on rebuilding these structures and has launched ambitious training programs for judges, prosecutors, defense attorneys, and municipal police forces. These training programs have mostly been conducted by international experts employed by private contractors specializing in justice reforms in Third World countries. This is for instance the case of the PAE group, a global security company specializing in military logistical support, but also running the U.S. State Department–sponsored Justice Sector Support Program (JSSP) in Afghanistan. Indeed, the borders between war and humanitarianism have become more porous over the past decades, making American military subcontractors the world's largest human rights training institutions in Third World countries (Kennedy 2004, 294).

As a U.S. State Department subcontractor, the JSSP trains prosecutors and investigative police through a combination of class instruction and mentoring. This training has been recently extended to judges and defense lawyers. In addition, more occasional mentoring of senior staff, such as provincial chief prosecutors and judges, is also carried out. The JSSP also runs various programs at the central level, including technical support, mentoring, and advising to the Ministry of Justice and the Attorney General's Office.

In his villa, guarded behind barbed-wire walls by Nepalese DynCorp[6] security guards, a JSSP legal expert was feeling cynical: "There are three things the international community is interested in doing: writing the laws, giving training, and building buildings. They appoint "experts" to give power point presentations. These experts are paid incredible salaries and most of them have no experience with the legal practices of this country. I remember one of these experts giving a presentation on an international convention Afghanistan hadn't even signed. This is how the money is going back to us. Take the example of the PAE group: we spent millions of dollars to train twenty police officers and ten prosecutors."[7]

Legal Imperialism

Brenda is a gender adviser/law enforcement officer within the JSSP. She is a tall and slender American woman in her mid-forties who wears a short-sleeved tunic, a helmet covered with a panther-print fabric, and a bulletproof jacket each time she ventures outside of her house. She had worked in the Balkans before coming to Afghanistan. With her military equipment and her two bold and heavily armed bodyguards, she looks as if she has been directly recruited from a Mad Max movie. She is a "postconflict" specialist who has seen her share of human horrors since she started her career. She had survived a suicide attack in Herat a few months before we first met and she was about to be sent to Iraq once her "mission" in Kabul was over. As we crisscrossed the city in an armored vehicle on our way to the Family Response Units located in the major police stations of the capital, she explained how she was given only a two-week "R&R" (U.S. military slang for "rest and relaxation") in a luxury hotel in Dubai after what she called "the incident." Brenda was "psychologically strong," as she liked to say, and she was convinced that the legal training of the Afghan policewomen was central to the establishment of gender justice in Afghanistan.[8]

In 2005, two American mercenaries employed by the private security company DynCorp, working as police advisers in police stations in Kabul, took the initiative to set up the first Family Response Unit (FRU). The objective was to provide training for the four policewomen employed at the station, involving a variety of low-level, nonpolice duties instructive in policing competencies, while providing policing services for those women in the communities who were the victims of family violence. The four policewomen were trained on "family violence" by the United Nations Assistance Mission in Afghanistan (UNAMA) gender adviser, while police techniques were taught by the American police advisers attached to the unit. In 2007, there were four FRUs available in the city of Kabul and nine FRUs available in the provinces (one in Baghlan, two in Herat, one in Jalalabad, one in Kunduz, three in Mazar-i-Sharif, and one in Takhar). Most of them had been installed in furnished containers given by the UNFPA. They each consisted of a reception area, an office, a separate interview room, and a washroom. Policewomen working in FRUs received on-the-job training and supervision by the DynCorp policewomen advisers, while Brenda covered the legal part of their training.

Our car finally reached the first FRU located in Kabul Central Police Station. Our two bodyguards stepped out first and took position on each side of the container, anxiously screening the surroundings from behind their black shades. Behind the Formica desk, the policewoman in chief was glancing through a pile of reports. Prior to this position, Mrs. Alkozai had worked for ten years as the head of the women's prison in Kabul. She had been in charge, among other tasks, of supervising (or guarding) the woman who was publicly executed at Kabul Stadium in November 1999.[9] She was assigned to the FRU when the Taliban regime fell.

As is often the case with regime changes, masks had been swapped and, from an officer in charge of implementing the Taliban's religious decrees, she had been turned into a policewoman in charge of protecting women victims of violence. During the interview I conducted with her, I realized that her new position did not mean much change in the way she understood the nature of her work. "I have a lot of experience," she said with self-confidence. "I know how to handle family problems. If these women ask for divorce, they know that there will be nothing left of them. Their family may accuse them of running away from home and they may even end up in prison. So I encourage them to talk to their husbands and their relatives and to become reasonable." Like most of the other policewomen who had been assigned responsibilities within the FRU program, the policewoman in chief was well aware of the distrust many Afghans had toward the police, who they saw as corrupt and tied to local power holders. Indeed, in the midst of this corruption that hides itself behind the flag of reconstruction/democratization, most Afghans remain skeptical toward both state legal institutions and local jirgas

and shuras whose political allegiances are constantly shifting. Having no-
where to go, the majority of Afghans have taken justice into their own hands
and use family mediation as a preferred strategy to resolve their disputes. This
privatized form of justice is, according to De Lauri (2012b), the direct result
of an "inaccessible normative pluralism."

Women who turned to the FRU in search of support often did so as a last
resort after the level of violence they endured had become unbearable. Reporting this violence to an official institution and revealing to the outside
world a family's secret was a risky gesture that could cause violent reactions.
Perceived as a challenge to the family's honor and reputation, reporting to
the police often leads to further mistreatments by male relatives ashamed of
the public scandal the woman has provoked. Furthermore, the various forces
within which the justice sector in Afghanistan was caught (the international
community, the government) powerfully constrained policing practices, forcing police agents to practice "a sort of negotiated justice, which did not fulfill
the needs of the citizens," but which reflected the necessity to negotiate between various normative systems (based on custom, sharia, state law, human
rights and Islamic principles) in order to preserve legitimacy (De Lauri 2010,
14). The main consequence of this privatization was that justice was traded
against the imperative of preserving community harmony and cohesion. Indeed, women's incapacity to be heard in both state courts and shuras was
proof that, in spite of the high hopes raised by the national liturgy of "rule of
law," the new legal order had created a second layer of injustice toward women.

I sat on a sofa and observed Brenda training the few policewomen, some
in uniforms and others wearing civilian clothes, present in the FRU. Brenda
asked me to take pictures of the session to be inserted later in the weekly activity report she had to send to her company's headquarters in the United
States. "Here is the Constitution of Afghanistan and here is the Civil Code,"
she said while the interpreter simultaneously translated her words and the
flash of my camera captured her frozen smile. "You have to study these two
books very carefully because I will come back and question you," she humor-
ously added. She pointed at sections of the books mostly relevant to the policewomen's mandate and concluded the session by asking questions related
to the cases they had received over the past month. She verified that the rec-
ords were properly kept and that the policewomen had referred their cases
to the relevant judicial bodies for further investigation. The vague and illu-
sive answers of the policewomen together with the filter produced by the interpreter's simultaneous translation transformed the task of verification into

a ritualistic performance. I discreetly asked Brenda whether all the police officers employed in the station were literate. Apparently, only the chief policewoman was. "That's annoying," commented Brenda worriedly, "I guess the ones who can read will have to read the Constitution and the Civil Code to the ones who cannot." Problem solved. We jumped back into the car and drove toward another police station.

The FRUs provided a structure for women victims of family violence, but the American DynCorp employee in charge of the mentoring, informed by their own professional experiences in U.S. emergency police units for abused women and by a depoliticized understanding of the functioning of the law, had difficulties appreciating the complex social environment in which the FRU staff had to perform their duty. One mentor was an African American woman who wore the DynCorp uniform, skintight fatigues and a T-shirt that emphasized her muscular body. A revolver was tucked in a removable pocket attached to her thigh. Her charismatic military manners, her body language, and her conception of the role of the police all colluded to place her in a universe totally removed from anything that the Afghan policewomen could possibly relate to. After a few months spent trying to teach them the procedures that were part of the "standard code of practice," she was about to give up. She complained about the policewomen's lack of empathy and about their incapacity to understand how to preserve confidentiality during interviews with clients. In addition to what she identified as a general lack of professionalism, broader structural constraints impinged on FRUs' staff to perform their assignments in a manner that could even remotely resemble police duties carried out in contexts where the state enjoys full sovereignty. Indeed, policewomen were regularly moved to other positions by their male superiors and were oftentimes deprived of access to vehicles to conduct investigations. Turnover of staff was a major barrier to their training and to the good functioning of the units as follow-ups to cases could not be properly conducted. When I shared my concerns with Brenda, she admitted that there was little that could be done to tackle these problems since political decisions were beyond her reach. "But we can still raise awareness and develop their sensitivity to and knowledge of women's rights," she added, as if trying to convince herself.

To understand the political complexities that cut across the Afghan legal field, one needs to take into consideration the networks of social relations in which it is embedded. In the current context, a series of factors—ones that cannot be simply summarized in terms of "lack of professionalism" as the narrative of the American police mentors suggests—have severely limited ordinary Afghans' capacity to find justice. According to De Lauri (2013, 266), these factors include:

> (1) the impossibility of accessing judicial institutions in an autonomous way; (2) the impact of international humanitarian policy on state institutions—in the sense that this "aid" is perceived as external interference; (3) the social hierarchies that both customary and state institutions tend to reproduce; (4) the link between state institutions and warlords' systems; (5) the corruption rampant in courts, prosecutors' offices, and among policemen; (6) the inefficiency of justice sector institutions as a result of limited human and infrastructural resources; (7) the radicalization of certain customary practices determined by the logic of violence; and (8) the extreme politicization of religious dogma and of legal claims.

Having to submit to greater "powers" (male police officers, commanders, religious figures, politicians) that challenged their authority on a daily basis, following procedures and applying the law was totally out of female police officers' reach. The only concrete option available to them was to apply a mixture of legal, moral, and customary rules in order to mediate problems since they lacked the concrete means to solve them in a formal way. During my visits to the FRU, I was able to observe a few cases of women who came to report abuses. One of them was a woman married to a man who had developed an addiction to heroin as a migrant worker in Iran. Since his return to Kabul, he had been unable to find work and had spent the modest savings of the household on purchasing drugs. The woman could barely afford to buy food for herself and her newborn baby and had to rely on neighbors and relatives' generosity for survival. Because her husband had become increasingly violent, she had turned to the FRU in a desperate attempt to find support. While the policewomen carefully listened to her testimony, they discussed with her the best strategy to adopt. Ironically, none of their advice involved the filing of a complaint at the police station. Rather, they encouraged her to approach her relatives and her husband's family and ask for their mediation.

After the woman left, I asked why they had sent the woman back to her violent husband. One policewoman answered: "As women and as police officers, most families believe that we have no authority to interfere in their internal affairs. Our intervention can create more problems. It is often better for women to have elders or male relatives help them solve their problems.

We have seen husbands coming here and threatening to kill us if we kept on asking questions. So it's a very delicate situation we are in. We have to be very careful."[10] This testimony echoed that of a female defense lawyer, Gul Ghotai Afzali, in charge of family affairs at the Legal Aid Organization of Afghanistan. At the time I met her, her organization, which was mandated to provide legal aid services to indigent people in criminal defense, family law, and some areas of civil law, had existed for less than a year. The profession of defense lawyer was quite new and lacked recognition from Afghan judges.

> Recently I had a woman who had escaped from her violent husband. He had pulled her nails out, cut her ears, attached her to the bed and hit her with cables. One evening, he had dug his wife's grave in the garden. The neighbors warned her that she would get killed and she escaped from the house. She ran to the police station and there she was kept in custody for several days, until she got referred to a shelter. The problem is that shelters cannot keep women for a long time, because they do not have enough capacity. A woman can usually stay for a period of six months. But according to our law, she has to wait for three years to obtain a divorce. The violent husband was not even arrested by the police because he is a rich man and he can bribe the police. The entire system is corrupt. And our laws are not in accordance with the evolution of our society. So what I can do as a defense lawyer is very limited.[11]

Because of the conflicting imperatives of protecting women and preserving marriage, the chief judge of Kabul Family Court hardly ever pronounced divorce unless men initiated it. Most of the cases she received were referred to local jirgas and shuras composed of elders and religious leaders who were considered as best suited for adjudicating these types of disputes. The shuras were asked to keep a record of their proceedings and present their decisions to a judge. Both parties were requested to sign a declaration once an agreement between the two families had been reached. If a husband refused to honor the decision of the jirga once the dispute was settled, the woman could in theory threaten to return to the court in order to obtain her due. Because most of the time these documents were kept by male relatives whose main concern was to preserve the family's reputation by avoiding public scandal, women were very rarely able to use them unless they obtained the support of male family members. The interconnections between different normative orders (customary, human rights, Islamic law, positive law) were surely already part of the legal field in Afghanistan and the judge only navigated these norms in a manner that demonstrated her desire to remain within a shared universe of values. In the meantime, her practice seemed guided more by a concern over "maintaining equilibrium amongst the various forms of power and mechanisms of social legitimization" (De Lauri 2010, 20) than by a desire to protect victims of violence and abuse. Her practice revealed a tragic tension between her duty to uphold the symbolic authority of the state and the practical need to preserve social stability in a context where the court did not represent an acknowledged site for the delivery of justice. In her view, this hybrid form of "court-supervised councils" was the only culturally relevant way to ensure the preservation of traditional values that Afghans held dear.

However, some women's rights activists did not share her view. If all of them recognized the necessity to conform to Islam in the practice of justice, they also considered shuras and jirgas as reproducers of misogynistic traditions like the bartering away of girls to settle debts, an often ill-informed idea of women's rights under Islamic law. Their perception was certainly right from a pragmatic point of view, but perhaps also too clear-cut to reflect the potentialities of these community-based dispute resolution mechanisms to which most people turned when other forms of family mediations had failed. On the other hand, the antagonistic posture of certain political leaders, mullahs, ulema, faction leaders, and government officials when it came to issues related to women found expression in cultural claims about "Afghan customs" largely reinvented to symbolically resist the hegemonic power of external forces.

These examples corroborate the findings of empirical studies conducted in other postconflict/reconstruction contexts where human rights, the "archetypal language of democratic transition" (Wilson 2001, 1), are exported by international institutions with a particular vision of social justice based on a neoliberal privileging of individual choice (Englund 2006). In Afghanistan, this particular vision has remained insensitive to the multilayered forms of injustices experienced by ordinary Afghans over the past forty years of foreign occupation, civil war, and Islamic fundamentalism during which the legal field has been taken over by the only social structures that did not entirely collapse, that is, tribe members or members of the same village or lineage (*qawm*). The framing discourse of the "rule of law" with its standard package of ready-made solutions has been divorced from the political, social, and ideological backgrounds that shape local understanding of justice. In this sense, Kamari Maxine Clarke and Mark Goodale's (2010) metaphor of justice as a mirror is particularly relevant to describe the complex dynamics of transparency and opaqueness, resistance and assimilation, imbedded within current legal practices in Afghanistan. The utopian idealism that guides liberal perceptions of justice as a mirror that perfectly reflects and reveals unfair situations to the public in order to provide reparation is poorly equipped to give insight into what this mirror may hide in terms of other, less visible forms of discrimination.

Women's Rights and the Sharia Field

If sharia law has always played an important role in Afghanistan, modernization efforts conducted under King Amanullah, King Zahir Shah, and the Communist regime have attempted to circumscribe the power of the ulema by turning them into salaried employees of the state. The re-Islamization of legal practices was a gradual process that started during the resistance war against the Soviets. The war allowed the emergence of a new political and religious class: the increased visibility of the sharia therefore reflects important social transformations.

Thomas Barfield (2008) explains that the withdrawal of the state from rural areas during the resistance war against the Soviets did not lead to total anarchy but left a vacuum filled by a new cadre of ulema whose authority stemmed from the Islamic prescription according to which the community should be protected by Islamic laws in times of jihad. "These clerics took advantage of the networks created by the political parties in order to gain clients through which they could impose themselves and *sharia* law on areas controlled by the resistance" (Barfield 2008, 364). Barfield compares the practices of the ulema during this period to premodern Islamic forms of justice delivery in which judges were largely independent from the state because the laws they used derived from religious sources and not from a government-legislated code. Because ulema were able to restrain military commanders from taking arbitrary action and because commanders feared the ulema's influence, sharia gradually took precedence over customary law, especially in non-Pashtun regions. The success of the type of sharia practiced by the ulema was mostly due to its immediate accessibility and its capacity to provide a protective shield against the tyranny of the powerful.

The Taliban, who considered customary law un-Islamic, reinforced this trend even though the religious leadership, which had been trained in Pakistani madrassas, often conflated Pashtun tribal culture with religious law (Barfield 2008, 367). The radical version of the sharia that they imposed was the result of the chaotic situation of the civil war and was as much alien to Afghans as the secular laws that the Communist PDPA had tried to impose on them.

For Afghan women's rights activists who have a historically informed understanding of justice as a social field tightly connected to existing norms, social structures, ideologies, and power hierarchies, one way to reconcile the antagonism between the competing normative orders that composed the legal landscape (human rights, customary law, and sharia) was to root women's rights within an Islamic framework and to distinguish between customs that enjoyed Islamic support and customs that were not Islamically grounded. This was, for instance, the position of Mary Akrami, the founder and director of the NGO Afghan Women's Skills Development Center, an organization that provided shelter and vocational training for women victims of violence: "After decades of war, the minds of the people have to be rebuilt. War has destroyed everything, people's minds included. Before, when education was accessible to a greater number of people, people used to respect women's position in Islam. We need to return to our Islamic traditions and to the values we had before the war, because the traditions that are being practiced now have nothing to do with Islam."[12] Among the traditions that she identified as contrary to Islam were forced and child marriage, the accusation of *zina* (extramarital sexual relationship) as a crime punishable by prison sentence (and in some cases, lashing, stoning, or death penalty) for women victims of rape, and the practice of *baad* that entails giving a woman belonging to the family of an individual who has wronged another family, as a form of compensation, to the family who has undergone the injury. These traditions were certainly based on distorted versions of Islamic law and therefore, because Islamic legal tradition encompasses notions of public interest, there was a possibility to invalidate such harmful practices within the bounds of its framework.

Abdullahi Ahmed An-Na'im (1995) argues that in order for human rights to be culturally legitimate they must fit into existing normative structures and ways of thinking. In Muslim countries, claims for rights have better chances to be positively received when they are based on sources of authority that enjoy wide popular recognition such as the Koran and the Sunna. An-Na'im advocates for a cross-cultural dialogue on human rights in order to identify areas of conflict and contradictions between Islamic practices and values and international human rights law. It is this intense and continuous dialogue, he contends, respectful of cultural differences and equally concerned with universal standards, that should guide human rights activists in their attempt at making human rights real in the world.

However, the question as to whether women's rights activists in Afghanistan can create the conditions for the possibility of such a renegotiation remains open because of the broad entanglement of women's rights with nationalist discourses that reinforce patriarchal versions of culture. Indeed, Sally Engle Merry (2005) argues that in order for human rights ideas to be effective they need to be translated into local terms and situated within local contexts of power and meaning. She calls this process of translation "vernacularization," a complex process through which human rights gain the local relevance that they initially lacked because of the "fault line" separating the transnational human rights community from local and national spaces. In Merry's view, civil society serves as a zone of mediation between the international and the local and therefore plays a central role in packaging human rights in familiar terms. However, the difficulty for activists is to preserve the emancipatory potential of rights—that is, their capacity to challenge existing assumptions about power and relationships—while remaining culturally audible.

This picture is further complicated in the case of Afghanistan by the fact that groups that constitute so-called civil society are in fact Western-sponsored NGOs acting as local entrepreneurs with an often very loose and problematic connection at the grassroots level. Liberal ethics guide the reconstruction, meaning that local NGOs are often put in a situation of competition (instead of collaboration) to access resources and therefore tend to tailor their programs according to standards and benchmarks set up by international donors. "Organized in what appear to be horizontal networks spanning national borders, these associations and their animators deploy a discourse of human rights, democracy, and legibility. The subtle and often not so subtle problem of their popular representation and legitimacy go unnoticed" (Monsutti 2012, 588).

The first type of reception of a global idea that occurred after the fall of the Taliban was the creation of social services for women. A dozen women's shelters, for instance, were established in Afghanistan's major cities. They accommodate women who have run away from their homes as a result of mistreatment. These institutions, broadly criticized by conservative religious and political leaders for challenging traditional family values, are under the constant threat of being shut down by the government. In June 2012, Justice Minister Habibullah Ghaleb claimed during a conference organized by the Women's Affairs Committee of the Afghan parliament that women in shelters are prostitutes and are encouraged to disobey their parents. Even though he later apologized for his unfortunate comment, this attack followed a legal proposal (which was finally abandoned) to put shelters under the direct supervision of the government with women runaways required to plead their case before an eight-member government panel, including members of the Supreme Court and Ministry of Justice.

The political antipathy toward shelters, together with the absence of a legal framework to punish perpetrators of violence, means that the "translation" work that is necessary to protect women is a particularly delicate task. Shelters are very discreet and accept clients through network referral rather than on an open-door basis. Trying to adapt their programs to the structural conditions in which they operate, the women's organizations running the shelters have put in place various strategies. Because a woman who leaves her abusive in-laws/husband for a shelter has few other housing options and must sooner or later go back to them, women's rights activists use the mediation of the legal department of the Ministry of Women's Affairs to negotiate women's conditions of return with families and, if necessary, with local shuras. In Kabul, this mediation often takes the form of official meetings held at the legal department of the Ministry of Women's Affairs with the runaway's male relatives, under the presence of sharia-trained defense lawyers and the head of the legal department, Fawzia Amini. If these meetings fail to guarantee appropriate conditions for a safe return, local shuras/jirgas are called to intervene. Contrary to the system of court-supervised shuras for which the head of the family court had opted, the Ministry of Women's Affairs called local elders and religious leaders directly to its own premises. This hybrid form of customary justice allowed the participation of new actors in the mediation process, such as defense lawyers and civil servants who could provide alternative interpretations of the sharia. In the meantime, women could remain in the safe environment of the shelter until guarantees for a safe return had been secured.

Women's rights activists are adamant that knowledge and command of sharia law is key to enhancing women's rights. They also highlight the importance of building alliances with men of authority and taking into consideration the structural and material conditions that impinge on women's ability to claim rights. As Anila Daulazai (2008, 432) argues:

Men are not only left unemployed, a condition that has serious psychological consequences anywhere in the world, but they have to live in an environment that is controlled by foreign agents who consider Afghan men to be inherently misogynistic and anachronistic. It therefore needs to be considered that the ways in which the international community determines the conditions of possibility under which Afghans, men and women alike, can or cannot make ends meet are not primarily perceived as liberating, but as very stringent, very limiting, and very arbitrary.

Aware of these issues, Mahbouba Seraj, a relative of Kings Habibullah and Amanullah, returned to Kabul after twenty-six years of exile in the United States with the objective of improving the situation of women. With the support of the NGO Equal Access, she established men and women's groups in the villages of various provinces to which she and her male colleagues taught human rights according to the Koran. Participants were selected through the intermediary of local leaders (mullahs, elders, and members of the Community Development Councils who administrate the National Solidarity Program) who played a key role in granting the good reception of the program at the local level. In Jalalabad, Mahbouba organized the meetings of one women's group in the premises of the Department of the Ministry of Women's Affairs. In the remote villages of the Dragon Valley (Hazarajat), these meetings were held in local teachers' or nurses' houses. There, women who had limited opportunities to meet each other otherwise not only learned about their rights in the Koran but were also able to discuss their problems and devise strategies to support each other. Just being able to share stories could be life changing for many of them.

In Panjao District located in an isolated valley of central Hazarajat, women sipped tea and nibbled biscuits, seated on red cushions aligned along the room's walls, while exchanging village news. One woman had been repudiated by her husband who had accused her of being infertile. He had sent her back to her parents who could not afford to keep her in their house because of their scarce resources. In tears, she explained that she did not know where else to go since her husband refused to negotiate with her relatives. Some women offered to use their proximity to the man's family to speak on her behalf. Others promised to look for a new husband in case reconciliation failed. In the absence of trustworthy legal institutions to turn to, women tried to join hands and have their voice heard in the various ad hoc bricolages that constituted the everydayness of justice-making. Very few of them developed a human rights consciousness in the process even though some may have widened their self-understanding as rights bearers in Islam. Overall, women's sense of injustice remained rooted in the existing norms of kinship according to which care is to be granted to women as daughters, mothers, and wives.

MAHBOUBA. I want to tell you a true story of a twenty-one-year-old woman from Khost. Her name was Hamina. She had five children. The youngest of her children was eight months. Her husband's brother and her father-in-law lived with them in the same house. In order to support her family, Hamina wove rugs with her daughter and the sons went to school. The sons and the father-in-law took some food with them when they went to work. Hamina with her daughters would be hungry until the husband came back home. Sometimes, when her husband had finished his work, he would not come back home and he would go to the *chaikhana* [teahouse]. In the *chaikhana*, he would talk with other villagers and sometimes he would go to the head of the village's house to watch TV. When Hamina had finished weaving the rugs, she would give them to her brother-in-law to sell on the market. When he received the money, he gave it to his brother. Now, tell me which right this woman is deprived of?

WOMAN. The husband did not provide food for her and her daughters.

ANOTHER WOMAN. The husband should give money to his wife because when the guests come, she should be able to welcome them.

MAHBOUBA. Yes, the attitude of the husband is violent toward his wife. Which other rights this woman did not receive? When she wove the rugs, what happened?

WOMAN. When she wove rugs, she did not receive any money. When her brother-in-law received the money, he gave it to his brother. This money was her property.

This conversation illustrates that the women of Panjao attributed Hamina's injuries to her relatives' failure to abide by the norms of kinship and care. Mahbouba encouraged them to see her injuries as violations of her rights as a kin and as a Muslim woman. Notions of justice were therefore embedded within the cultural and moral environment in which Panjao women were

Figure 13. Koran class in Panjao, Hazarajat, 2007. Photo by Julie Billaud.

rooted. Through these discussions, women developed a sense of self-worth and dignity that encouraged them to support each other and carve out discursive strategies in order to confront everyday forms of injustice. In their struggle to achieve greater equity, these women did not take a new social position but rather reinforced their identities as wives, as members of a kinship network, and as Muslim women.

Conclusion

The discrepancy between the public face of justice in the "post-Taliban" era and the actual state of lawlessness that marks this period has increased Afghans' resentment toward the central government and has reinforced conservative interpretations of sharia. Afghans' lack of trust in formal and informal institutions of justice delivery has meant in practice that people have taken justice into their own hands and that families and local shuras have become entirely responsible for delivering justice. These developments have rendered women more vulnerable to distorted versions of Islamic law even though activists have also been able to open marginal room for contestation.

The reasons for the type of religious orthodoxy that is prevalent in the post-Taliban period are multiple. As we will see in the chapters to follow, they mostly pertain to the nationalist revival that has erupted in response to the occupation. The discrimination, violence, and abuse that many women continue to face illustrate the political (and therefore communicative) dimension of gender-based violence in contemporary Afghanistan. While the occupation asserts the hegemonic power of foreign forces over a judiciary apparatus from which Afghans have been totally dispossessed, the proliferation of acts of sexual violence emerges as evidence of the blockage and failure of an externally imposed "rule of law" project. Because the sexual is the domain in which violence achieves to the highest degree its communicative dimension, these types of crimes are to be read as discourses of agency pronounced by those who have been alienated from the languages of power (Morris 2006).

This form of violence has become an integral part of women's "poisonous knowledge" (Das 2000) to the extent that seeking justice often means acquiescing to forms of subjugation that have been conducive to violence in the first place. Veena Das suggests that "the mutual shadowing of the ordinary and skepticism" is what "defines the character of everyday, so that to secure the everyday, far from being something we can take for granted, might be thought as an achievement" (Das 2010, 376; Das 1998; Das 2007). In anthropological debates, agency is often conceptualized in terms of escape from the ordinary—or at least as a (more or less aware) reaction to what distresses the ordinary. However, everyday practices of people who have to endure the various forms of violence triggered by the occupation and whose social world has been turned upside down by war and displacement highlight forms of agency that consist in a descent into the ordinary, that is, a quest for maintaining meaningful social relationships.

It is precisely through this framework that the practices I have described in the last part of this chapter have to be understood. What Das identifies as the descent into the ordinary is this process through which individuals remake social life out of events that threw the very idea of the social into question. Women's attempts at maintaining relationships in situations where responsibilities expected from kinship ties have been disrupted by war and poverty is an achievement for the sense of continuity it seeks to maintain in the midst of chaotic life conditions.

PART II

Bodies of Resistance

CHAPTER 4

Moral Panics, Indian Soaps, and Cosmetics:
Writing the Nation on Women's Bodies

In March 2007, an article entitled "Zanan az democracy soy istefada miku-nand" ("Women Misuse Democracy") was published in *Arman-e-Milli*, a na-tional weekly newspaper.[1] The article reported that the director of the Department of Women's Affairs of Balkh Province had complained about "the semi-naked [*sic*] and skimpy clothes worn by women at wedding parties and other ceremonies in the province." In the interview she gave to the newspa-per, Feriba Majid expressed her concern about what she thought was a mis-understanding of women's rights and democracy. She commented that "we know that everyone interprets democracy in his own way, but some women are shaming other women by showing up half naked at parties. This is quite wrong and Islam condemns it." She also announced that female security of-ficials would be hired to check women's appearance on specific occasions like weddings and other ceremonies.

The publication of an article like this was not an isolated occurrence in public debates. During the same year (2007) a number of similar articles were published in the press, waving the threat of cultural dilution and loss of Is-lamic values. Because of their recurrence, the sensationalized tone used by journalists, and the political reactions that ensued, this phenomenon can be described as a "moral panic" (Cohen 2002): a threat created through the col-lusion of the media and conservative political leaders in order to stir up pop-ular fears and construct a new national identity.

Indeed, after the fall of the Taliban regime polemics emerged around the increased Western influence and its perceived negative impact on Afghan cul-ture. Western-style modernity, with new modes of consumption and lifestyles, was perceived in the press and in political circles as a threat to conventional

Figure 14. Bride being photographed in a wedding hall, Kabul, 2007. Photo by
Alexandra Estève.

morality where women's modesty was generally understood as key to social
order. This occurred in a context of growing resentment toward the presence
of international military troops, NGOs, and foreign companies, which were
broadly perceived as "polluting" religious values. Building on popular discontent, conservative political groups turned up the heat on identity issues
and started to make legal proposals for banning the broadcast of popular television series, the use of cosmetics, and the wearing of Western clothes, and
for the reestablishment of the religious police. These measures targeted segments of the population traditionally considered as the most impressionable:
the youth in general and young women in particular.

This chapter unpacks the complex meanings of these popular anxieties
crystallized around the position of young women in the "new Afghanistan."
It uncovers the ways in which these panics affect young women's perceptions
of selfhood by exploring the negotiations they undertake in order to find their
own feminine expression. The Women's National Dormitory located on Kabul
University campus was a particularly interesting entry point to observe
these dynamics because the female students who resided there were at the

forefront of a symbolic battle between competing standards of modernity and values of acceptability, success, citizenship, and nationhood.

An analysis of the context in which these panics erupted reveals that anxieties about Westernization and national identity are tightly connected to feelings of dispossession and disempowerment that have emerged as a result of the occupation. For Afghan female university students, the desire to physically appear "modern" while respecting their Muslim faith has forced them to engage in other forms of self-discipline in order to maintain status and reputation. Young women's creative and ambiguous responses to dominant discourses on their bodies can be understood as attempts to renegotiate Islamic norms of modesty while preserving a shared universe of meanings and moral values.

Room 42 of the Women's National Dormitory

Kabul University is an immense construction site. Here and there new buildings have started to grow, all built on the same Soviet-style architectural model: solid parallelepiped blocks of concrete and bricks piled up on top of each other. It is the middle of winter and the campus is deserted. Holidays have begun with the arrival of snow when it eventually became impossible to study in classrooms deprived of heating systems. At the end of an alley one can distinguish a three-story building composed of four wings: the Women's National Dormitory. The relatively new aspect of the building contrasts with the men's dormitory located a few hundred meters away. Whereas female students benefit from constant electricity, hot showers, and a room equipped with new Dell computers and Internet access, boys crowd in freezing and filthy rooms that have remained untouched since their construction in the late 1970s.[2]

The women's dormitory, like all reconstruction projects in Afghanistan, is a political business. Rehabilitated with the financial support the United States Agency for International Development (USAID), the women's dormitory was the personal project of America's first lady. Ironically, and perhaps without being aware of it, Laura Bush's project placed her in the same proactive gender policies previously put in place during the Communist regime. Indeed, the first women's dormitory was opened in 1980 (Zulfacar 2006) as part of a broader package of programs aimed at justifying the Red Army's occupation of the country. It is in a similar spirit that on the day the dormitory was inaugurated, Laura Bush announced: "There is much more to this place than the bricks and mortar you see around us. The ordinary business that will take place here is, in fact, a symbol itself of the extraordinary leap forward Afghan women have taken" (Herman 2005).

Surrounded by high walls topped by barbed wire, the dormitory is under strict security rules: armed guards are posted at the entrance gate twenty-four hours a day, residents can only receive female visitors, and times of entrance and exit are strictly regulated and monitored. With elderly female guards pacing up and down the corridors, entering rooms by surprise, and sometimes sitting in silence in a corner of a room without invitation, the living conditions are reminiscent of a milder form of what Erving Goffman could have identified as a "total institution" (Goffman 1968). The confinement that comes with this project of women's emancipation is emblematic of the paradoxes that arise when "freedom" is imagined along universal parameters and is concretized through standard "toolkits," where aesthetics matters more than outcomes (Apthorpe 2012, 1548).

Dormitories built in Kandahar, Jalalabad, and other Afghan cities to accommodate female students were eventually used to host men for lack of female volunteers. In spite of obvious social mistrust toward the ability of the state and its foreign sponsors to care for women, donors continued to support such initiatives. While the National Women's Dormitory remained half empty, another one was being built next to the Faculty of Medicine, as if donors, in their competition for the most visible act of generosity toward Afghan women, had remained blind to the fact that very few girls were in attendance at the school. These precarious spaces offered as a gift to Afghan women portrayed as victims of fundamentalism in the moral grammar mobilized to justify the war bear witness to the irreducible dead ends of the reconstruction project. The inconsistencies of the dormitory project illustrate the abject[3] nature of "normality" in the post-Taliban era. In the same way as Joshua Comaroff (2007) describes Guantanamo as an emblematic "space of contradictions" where the tale of the "war on terror" can materialize, the dormitory captures its reverse and complementary side by providing the "free world" with a site where the fruits of its military-humanitarian intervention (the "carnival of postwar") can be represented.

It is winter and the 188 available rooms in the building are empty. Only a dozen girls unable to return to their province of origin due to heavy snowfalls that have blocked the roads have had to stay in the dormitory, which is half empty during the rest of the year anyway. On the walls of the long cold corridors dimly lit with white fluorescent lights, posters of the women's rights movement in the United States hang unnoted. Suffragettes and early feminists' names and slogans appear on sepia prints to which none of the girls seem to pay much attention. Instead, behind their closed doors, girls' dreams are fueled with the commercial version of the "American dream": Leonardo DiCaprio starring in *Titanic*, Bollywood movie star Aishwarya Rai, white babies with blue eyes and teddy bears holding pink hearts in their arms. The contrast between the interior decoration of the rooms and the outside corridors covered with posters of suffragettes simultaneously captures the various versions of modernity at work in this institution, established with the objective of producing the new feminine elite of the nation. It bears witness to the multiple imaginaries that fashion and shape these young women's aspirations, desires, and dreams.

Unaccustomed to sleeping on bunk beds, students have recreated their traditional bedrooms with mattresses displayed along the white walls around a large central piece of carpet, provoking the exasperation of the director of the dormitory.[4] Employed by the United Nations Office for Project Services (UNOPS) to administrate this girls-only institution, the Tajik woman in her late forties thinks that the dormitory is more than a simple hostel. "Girls from different ethnic backgrounds are mixing for the first time. Not only do they learn how to live together away from their families but they also learn basic principles of hygiene that are seriously lacking in their education," she told me when I first met her.[5]

In the corner of room 42, sitting on her mattress, twenty-two-year-old Fawzia applies makeup to her face, getting ready to go to work at Bagh-e Zanana, the women's park. Fawzia is Hazara and she shares a room with Ramzia, a Pachai girl from Kapisa Province, Rokia and Maryam, two Tajik sisters from Kabul, and Mariam, another Hazara girl from Mazar-i-Sharif. Rooms shared between girls from different ethnic origins are rare but the girls of room 42 get on well. All of them have spent most of their lives in exile, in Iran and in Pakistan, and have returned to Kabul shortly after the "liberation" in order to continue their studies. They have brought with them habits, attitudes, and consumer items, a slightly different set of experiences from the other young women whose families have remained in Afghanistan during the war. Residents of room 42 are second-year students in different faculties but are also an important source of income in their families. They share their time between the foreign organizations in which they are employed and the university campus. As returnees, girls from room 42, like other girls who have been raised abroad, consider themselves more modern and open-minded than the others.

The young women to whom I became the closest during my four-month stay as an English and French teacher in the dormitory were predominantly among this group. While the other dormitory girls were rather suspicious toward my intentions and remained somewhat distant, the girls of room 42 demonstrated a great eagerness to learn about the West. My presence among them probably served to reinforce their desire to present themselves as progressive, hence capable of making friends with foreigners. To a certain extent, my position as an outsider mirrored their own social "disembeddedness" as returnees to a country about which they knew little. The way they spoke Dari with a slightly foreign accent, the way they dressed, and their general attitudes distinguished them from the other girls who called them, with a touch of contempt and jealousy, *khariji* (foreigner), or *Irani* (Iranian) for the ones who spoke Farsi. Many of these girls studied foreign languages. Some of them were hired in part-time jobs and were more or less financially autonomous. As a result, they were able to purchase consumer goods such as mobile phones and fashion accessories that were part of the attributes of a social class to which many dormitory residents aspired to belong. The five young women of room 42 introduced me to some of their friends and relatives, and I was often used as a token of their cosmopolitanism and open-mindedness. I was introduced as the *dokhtar-e Fransawi* (French girl) who had come to Afghanistan to study "women and culture."

The time I spent with the young women of the National Dormitory will remain one of my most vivid and pleasurable memories of my stay in Afghanistan. Behind the four walls of room 42, free from outside supervision, we discussed their studies and their hopes for the future. We shared stories, pieces of poetry, memories of exile as well as cosmetics and fashion accessories. The dormitory, and room 42 in particular, was a microcosm that both reflected the tensions that cut across contemporary Afghan society and opened an experimental space for subject formation and the subversive "resignification" of norms. Indeed, like the prison, the asylum, or the hospital studied by Michel Foucault, the dormitory as an institution had a similar disciplinary power. However, the various organizations in charge of its supervision (the Afghan Ministry of Higher Education, UNOPS, and the USAID sponsor) competed to promote their own vision of the "new Afghan woman." Caught in the middle of these various forces and exposed to idealized models of femininity, these young women strove to find their own feminine expression. In the section that follows, I describe the "moral culture of alarm" (Navaro-Yashin 2002, 6) that came to serve as an articulator of tensions around young women's bodies and nationhood.

"Women Misuse Democracy"

After the fall of the Taliban, a collective composed of international aid organizations, capitalist institutions, and modernizing elites started to promote new standards of womanhood and desirability. In 2006, a fashion show was organized in a luxury hotel in Kabul. It showcased a model under a *chadari* (burka), lifting her veil at the end of the catwalk. The designer was an Afghan woman from the diaspora in exile in the United States who had recently returned to Kabul; most of the audience were foreigners. The image was strong and the event soon made the headlines of Western newspapers (BBC News 2006) with many journalists making comments on the important signs of progress and "normalization" the fashion show represented in the war-torn country. Ironically, because of the volatile security conditions and an extremely tense political climate, not a single Afghan model had ventured onto the catwalk.

The fashion show experiment was one among many projects that aimed at fashioning the "new Afghan woman" and convincing the world that Afghanistan had arrived on the global stage as a civilized and modern country. In 2003, a beauty school was opened in the Ministry of Women's Affairs. Sponsored by *Vogue* and *Marie Claire* magazines, supported by product donations (Estée Lauder, Paul Mitchell), and staffed by a group of volunteer American beauticians, "the project would later become known as 'Beauty Without Borders,' implying that salon treatments are like medicine for the ill" (McLarney 2009, 6). Because of the controversies that the beauty academy triggered, the minister of women's affairs could not support the project for more than a year and, after the first class of beauticians graduated, the academy was removed from the ministry's program. More than mere commercial attempts at opening a new market for fashion and beauty products, the fashion show and the beauty academy were part of transnational circuits of fantasies whereby Afghan women's bodies could finally be revealed and accessed after years of hiding under the burka. As in many other developing countries seeking international recognition, beauty pageants and fashion

shows are important forms of nationalist expression and powerful and contested symbols of progress and normalization as well as economic and social
liberalization (Ahmed-Ghosh 2003b; Balogun 2012; Shissler 2004). In Afghanistan, these projects have become the subject of intense polemics, revealing
the heightened concern over the standards of modernity that the new Islamic
republic would impose.

In media outlets and political discourses, this symbolic battle articulated
itself in terms of a radical opposition between the authentic Afghan culture
and a corrupt West, producing public fantasies "in a manner analogous with
the play of gossip and reputation in the local community" (Navaro-Yashin
2002, 6). The contours of what constituted "corrupt Western modernity" were
not easily identifiable. However, in commenting on the West, journalists and
politicians redrew the boundaries around their imagined community. They
defined what Afghan culture and the Afghan state had to be distinguished
from. An analysis of these moral panics allows one to explore the nonrational
dimensions of the political in public life, the kinds of fantasies that shape
local structures of feelings.

Since the fall of the Taliban regime, columns in the papers denouncing
the loosening of women's sense of modesty and warning against the dangers
of widespread moral corruption have become more and more common. These
moral panics, I argue, reveal the conflicting relation of Afghan society with
what could be categorized under the broad label of "modernity." I use here
the word "modern" in reference to a Western set of values (individualism, secularism, and equality) produced by the Enlightenment, the industrial revolution, and pluralistic democracy (Göle 1996, 7). The word has a few Dari
equivalents (*emrûzi*, modern), but, most important, it has a historical anchorage in the "modernization" projects that marked the reigns of King Amanullah in the 1920s, King Zahir Shah in the 1960s and 1970s, and, later on, the
Communist regime in the 1980s. These different waves of modernization inspired by Western ideas of progress, social engineering, and economic growth
were designed with the view of overcoming the lag in scientific, economic,
and political development. Under the Communist regime, "modernization"
became the justification for the pursuit of imperialist domination (see Chapter 1). The idea of "modernization" mobilized by the political elite was used
to legitimize regimes that lacked democratic grounding. The attention paid
to "the women question" in this process played a key role in bolstering the
idea of progress for the country's foreign supporters and for the urban cosmopolitan upper class that benefited the most from modernization efforts

(Ahmed-Ghosh 2003a; N. H. Dupree 1984). The counterreactions these projects provoked among the rural, tribal, and religious segments of Afghan society underline the historical recurrence of conflicts over the ownership of nationhood as symbolically embodied in women (Yuval-Davis 1997).

Since nation building has been from the outset a highly internationalized process, these dynamics of resistance have been reactivated. In July 2007, the following article was published in the Dari-language newspaper *Cheragh*,[6] under the title "Tahajum farhangui ajib-o-gharib dar hozour numayendagan e ma" ("Strange Cultural Invasion with Officials as Watchers"):

> If a number of countries seek to impose their culture on Afghanistan using propaganda and if they intend—in this way—to divert our young generations—who are the backbone of society—from the right path by pulling them toward ethical corruption in order to lead our society to destruction and to implement their policies in Afghanistan, then we should mention that as our society is an Islamic society and most of our people are faithful to Islamic principles, then we will disagree with those who have been sold to foreign culture. There is no compatibility between these two cultures, and conflicts will erupt between these two ways of thought. The intensification of the foreign invasion will automatically lead to the intensification of the resistance from the forces opposed to the government of Afghanistan. (*Cheragh* 2007c)

In the rest of the column, the journalist advised the government to take every means at its disposal in order to make foreigners "observe Islamic customs" and wear modest clothes ("foreigners walking around in the city and bazaars wearing semi-naked (sic) clothes will provoke the hatred of the people"). He also insisted on the necessity for foreigners to respect "Islamic *hijab*" ("we see that some foreign countries cannot tolerate the Islamic *hijab* of a Muslim student"). The Ministry of Hajj and Religious Affairs was urged to investigate the "exact nature of the foreign invaders' plot" in order to identify ways to prevent it. The author finally recommended the reestablishment of the Ministry for the Prevention of Vice and the Promotion of Virtue.

In this article, like many others published during the same period, the perceived "external threat" was articulated in divisive and irreconcilable cultural terms. The journalist emphasized the need to protect "culture," yet the fundamental characteristics of what was referred to as "Afghan culture" remained quite vague, with the author tentatively equating culture to religion.

Islamic values, mostly determined through Islamic dress code, were put in radical opposition to foreign values, reinforcing the idea that no understanding could exist between what was perceived as two opposite "models of thought." By intensifying opposition between "us" and "them" and by reactivating the fear of a "cultural invasion," the media supported the dominant conservative views of the political apparatus. The youth, especially young women, were perceived as a particularly vulnerable and influential group in need of protection.

Similar views were expressed in another article entitled "Democracy ba mani be hejabi nist" ("Being Unveiled Is Not the Meaning of Democracy") published in the same newspaper in April 2007 (*Cheragh* 2007a). In this article, the author explicitly stated the need to control women's dressing habits. He denounced "girls who go to school or university wearing clothes that are better suited for wedding parties" and encouraged the government to reinforce "Islamic principles" by monitoring women's veiling in public spaces.

These controversies present the three major characteristics of moral panics as defined by Stanley Cohen (2002): a high concern over the behavior of a certain group or category of people; an increased level of hostility toward the group regarded as a threat; a disproportionate assessment of the threat or danger. Indeed, the series of articles published in the national press depicted the foreign presence in the country as a threat to "culture," using terms such as "invasion," "flood," and "ethical corruption" to highlight the intensity of the phenomenon. Using the argument that internationals were trying to impose not only their military presence in Afghanistan but also their "loose morals," the media requested more governmental control over their behavior as well as restrictions on programs broadcast by private television channels and that greater attention be paid to "un-Islamic" practices among youth and young women in particular.

Confronting the information delivered in the columns of local newspapers with my personal experience as a European in Afghanistan, it became clear that journalists were inventing a threat rather than simply reporting one. My first walk in a bazaar of Kabul with Afghan friends was a revealing experience in this respect: I was definitely the only foreigner there and the way I was dressed drew amused comments from my friends. "You look more Afghan than an Afghan girl," my friend Mustafa told me, pointing at my long veil and large *shalwar kameez*. Girls at the dormitory often found my clothes too "traditional" and "rural" for their liking and offered me their personal assistance in shopping in local clothing stores on several occasions.

Figure 15. Entrance to a beauty parlor on Flower Street, Kabul, 2007. Photo by Julie Billaud.

I was therefore surprised to read reports about "foreigners walking around half naked in the city," not only because the foreigners I knew lived under such strict security regimes that a simple walk in the streets of Kabul was forbidden to them, but also since the majority of them were putting quite an effort into trying to camouflage themselves under large clothes (at least during the day) for these same security reasons. I was actually more shocked by what was happening at night behind closed doors in places reserved for foreigners than by their attitudes in public.

For those who have never been there, Kabul is what it must have been like in a boom town in the American Wild West, a surreal world of DJ disco house parties with bars of free, flowing drinks, Chinese teahouses (you're not going for the tea), and stacks of AK-47s. Foreigners were not walking the streets of Kabul half naked, for sure, but they were certainly drinking alcohol, listening to electronic music, and visiting Chinese prostitutes in places created exclusively for these new types of consumers shortly after the NATO intervention.

To help the internationals escape the anxiety of being cooped up in compounds, social mixers and parties were often organized. Some of these parties could sometimes involve a hundred internationals, dancing in a lighted

garden to DJ mixes from around the world with the foreign mixture of fla-
vors, camels, and guns that left your senses buzzing. It was actually like you
were transported to a borderland dream world that had a home neither in
Afghanistan nor in the West. In this strange "carnival of war," humanitarian workers, construction contractors, and private security guards were mingling and sharing the same dance floor at night while meticulously ignoring
each other during the day in an attempt to reassert the radically different nature and purpose of the work they did. The carnivalesque nature of these encounters, during which masks were constantly swapped and subject positions
constantly displaced, was certainly emblematic of a transition period marked
by opportunism and uncertainty.

Many of these house parties and other establishments where internationals socialized did not allow Afghans to enter unless they had a foreign passport or were accompanied by a Westerner for various reasons—alcohol being
the main one. This segregation led some Afghans to view the international
community as wasting resources needed for the reconstruction of their country. In *Afghan Scene*, a free magazine distributed in NGOs, international agencies' offices, and venues reserved for internationals, photographs of the latest
expatriate parties in town were published. Rumors ran wild among Afghans
about what was going on behind the compound walls.

Was this the behavior journalists wanted to denounce when they discussed
the "negative influence of foreigners" and when they advocated for the reestablishment of the moral police? Or was it a broader popular feeling of alienation and dispossession that was to be read between the lines of these press
releases?

Whatever the motives behind journalists' accusations, it was clear that
debates intensified both in the press and at the political level as to whether
the freedom allowed by democracy should be promoted at the expense of religious ethics. In the National Assembly, conservative MPs started to question the moral content of Indian soap operas broadcast on the private TV
channels that had flourished shortly after the downfall of the Taliban regime
as well as movies produced by Afghan directors.

In September 2007, a movie critic from the daily newspaper *Cheragh* vividly criticized the newly released *Dokhtar-e-Afghan* (Afghan Girl), a romantic movie produced by Afghan film director Yousouf Rouyan, in which the
main female character, played by Afghan actress Sana Tabasum, faced the
moral dilemma of being in love with two men at the same time (*Cheragh*
2007b). The article mentioned that the movie was "the lowest example of West-

ern debauchery" and went on to add that the production of such a movie sig-
nified "the loss and violation of the complete dignity of the Afghan culture."

As prime-time viewing slowly became a battleground between Afghanistan's liberals and conservatives, the government could not continue to ignore the issue. In May 2008 the Ministry of Culture and Information officially
banned five Indian series from broadcast on private television stations. These
debates had put President Hamid Karzai in a bind as he was continuing to
lose popularity. If he rejected the ban, he risked alienating Afghanistan's clerics and their conservative supporters while giving Taliban-led insurgents fod-
der for antigovernment propaganda; if he supported the ban, he risked
alienating his Western supporters. Karzai ended up supporting the ban and
the influential conservative clerics who pushed it. In one public comment on
the matter he declared "that media freedom would be maintained but added
that unsuitable material should not be broadcast" (K. Barker 2008).

What captivated my interest the most while these debates were taking place
was the fact that the television series and movies that had monopolized leg-
islators' attention had one common denominator: all of them were starring
actresses playing the main character in the storyline. These soaps were quite
traditional in many ways, showing prototypic female characters: evil tempt-
resses against dutiful daughters and self-sacrificing mothers. But if gender
stereotypes were somehow reinforced, the series also fueled the audience with
ideals of romantic love, a needed catharsis of feelings and emotions after the
austerity and rigidity that had marked the Taliban period.

These series were doing more than simply feeding the masses with romance. *Tulsi* and *Perina*, the two most popular Indian series, were also addressing issues to which most Afghan families could relate: the difficult
relationships between mothers-in-law and daughters-in-law, arranged marriage, and a family's honor. These series also challenged some social taboos.
Tulsi, the main character in the most popular soap, which was officially entitled "Zaman-e-khosho ham arous bod" ("Because the Mother-in-Law Was
Once the Daughter-in-Law") and which was aired on Tolo TV, had certainly
met with her share of un-Islamic adversity. Her husband fathered a child with
another woman while he had amnesia. Tulsi herself nearly got married to another man twice—once when she was out of her mind and once when she
thought her husband was dead. As for Perina, not only had she conceived a
child with her secret lover Anurak without being married to him, but she also
became a rich and successful businesswoman, a status that remains quite un-
common in the Afghan social imagination.

For the clerics, the reasons for banning the Indian soaps despite their popularity were unquestionable. *Perina* and *Tulsi* showed unveiled women wearing makeup and dresses that revealed their waists, arms, and shoulders, as well as romantic scenes in which lovers danced, courted, and embraced each other. This was enough to get the members of the Council of Clerics sitting on the Supreme Court more than angry toward Tolo and Afghan TV. In an interview he gave to *Al Jazeera* reporter Zeina Khodr, a religious leader explained, "These programs have changed the behaviors of our children and women" (Khodr 2008). This comment echoed opinions I often heard in Afghan families: democracy with the liberalities associated with it meant that girls and women would become uncontrollable, that they would start wearing makeup and inappropriate clothes, that they would demand greater freedoms and, by doing so, bring shame and challenge the reputation of their families.

Crafting Modern Subjects Through Television Serials

The competition between these contrasting views was perhaps best exemplified in debates on free speech that accompanied media reconstruction in Afghanistan. Color television broadcasting reached Afghanistan in 1978. Radio Television Afghanistan, the national state-owned TV broadcaster, was created under the Communist regime as a means to inform people about the achievements of the revolution. When the Taliban took over Kabul in 1996, television was banned and Radio Afghanistan was renamed Sada-e Sharia (Voice of Sharia), the only authorized radio station in the country. The religious police smashed privately owned television sets and strung up videocassettes in trees in a form of symbolic execution by hanging. Anyone found harboring a television set was subject to punishments of flogging and incarceration.

Shortly after the invasion of Afghanistan, the reconstruction of Afghanistan's media outlets under U.S. direction promptly began. Responsibility for overseeing the media development in Afghanistan rested primarily with the Office of Transition Initiatives (OTI), which maintains an important position in the U.S. democracy-promoting apparatus, sitting within USAID's Bureau for Democracy, Conflict, and Humanitarian Assistance (M. J. Barker 2008). Besides supporting the development of "independent" nonprofit print media, radio, and TV stations, the OTI also supported for-profit media. A \$2.2 million grant went to two Afghan-Australian brothers to create Afghanistan's first private media outlets, Radio Arman and Tolo TV (M. J. Barker 2008, 116).

Western support to media outlets, especially radio and TV channels, in Third World countries where the majority of the population is illiterate is not a new phenomenon. During the Cold War, modernization theorists asserted that for the seeds of democracy to grow the Third World had to extricate itself from the disabling claws of tradition and become modern. Mass media was the most efficient means to open traditional minds by introducing them to difference. It encouraged opinions and political participation and fostered people's mobility. Media was considered a primordial tool to create the modern citizen. The international community's urge to promote the reconstruction of media in Afghanistan shortly after the downfall of the Taliban shows that donors' concerns with promoting democracy are still influenced by these views.

However, the main difference between early modernizers and the new generation of those who are sent to postwar or developing countries is that they no longer consider the state as a reliable entity to create the conditions for democracy. As a result, civil society and private entrepreneurs have become privileged stakeholders in democracy building for the values of diversity and autonomy they are supposed to represent. Indeed, USAID, as the main funding body for media projects in Afghanistan, insisted that media should be "*truly* independent," that is, "autonomous" from state support and market driven (M. J. Barker 2008). The creation of Tolo TV in 2004 is a good example of this shift in policy.

As a commercial TV channel, Tolo TV derives all its income from sales of advertising and production of programming content. Tolo TV primarily broadcasts live shows, music programs, foreign movies, comedies, and soap operas. It produces and broadcasts *Afghan Star*, one of Afghanistan's most popular television series. *Afghan Star* is of a similar format to *American Idol* and is billed as Afghanistan's biggest talent search. Tolo also broadcasts *Tulsi*, one of the five Indian soaps that were banned by the government in May 2008. Tolo director Saad Mohseni rejected the ban, calling the government's intervention a breach of the constitution and of media freedom.

Since its creation, Tolo has been the target of heavy criticisms from the government and the National Assembly. The channel is regularly accused of broadcasting programs of poor informational and educational content, of promoting lifestyles in contradiction to Islamic principles, and of creating polemics by discrediting members of the parliament. The strongest condemnations come from conservative segments of the National Assembly like Abdurrasul Sayaf, a deputy and former mujahideen, who accuses Tolo of being an entry point for "foreign conspiracies" (Najibullah 2008).

The power of television stands in its capacity to bring nonlocal or temporally remote experiences to the heart of the most local situations: the home. Access to television in Afghanistan is limited to major city centers but wherever TV sets and electricity are available, watching TV becomes a major source of entertainment. Invited once for dinner at a friend's place, I was astonished to discover that the TV set had been installed on the rooftop of the family's house especially for the occasion. As we ate in silence seated on carpets spread on the floor, watching an Afghan black-and-white movie from the 1960s aired on Aryana TV, my friend Fahair, a twenty-two-year-old car driver from Penjshir, suddenly asked: "Where is this movie from? This cannot be Afghanistan." The scene was showing unveiled women wearing short dresses dancing and chatting with long-haired men during a private house party in Wazir Akbar Khan, the upper-class district of Kabul in the 1960s and 1970s, now occupied by the headquarters of various UN and international organizations. For Fahair, who was born during the war and whose male family members had all fought beside Commandant Masood, it was hard to imagine that such a lighthearted lifestyle had once existed in his country. Despite my repetitive attempts at convincing him that this was Afghanistan, pointing at settings that were still recognizable, Fahair was stubbornly shaking his head in disapproval: "This was shot in a foreign country! This is not Afghanistan! This is foreign, foreign!" he protested while I pointed at Gargha Lake where a black and white couple was walking hand in hand to a romantic song.

In post-Taliban Afghanistan, a well-intentioned conglomerate of media professionals sponsored by Western governments has constructed out of people like Fahair in general, and of women in particular, a subaltern subject in need of enlightenment. Influenced by Western liberal ideas, they feel endowed with the mission to alleviate ignorance, educate citizens, and spread the seeds of a modern nation. When interviewed by Reuters journalist Sayed Salahuddin, Farzana Samimi, a presenter of the woman's program *Banu* for Tolo TV, emphasized the educational purpose of the soaps (Salahuddin 2006). "It enlightens the minds of people in the family, not only of brides or mothers-in-laws, but others too," said the twenty-sevm-year-old psychology major turned TV presenter in defense of the Indian soaps threatened by censorship. Similarly, the TV and radio spots produced by Sayara Media and Communication, the communication agency for which I worked at the beginning of my fieldwork, delivered messages about the importance of education, the evils of poppy production and consumption, and the role of the Afghan National Police in bringing security to the population. The agency and its clients (NGOs, international organizations, Afghan ministries) who ordered such communication products worked with the aim of educating the public, holding the view that positive change would occur at the national level only if Afghan individuals at the grass roots changed and became more socially and civically aware.

In March 2007, a conference organized by the Media and Civil Society Forum was held in Kabul Intercontinental Hotel under the slogan, "Media *Is* Development" (original emphasis). In the middle of the luxurious room where the conference was taking place, an Afghan camerawoman, whose face was totally concealed under a black chador (headscarf) that left only a thin slit for her eyes, was filming the event. The conference was headed by the Killid Group (TKG), a media group founded in 2002 with the financial support of the OTI and the European Union (M. J. Barker 2008, 115). In the report that was published following the conference one could read the following: "Neither democracy nor sustainable development can work unless people are driving the process and feel that they are involved. A free and accessible media can provide the link between the people and state which is needed for enhancing ownership and involvement in the process" (TKG 2007).

There was a certain irony in the conference organizers' reiteration of the commonplace idea that free media was pivotal to establishing participatory democracy. Indeed, since their creation, TKG and other media groups sponsored by the United States as part of its "democracy promotion" agenda have deeply jeopardized smaller provincial media outlets. Provincial media outlets, run by small indigenous civil society organizations and political parties, were no longer able to compete for funding with giants like the Killid Group. In this respect, the comment made during the conference by MP Hadji Mohammad Mohaqiq, chairman of the Media, Culture, and Religious Affairs Committee of the National Assembly, was revealing of his political awareness of the double standards applied in the domain of "press freedom." "Is the press freedom in the country driven by the presence of the international community or does it really reflect the degree of openness of the Afghan society?" the MP asked.

If *Tulsi* and *Perina* evidently won a certain success among the urban population of Afghanistan's major cities, the effects of broadcasting such series in conservative rural areas where fighting and NATO bombings were still going on might have been less positive than what Tolo director Saad Mohseni argued. Additionally, if television was to be a guide to "modernity," one could ask who was to be accountable for defining the benchmarks upon which the progress of democracy would be measured. So-called independent media sponsored by Western governments and international organizations, even if well intentioned in their claims to "educate" the Afghan public, undeniably reflected some of the ideas, values, and aspirations of the development agencies that funded them. The Mohseni brothers (owners of Tolo TV), Atiq Rahimi, the Afghan filmmaker who had been selected by Tolo to direct the first Afghan soap opera, the TV presenters who ran prime-time shows had this in common: many of them had lived in exile for a long period of time and had brought with them new ideas about "modernity." They were educated and could speak foreign languages. As members of the cosmopolitan middle class, they shared relatively liberal views. Most of them had never experienced the hardship of their Afghan compatriots who had not been able to flee during the wars, and they remained remote from the reality of provincial life. Their views on how women's lives could be improved and on the kind of knowledge women should gain in order to be empowered were inspired by the humanist ideas to which they had been exposed during their exile. They believed in the universal human capacity to break free from structures of subordination despite the political and economic constraints that determined the everyday life of ordinary Afghans.

The Subjective Meanings of the Soaps

TV stations, the funding agencies, and the advertising companies that support them are powerful tools to shape public opinions and promote lifestyles. "Television audiences are one among several sites in which local negotiations of meaning are suffused by translocal relations of knowledge and power" (Mankekar 1998, 32). But if television creates a global community of viewers, the same soap opera may be differently received in different parts of the world. In the dormitory, young women's interpretations of the soaps were located at the crossroads of these various instances of power but were also the product of their specific position within Afghan society as well as the individual experiences that had marked their lives. The soaps were conversational objects that exposed the problems inherent within the nature of the family as an institution pivotal to maintaining social stability.

For Ramzia, who had lived with her uncle in Pakistan during the war and who unlike the majority of the girls from her generation had received an uninterrupted education in the Franco-Afghan secondary school in Peshawar, the feminine models proposed in *Tulsi* and *Perina* were highly inspirational in comparison to the hopelessness that, in her opinion, marked the majority of Afghan women's lives. "Tulsi and Perina are not Muslim but they face problems similar to those of Afghan women: unhappy marriages, difficult relationships with mothers-in-law. . . . The difference is that they are brave and independent. These women don't show weaknesses when they face difficulties. They are strong, independent women," she explained.[7] Notions of independence, autonomy, and strength to which Ramzia referred were further explained in relation to a traumatic event that had occurred in her family.

Ramzia's sister, Nafisa, had been kidnapped by a man from her village named Raouf whose marriage offers she had rejected numerous times. Raouf took Nafisa to Iran, where his family had found him a job. Nafisa disappeared for a few months until she managed to convince him to return to Afghanistan. In order to preserve her family's honor, Nafisa had had to marry her abductor. After she delivered her second baby, Nafisa, who was leading an unhappy life with a husband with whom she continuously argued, approached the village's shura (council of elders) in an attempt to obtain a divorce. The divorce was eventually granted but Nafisa was refused the custody of her children who, according to local interpretations of sharia law, belonged to her husband. The pain of being separated from her children made her rescind her decision. She stayed with Raouf and a year later gave birth to a third baby. Nafisa had turned into, in Ramzia's words, "a prisoner in her own home." Ramzia blamed not only Nafisa's husband for her sister's unhappiness but also her grandmother who had lobbied in favor of this marriage based on the argument that the family, mostly composed of women, with an aging father at its head needed the support of another man. Unfortunately, Nafisa's husband revealed himself to be a mediocre businessman, and Ramzia's family never really benefited from this new connection.

It is within the context of this life event that Ramzia commented on the Indian soaps. When I asked her how she reconciled the fact that Perina had conceived a child outside of marriage with the values of Islam, she simply replied, "These kinds of things happen all the time in our society as well. The thing is that it is taboo to talk about it. Perina and Tulsi are free women. If these series are so popular, it is because everyone would like to be free like the characters in the series. Everyone likes freedom."[8] Ramzia associated freedom with love because her sister Nafisa's forced marriage to a husband who had kidnapped and abused her was, to her understanding, equivalent to a life sentence. In this marriage, Nafisa's sacrifice had brought nothing to the family except a strong sense of waste and treason. Perina could be blamed for having an illicit child but "her love for Anurak was real and her heart was pure," she explained. The shameful stamp of treachery did not mark Anurak and Perina's story. Besides, Perina was educated and had proved her worth by becoming a successful businesswoman. Nafisa's experience had traumatized the family to such an extent that the parents had promised Ramzia that she would be able to marry a man she would choose for herself. But this privilege was also granted to Ramzia because, like Perina, she was the main family provider and she "had a brain," as she liked to say.

The value of love in the face of social pressure was understood by the young women of room 42 as a universally applicable alternative to marriages arranged by families for financial and strategic reasons. To them, love not only enhanced women's status and lives but was also an aspiration they could afford to have as educated women. The soaps did not simply sell "foreign ideas" to the dormitory girls. As the example of Ramzia shows, girls were actively engaged in negotiating and interpreting these ideas in the specific and culturally located context of their lives. Of course, to some extent girls' perceptions of and ideas about marriage and the family were the product of cultural hybridizations that had marked their lives as emigrants in Iran and elsewhere. They were also the reflection of the relative liberalism and cosmopolitanism that had suddenly reached Kabul after years of isolation due to war and civil unrest. But these ideas were not mere foreign transplants. The soaps were in many ways mirroring the lives of the girls, questioning some of their assumptions and making some of them challenge the boundaries of the social order.

For Massoma, who was an ethnic Hazara,[9] the ethnic group that suffered and is still suffering the most from discrimination, the upward mobility promised in love relationships could not apply to the people of her group. Among the residents of room 42 Massoma was undeniably from the poorest family. She had one sister and three brothers, one of whom suffered from mental health problems, another who had illegally migrated to France and was kept in a detention center next to Calais, and the youngest, who was only fourteen years old and still attending school. The destitution in which her family lived, occupying a fifteen-square-meters room in an impoverished neighborhood on the outskirt of Kabul, made her feel particularly responsible for maintaining her status as a loyal, self-sacrificing, and dutiful daughter. Indeed,

Massoma's father was old, sick, and jobless. Massoma was able to support the family thanks to the modest amount she earned as a part-time NGO employee, but she was also aware that getting married could be a more profitable and sustainable option for the supportive connections it could create with another family.

The ideal of "autonomy" to which the girls of room 42 aspired was therefore never discussed outside of the kinship bounds and the material reality in which their lives were entangled. Dreaming was still allowed, after all. And while Massoma was getting ready to take off for work, Maryam and Rokia returned to their mirror to add some extra makeup to their eyes. This was perhaps what the soaps achieved the most effectively: the modeling of these young women's bodies on their favorite Indian actresses. This was a comment I heard once from a female civil servant at the Ministry of Women's Affairs: "With all these new products and these Indian series, women have become more greedy and it creates troubles in families. Their husbands cannot always afford to buy them everything they want and then they argue and men become violent." In her opinion, futile consumer desires among women were a fundamental explanation for increased domestic violence.[10]

Going shopping for clothes and cosmetics was indeed a major Friday afternoon activity. We would usually take the bus to Kute Sangi and crawl into one of the big malls that had survived the bombings. In what would be better described as Ali Baba's cave, girls would buy for each other lipstick, eye shadow, creams, and scarves. The gifts they made to their friends were not only means to consolidate their friendships, show their loyalty, and strengthen their ties between group members but also practices that defined them as "modern" and "independent," yet also honorable Muslims.

In Afghanistan, men and women's public spheres of sociability are segregated and women's public sphere consists of women's gatherings in family homes. Because hospitality is considered an important Islamic value, women's capacity to invite each other to their houses is central to maintain a family's reputation within the broader community. As a result, such gatherings were regularly taking place in the dormitory, with residents inviting each other for tea in their rooms, wearing fashionable clothes and makeup for the occasion, and giving gifts (perfumes, veils, cosmetics) to each other. Despite the little money Massoma carefully saved for her family, she could not extract herself from the gift economy. If she was offered a chador, she had to make sure she could return the gift at some point. Her incapacity to do so would damage her status within the group and make her more vulnerable to gossip, backbiting, and other criticisms that were commonly perceived as the worst and most dangerous feminine weapons. As a Hazara and a Shia, Massoma was already more exposed to all sorts of mean criticisms than girls from other ethnic groups.

As a matter of fact, the Indian series played a crucial role in creating desires and anxieties pertaining to different forms of modernity. For the most part, the meanings imputed to modernity were neither anchored in the West nor assumed as self-evident but were, in fact, constituted and contested through Tulsi and Perina's discourses on gender and class. A "modern" woman would assert her class status by consuming dresses of bright colors and makeup and allowing herself to "fall in love" (most of the time in a platonic manner), but would also remain unconditionally faithful to her kin and family by making sure that harmonious relationships with her relatives were maintained.

The Indian soaps have therefore allowed a public culture to emerge in which new kinds of speech could be generated, creating new aspirations for love, companionship, and consumption. However, in a context where the norm of the "harmonious family" prevails and where kinship relations represent the most reliable means to maintain a sense of safety and protection, these aspirations cannot be expressed in a way that would make them appear as threats to the social order. Young women's understandings of autonomy and independence are tightly entangled within a set of relations that form the very conditions of their possibility.

In the process of interpreting the soaps, the young women of room 42 were not radically opposing structures of subordination for the simple reason that these very structures, despite the gender hierarchies they induced, were also providing them with a sense of safety that could not be found anywhere else. As the example of the soaps in Afghanistan shows, notions of freedom and autonomy are discussed within the broader economy of relations that women see as important to preserve. Besides gender, other forms of social stratification such as class and ethnicity are determinant factors in shaping desires and aspirations.

The Cosmetic Cover of Nationalist Anxieties

Self-beautification did not just disappear under the Taliban. During their rule, women ran clandestine beauty salons in their homes, using cosmetics smuggled from Pakistan. Their pursuit of beauty was a means to preserve a

Figure 16. Young woman applying makeup, Women's National Dormitory, Kabul, 2007. Photo by Julie Billaud.

sense of self-worth and continuity in an environment where their lives had been severely restricted. These underground activities were also about maintaining spaces of sociability in a universe where such social possibilities had dramatically shrunk. As for men, personalizing their bodies by lifting weights and pumping up their muscles in underground gym clubs was common practice. However, after the intervention of the NATO forces and the anarchic liberalization of the economy, beauty became a public matter that crystallized anxieties about globalization, gender, morality, and nationhood.

With the rapid opening of the economy and the rise of consumerism the conformism that dominated during the Taliban, which forced both men and women to follow a strict dress code in public, slightly loosened. Permissive spaces, often related to consumption spaces, started to appear in the city. The youth, starving for entertainment after years of austerity imposed by the mullahs' regime, started to test the boundaries of the permissible. In cities, young men let their hair grow and exchanged their traditional *peran tomban* for blue jeans and slinky T-shirts, trying to fashion their appearance on their favorite

Bollywood movie stars. With the renewal of the marriage industry, extravagant wedding halls with exotic names mushroomed on the outskirts of major Afghan cities. In Kabul, Sham-e Paris (Parisian Night), with its replica of the Eiffel Tower illuminated on the forecourt, was a luxurious and exuberant complex composed of reception halls, beauty salons, cocktail dress shops, and photography studios. This overt exhibition of private wealth in the middle of overwhelming public poverty exemplified in a powerful way the contradictions inherent in the transition toward democracy.

In the beauty salons of Kabul, the walls were plastered with posters of heavily made-up Indian actresses. On special occasions such as wedding parties, Afghan women modeled themselves on these women whom they perceived as beautiful and liberated. Inside the salons, women were dyeing their hair, plucking their eyebrows, and brushing colored shadow on their eyelids only to eventually hide their hard work under their *chadari* as soon as they returned to the street. A wedding has no price in Afghanistan. On this occasion, the groom's family can spend up to U.S.$20,000, a small fortune when more than half of the population is living below the poverty line. The success of a marriage is measured by the number of guests a family can afford to invite. In a country where security is seriously lacking, a wedding is a powerful means to develop coalitions and to strengthen ties with relatives and the broader community. The bride is never beautiful enough on her wedding day. She usually changes dresses up to three times during the party, disappearing for an hour only to reappear, as in a fashion show, under a completely new face in front of the guests. The first dress she wears is traditionally white, the second green, and the last either red or blue. Makeup and hair design should match her dress color, which keeps hair dressers and beauticians busy for most of the night.

A wedding is about much more than just the bride's beauty. It is an institution through which families display wealth and tighten connections. The issue of women's dress at weddings implicates whole families, not just the individual women concerned. Before the wedding party, women from both families traditionally spend the day together in a beauty salon. The bride's body is entirely waxed, her feet and hands are dyed with henna, and her face receives a thick layer of makeup: all this is performed under the attentive gaze of her female relatives. Through this ritual, the bride's body becomes the symbolic *trait d'union* between two families. The beautification of the bride through hair design, makeup, and dresses is the body work through which two families engage in a fruitful and rewarding union.

Calls to reestablish public order by controlling women's appearance at wedding parties, banning cosmetics and "Western" clothes as well as the most popular Indian TV series have to be placed in this context where increased consumerism has disrupted ideals of Islamic lifestyle. This kind of consumption, it was said, was an open invitation to sexualized self-exhibition, a visible sign of moral depravation and cultural dilution from which society and the youth in particular had to be protected. "Kabul has seen a wave of liberal, unwelcome influences," explained Qazi Nazir Ahmad, an MP from Herat Province who supported the law. "There are young women who have abandoned their *hijab* and now prostitution can be found openly in the streets of our cities. Our job is to protect the Afghan people," he added.[11] Consumerism, in his view, necessarily led to the commoditization of women's bodies and uncontrolled sexuality. The "politics of opposition" that he supported attempted to reestablish "the contours of the nation" and the responsibility of the nation-state "in a period when the sanctity of boundaries were perceived to be under threat" (Oza 2001, 1086).

As luxury shopping malls were erected in the city center while the rural poor in search of jobs and security poured into the slums surrounding Kabul, opposition groups and the media outlets they owned accused the government of encouraging private luxury consumption, a lifestyle perceived as contrary to the Islamic ideals of modesty, asceticism, and abstention from worldly pleasures. The opposition between Islam and consumerism constructed throughout these narratives challenged the stability of commonly shared Islamic values. Consumerism promised a range of possible lifestyles and behaviors that suddenly competed with or contradicted the uniform lifestyle demanded by Islamic conservatism, reinforcing contestations around "culture."

These dynamics were revealed to me when Soheila, a young woman boarding in the dormitory, invited me to accompany her on a visit to her sister who lived in a working-class suburb of Kabul. Soheila's mother had traveled from her village in Kapisa to meet her daughter's newborn baby boy. When Soheila entered the two-room flat, her mother looked at her and commented: "What kind of clothes are you wearing, my daughter? Is this democracy?" She shook her head in disapproval. Soheila wore beige trousers under a tight safari jacket, with a square veil tied under her chin in the style of most female students on Kabul University campus. For Nasima, Soheila's mother, who had spent her entire life in an isolated village in Kapisa and who had only attended primary school, her daughter's clothes clashed with common standards of feminine modesty. As much as she was proud to see her daughter having access to education, she could not consent to the type of femininity she embodied. In her understanding, "democracy" was associated with a self-driven individualistic type of femininity and was contrary to the Muslim way of life according to which respectable women wore with pride "traditional" Afghan clothes and primarily cared for the reputation of their family.

The current making of the Afghan nation under the particular circumstances of foreign-led democratization and market liberalization is a deeply gendered process through which contrasted views of the "public good" come into conflict. The postwar period has provided individuals with new opportunities to explore and experiment with social boundaries. Young women who have turned to styles of dress that do not correspond with traditional ideas of feminine modesty are perceived as threatening because as women their bodies are bearers and reproducers of collective values. As in India where, according to Emma Tarlo (1996, 17), social, religious, and regional stratifications are still strongly expressed and where the fashion industry is still relatively young, a change of dress in Afghanistan is likely to be interpreted "as an act of desertion or a change of affiliation." Conservative demands for stricter control over women's appearances in public as a means to preserve Islamic morality against liberal encouragement for a model of emancipated femininity embedded within a global consumerist culture illustrate the centrality of women's bodies in defining the nation's destiny.

The sartorial anxieties so vivid in post-Taliban Kabul are not new phenomena. The sensitive question of what to wear has been a recurrent issue throughout Afghan history. In the late 1920s, King Amanullah made it compulsory for men to wear European suits when entering Kabul. In the civil service, suits became standard attire for men, while women were encouraged to remove their chadors. In the countryside, pictures of the king's wife, Queen Soraya, unveiled and dressed in Western clothes, were used as propaganda against the government that was perceived as corrupt and "sold to the West" (L. Dupree 1973). In the 1960s and 1970s, at a time of important economic growth and industrialization, Afghanistan strove to present itself to the outside world as a modern liberal country. Women's fashion played a central role in showcasing such an image. But far from being unanimously endorsed, women's modern dresses remained the material focus of widespread tensions.

The fashion in vogue in Kabul in the late 1960s was not a mere reproduction of European designs, but distinguished itself by a drive to refresh and modernize traditional Afghan clothing. In her Kabul Studio, fashion designer

Safia Tarzi used Afghanistan's delicate and colorful embroideries, fabrics, and furs on patterns that blurred clear-cut distinctions between feminine and masculine, urban and rural, Western and Oriental clothes. Tarzi wore feminized turbans and waistcoats in an attempt to reinvent and reinterpret traditional clothing classifications. Her work was an arresting illustration of the cross-cultural fertilization processes at work within the broader society.

As in late colonial India when Gandhi called for a return to *khadi* fabric and caps for men as a form of symbolic resistance against the British occupiers (Tarlo 1991 and 1996), debates around which clothes constitute proper Islamic dress in contemporary Afghanistan have to be understood as a collective effort to assert identity and sovereignty. That everyone agrees with the fact that Islam is a central source of guidance when it comes to deciding what to wear but that no consensus can be reached on which pieces of clothing are acceptable is a powerful reminder that wearing a certain type of dress is a creative act. Because dress codes are enmeshed in wider issues concerning modesty, honor, and respect, clashes between different styles of clothing are often symbolic of wider discord between different cultural and social values and norms.

"Taliban Girls" and "Modern Girls"

Applying makeup and selecting clothes were part of the girls' everyday rituals in room 42. Quantity and colors of makeup and choice of clothes were highly situational. They varied according to the place they went, to the people they met, and of course by the money they had to purchase what are considered luxury products in Afghanistan. The motivations behind some of the dormitory girls' pursuit of beauty against dominant discourses reaffirming women's modesty as a fundamental principle of Islam have to be explored and questioned. Why were some female students refusing to follow the classic dress code when the potential repercussions (gossip, sexual harassment, arguments with relatives, comments in the streets) for their nonconformity were so harsh? Were they trying to make a public statement on Fridays when they made their way through the narrow alleys of the bazaar wearing lipstick and bright colored veils? Or were their bodies simply the passive objects of globalization and its standardized consumer items?

Girls who displayed their pampered and fashionable appearance most consistently and across most contexts were the ones who had recently returned

Figure 17. "Afghan karakul is coveted at home and abroad" (original caption).
From *Afghanistan: Ancient Land with Modern Ways* (Afghan Ministry of
Planning, 1969), 142.

to Afghanistan and who knew very little about their country. Some of them
were even born abroad, in Iran, Pakistan, or farther afield. This was the case
for Habiba and Farida, two sisters who studied foreign languages at the University of Kabul and worked part-time in a shop on a NATO military base
located on the road to Jalalabad. Farida and Habiba's father, a military officer, fled to Iran when the Soviets invaded the country. The two sisters had
never visited Afghanistan prior to their family's return in 2002. Even if they

had heard about the Taliban and their imaginations were filled with the horror stories they had heard in the foreign press and through friends and relatives, girls who had been brought up abroad had never personally experienced the fear, beatings, and humiliations of the other girls who stayed in Afghanistan during their rule. This radically different life experience explained in large part their capacity to reinterpret the dominant dress code.

Farida and Habiba's parents had longed to return home, but Afghanistan was obviously not "home" for their daughters who had grown up abroad. Their work with foreign soldiers, their use of Farsi expressions when they talked, and more significantly the veils and clothes they wore distinguished them from the other dormitory girls. Farida and Habiba wore colorful square chadors tied up under their chins, bright-colored T-shirts under tight black blouses, jeans, and sneakers. They drew black eyeliner around the contours of their eyes and plucked their eyebrows in a straight shape. But even though both of them were targets of ferocious gossip by other dormitory girls, people from their neighborhood, and relatives, being singled out as *khariji* (foreigners), Farida and Habiba kept on wearing makeup, trendy headscarves, and the clothes they brought with them from Iran.[12] When I asked them why they did not try to change some of their habits in order to avoid harmful comments, Farida replied:

> Girls at the dorm are totally ignorant. You know, the relationships that we have with foreigners are much easier than the relationships we have with Afghans. We feel that we are Afghans but with a superior culture. You know, in foreign countries, when a girl is working and is financially independent, it is perceived as something positive. Foreigners have a different culture and a different religion, but they think the same way as us. Here, it is not the same. It is very difficult for us to feel like foreigners in our own country. But it's like that. If we don't live here, where can we go? Afghanistan will develop one day and people will change their mind.

Convinced as they were of belonging to a "superior culture," the two sisters were not willing to be associated with the more traditional-looking dormitory residents who wore large chadors and loose *shalwar kameez* and whom they jokingly called "Taliban." It seemed therefore natural to them to embody what they considered a modern identity and to reject dressing practices they regarded as backward. They turned the rejection they experienced into a sign of their own "distinction." Our bodies and actions, according to Pierre Bourdieu (1984), rather than being primarily cognitive models, encode cultural meanings. We bring forth worlds or make our lives meaningful not only with language, rituals, and works, but also in and on our very bodies. Bourdieu claims that how one chooses to present one's social space to the world, one's aesthetic dispositions, depicts one's status and one's desire to maintain distance from other groups.

However, as much as the girls of room 42 and their friends strove to mark their belonging to an educated upper class, their performances were not unaffected by others' judgments. What they "gave," the verbal symbols and attitudes they used to convey information about themselves and prevent false expectations, contradicted what they physically "gave off" in public (Goffman 1969). In other words, girls were constantly involved in negotiating their appearance by using discursive justifications and disciplining their body in other ways in order to maintain their reputation. In public, their physical nonconformity was counterbalanced by a strict moral conformity to Islamic norms of modesty. When I walked in the street with Fawzia, for instance, she often reminded me not to laugh or speak too loudly. A girl laughing in public is perceived in Afghanistan as wanting to attract men's attention. Such an attitude is understood as a form of "openness," a sign of availability that goes against social expectations of female modesty. Under the *chadari*, women's "closedness," containment, and modesty were materially visible. I was often surprised to hear the lively conversations women had in bazaars, talking to each other through their *chadari* and bargaining with merchants. In the absence of this sartorial device, the young women of room 42 had to make extra efforts to conform to the ideal of female closedness and modesty (Meneley 2007; Makhlouf 1979; Popenoe 2004). This meant, in practice, walking straight without glancing at others, looking determined in order to prevent being seen as a loiterer, and avoiding any facial expression that could be read as having a good time: girls had to show that they were walking with a purpose. Their personal bodies, despite appearances, did not exist outside the social context in which they lived. Girls, indeed, had to overperform closedness and shyness (*sharmanda*) since their bodies were displaying opposite meanings.

However, by getting involved in such complex performances, these young women both reproduced and subverted the dominant gender ideology. Indeed, these tactics were mostly a means to prove to themselves and to their immediate surroundings that they were good and moral Muslim girls as external observers were hardly able to read these signs. The constant comments to which they were subjected when walking the streets proved that local interpretations of female modesty and shyness as primarily displayed through "proper" Islamic clothing were dominant. It was not rare to hear women in buses commenting aloud on their clothes. Colorful clothes and makeup were indeed corporeal ornaments considered as appropriate only within the intimate sphere of the home or at wedding parties, which were most of the time segregated along gender lines. But as consumers in their own right, wanting to wear jeans and other Western-style garments, these young women challenged household and community claims on their sexuality and income (Hansen 2004, 383). As a result of their education abroad and their financial independence, the girls of room 42 had a very different understanding of the principles of "shyness" (*sharmanda*) and "closedness" that were meant to apply to their sex. Despite their efforts to perform "shyness" through other means, the girls of room 42 were read as provocative transgressors. "I obey my parents and I work hard. They [her parents] know that my heart is pure and that I will never lie or deceive them," Habiba told me once in a bus after two older ladies had reprimanded her on her appearance.

In a context of rapid political, economic, and cultural changes about which there already existed anxieties about the corrupting impact of globalization, conservative groups effectively mobilized sympathy around their concerns for threatened Afghan culture. With the sanctity of the national boundaries being challenged by the military occupation and market liberalization, the public sphere became imagined as a site for the implementation of a religious and "traditional" way of life and women's corporeal visibility and social mixing in men's spaces all counted as "foreign" and contrary to Islamic values. However, when nationalist discourses associated modernity with Westernization, these young women's body work offered a self-crafted model of modernity: embedded neither in the liberal West nor in an authentic Islamic or Afghan tradition.

By wearing headscarves of different shapes, colors, and patterns, the girls of room 42 were slightly changing its meaning: from a garment originally seen as purely functional, their veils were turned into fashion accessories. Their makeup matched the color of their veils and by putting such an effort into these selections and arrangements, the girls answered their personal desire to appear beautiful, fashionable, and modern. "I cannot dress the way women dress in my village. Village clothes are not convenient for the city. Some of my relatives say I became like an American woman but they say this because they don't know what American women wear. I don't want to be an American woman. To me, my family is everything. I wear *hijab*. I am well covered. It is practical and chic," Zoora explained. In the girls' opinion, these dressing practices did not contradict religious values. The young women of room 42 were constantly reminding each other that they were Muslims and that, as such, they had to behave in a particular way. They justified their attention to how they looked by citing the Islamic principle stipulating that believers should have a pleasant and beautiful appearance. They considered Aisha, the "mother of believers," a model of educated femininity. Rather than transgressions, girls' beauty practices revealed the tensions and frictions between the various systems of values in which they were caught.

The young women whom they mocked by calling them "Taliban" were not totally immune to the influence of fashion and consumerism either. They too watched Indian soap operas, listened to Pakistani pop music, and played with makeup among themselves in the safe space of their bedrooms. Their beauty rituals, however, were restricted to the semipublic space of the dormitory where they sometimes organized parties to celebrate other girls' engagements and competed for the most beautiful makeup, dress, and hairstyle. These hidden "spaces [. . .] saturated with memories, that echo the lost worlds and the cracked sounds of pleasure and enjoyment" (Pile and Keith 1997, 16) were in sharp contrast to the austere appearance they adopted when they stepped outside the dormitory. Even though these young women were convinced believers, their conservative appearance was not motivated by a religious ideal. Young women wearing traditional chadors were not invested in practicing piety through body discipline (Mahmood 2005) but were rather concerned with showing their adherence to Afghan culture and tradition (Moors 2003). Most of them had struggled hard to convince their families—most of whom lived in rural areas—to let them attend university in the capital city, a place seen from the outside as both the center of moral corruption and social opportunities. The trust their families had granted them implied that they should concentrate on their studies. They regarded girls who overtly engaged with fashion as superficial and as "bad Muslims."

The pressure to look beautiful and fashionable that the young women of room 42 experienced mostly came from their workplace where internationals tended to value Afghan women who displayed an emancipated self. At work, the modern gendered subject was constituted through women role models and repetitive performances, including language styles and dress codes. This external pressure was revealed to me when Naheed, a dormitory resident working part-time in a local women's organization in Kabul, told me how her application to a position in a foreign embassy was turned down because of her wearing an *abaya,* a long overcoat and a headscarf covering everything except the face and hands. "They made me understand that if I wanted the job, I had to make an effort in the way I dressed," she said. She then went on to explain, that her family was happy for her to work outside of the house in tandem with her studies as long as she wore proper Islamic clothes. It is difficult to know whether this was common practice among foreign employers, but it remained a tacit rule to give advantage to women who could represent the ideal of a liberated femininity the international community was eager to promote.

By tying up their chadors differently and choosing different patterns, fabrics, sizes, shapes, and designs, the girls of room 42, like many other young Afghan women employed or seeking employment opportunities, were exploring and negotiating its symbolic potentiality. Their head covering practices reflected their struggle between remaining faithful to the Koranic principles on religiously appropriate dress and constructing a fashionable, beautiful, and modern appearance. Residents of room 42 and their friends spent a considerable amount of time in shops looking at the latest arrivals of chadors, usually buying a few of them at once to match their different dresses and the color of their skin or to offer as presents to their friends. Choices of colors, patterns, and shapes were influenced by a variety of factors: female TV presenters, Indian movie stars, advertisements, comments from others, and their own personal understanding of "appropriate Islamic clothes." Soheila, for instance, mostly wore a black square chador tied up under the chin as she considered black a decent and "chic" color and the square chador practical. Farida often wore the hood she had brought from Iran for similar practical reasons; she enjoyed the fact that she did not have to think about fixing it all the time, as once it was on her head it would not move. Habiba and Farida were more fashion-oriented as a result of their greater exposure to the feminine press and the fashion industry during their years of exile in Iran.

However, achieving a beautiful yet not sexually attractive look was a complex task that required a lot of calculation and beauty work. Young women would generally comment on each others' scarves, go shopping for chadors in small groups, and be attentive to each others' advice. Girls were also very susceptible to comments they received from others. They spent considerable time and effort to have their veil look straight and symmetrical on their heads. In scarf shops, the girls tried on several in front of a mirror, checking the comfort quality of the fabric, the positioning of motives, and the matching of colors with their own skin. They also took particular care of their veils, washing, ironing, and storing them with great meticulousness. The time and effort expended on daily head covering practices and the signification of beauty that they represented had many similarities with hair styling under-taken by women in other countries.

For working women like Habiba, Farida, Massoma, and Soheila, and for those who had lived abroad during the war in general, women in *chadari* were symbols of the oppressed Other excluded from modernity. In their under-standing, female students wearing the traditional chador today were the ones who would accept the *chadari* tomorrow if their husbands and in-laws asked for it. In contrast, dormitory girls who were sympathetic to longer chadors felt they were closer to religious principles of modesty by being resistant to luxury consumerism. By wearing formal chadors, they showed their entire dedication to the quest for knowledge, a central pillar of Islam and the pri-mary purpose of their presence in the dormitory. The girls of room 42 on the other hand despised such girls quite overtly, calling them "Taliban" and mock-ing their "old-fashioned" style. "These girls have never been abroad and they have never worked," Habiba told me once. "The only thing they know is their village and what the mullah has taught them. They think women should lis-ten to men and do whatever they say."

The actual sartorial practices of the urban educated and working women that I observed in the dormitory contest the stereotypical discourses and im-ages about covered women, complicating the tension between Islam and con-sumerism (Sandikci and Ger 2005). The aesthetics and politics of the veil that I have described in this section show that Islamic veiling in contemporary Kabul has become an unstable sign, a cultural codifier of the tensions and promises of modernity. The veil as a fashion accessory connotes a political posture but also a rank and an identity. Urban educated working women like the residents of room 42, striving to look modern as well as Muslim, are not mere symbolic repositories of the tensions between Islam and consumerism. The selection and wearing of veils entails an elaborate process that requires invocation of economic and cultural capital. The actual practices and dis-courses of these young women indicate the personalized nature of Islamic covering. Personalization and body work together create a sense of modern agency that is free to choose and shape while participating in a shared moral universe. Through their continual attention to their physical appearance, res-idents of room 42 were not simply the symbolic repositories of the conflict-ing interpretation of culture/religion but they were actively involved in making or in renegotiating culture/religion. In their capacity for transformation, these young women's bodies became tools or templates for reinterpreting culture.

Bodies as Sites of Anticolonial Contestation

In the limbo that marked the post-Taliban period, the girls of room 42 tested the boundaries of the social order with all the means they had at their disposal. They used their bodies as templates to project their views regarding religion and beauty and construct a modern Islamic identity and class status. In the merging of their bodies' agential and symbolic capacities, their beauty practices blurred traditional social conceptions of ideal femininity. It can be argued that these simple forms of feminine "anti-discipline" (Certeau 1984) were tactics that combined both elements of compliance to gender hierarchies and elements of subversion of these hierarchies. Indeed, the young women of room 42 were less invested in resisting structural relations on face-to-face grounds than in diverting them in subtle and creative ways. In an essentially male-dominated culture, girls' control of their own bodies becomes one of the few means by which they can assert their wishes and desires.

Despite these young women's claims to independence and autonomy, the social norm of male control over female presence in public spaces kept its primacy over women's control over their bodies. This gender ideology was pertinent not only for covered girls who simply wore more classic forms of Islamic clothes but for young women overtly involved in fashion and beauty work as well. While the latter felt a sense of empowerment provided by the personalization of their appearance, the efforts they made to project their aesthetic judgments, religious interpretations, and social position on their own bodies revealed the new forms of self-discipline that came to regiment their lives. Through these creative and skillful reinterpretations of ideals of beauty and fashion within an Islamic framework, these young women attempted to enlarge the scope of their possibilities. Paradoxically, this entailed both possibilities and limitations since increased visibility often meant they had to make extra efforts to socially communicate their Muslim selves.

That the dispute over what to wear crystallized around items such as blue jeans, cosmetics, Indian soap operas, and headscarves considered as "Western" or un-Islamic is not surprising. As in other parts of Asia that bear the scars of colonial domination, the issue of women's clothes is part of a long historical confrontation between opposing cultural values (Tarlo 1996, 200).

If this dispute tended to be framed in terms of an opposition between "traditional" village values and "educated" urban ones, ideas about the latter were informed by the values of a cosmopolitan Afghan elite who were the closest followers of European lifestyles in the 1960s and 1970s and of Soviet behaviors in the 1980s. As Tarlo argues, "colonial values are not only *in*vasive but also *per*vasive. Part of the very forcefulness of the colonial encounter was the infusion of alien cultural ideas in such a way that they can no longer be disentangled from [local] thought" (1996, 200).

In the context of the military occupation and rapid economic and social changes, women's bodies have become a symbolic site of struggle over national identity. The beauty work that I have described in this chapter reveals the difficulty for young women to override the emotional glue of nationalist ideas and symbols that the presence of foreign forces has revived. If some of them dare reinterpreting dominant norms in order to make them conform with their desire to express their belonging to a modern and educated class, the sartorial practices of both groups illustrate an effort to preserve Islamic norms and remain within a shared moral universe. The conformism that dominates the Afghan public sphere should not be interpreted in essentialist cultural terms; as in other colonial encounters, the preservation of the social body through the control of women's public appearance has to be read as a symbolic form of resistance to Western domination. In the current context of the occupation, women's bodies have become a symbol of social connectedness that carries the power to display the nurturing of the larger community. However, women's bodies are not mere repositories of nationalist ideologies but rather sites of colonial contestation (Jean Comaroff 1985) that women themselves creatively use to assert both autonomy from and solidarity with the broader national community.

=====

CHAPTER 5

Strategic Decoration: Dissimulation, Performance, and Agency in an Islamic Public Space

Khâ l na-shawi raswâ amrang-ejamâ'at bâsh.
Not to be considered strange, conform to the crowd.
—Persian proverb

The bus was making its way through a dust storm. The dust was blinding us, entering our noses and throats, making us cough like asthmatic patients, reaching under the layers of our clothing. Women veiled under their *chadari* who were seated in the front of the bus were covering their babies under their long blue enveloping robes in an attempt to protect them from the polluted air. "*Chadari* are sometimes practical," commented Fawzia, who had invited me on that day to her parents' home in Dasht-e Bashri, a poor and desolate suburb located to the southwest of Kabul.

Seeing Massoma dressed up with her semilong black blouse, her polished shoes, and her black trousers walking in the muddy alleys of Dasht-e Bashri in which latrine waste was overflowing had something of a surreal air. The contrast between her pampered appearance and the desolation that surrounded us was simply too sharp. "Now you understand why I prefer staying at the dormitory," she commented while pushing open the front gate of the compound where her parents lived.

Massoma's family shared a house with three other Hazara families recently returned from Iran, each of them occupying one room. The carpets spread on the floor and the *toshak* (mattresses) and cushions displayed along the walls

Figure 18. *Chadari* (burka) seller in Herat, 2007. Photo by Julie Billaud.

were the only pieces of furniture available. Massoma's parents, her three brothers, and her sister had piled up in this place for the past three years waiting
for their financial situation to improve in order to find a better place to live.
But jobs were scarce in Kabul and Massoma's father was old and sick. After
long consideration, they had eventually encouraged their eldest son, Farid,
to leave the country and find work abroad. Their last savings had been invested in a smuggler who organized Farid's long journey to Europe. According to the latest news, Farid had reached France after a few months spent
working illegally on some farms located somewhere in northern Greece. He
was now kept in a detention center next to Calais, waiting for his asylum claim
to be reviewed. He had told the French authorities that members of his family were Taliban supporters who pressured him to take part in terrorist activities, which he had constantly refused until he had made the decision to
escape and seek asylum in Europe where he thought he would be safe. To support his case, Farid had asked Massoma to send a picture of the family dressed
as "terrorists." My mission on that day was to take some pictures of the "terrorist" family and make sure they would arrive in France on time before the
French Office for the Protection of Refugees and Stateless Persons (OFPRA)
had deliberated upon Farid's case.

In spite of my attempts to explain to Massoma that, because of his Hazara ethnicity,[1] Farid's story had limited chances of being taken seriously, she had insisted and here I was now, observing the boys applying thick layers of kohl under their eyes "to look more scary."

"Madarjan, you need to wear *chadari* if Dad is a Taleb," Massoma noted, unconvinced by her mother's look.

"I never had one . . . but I think our neighbor has. Let me see if I can borrow it from her!" she said playfully while running to the room next door.

She came back giggling, holding the blue piece of cloth in one hand, raising it to the sky as a sign of victory. Everyone was ready now: boys had their turbans around their heads and kohl under their eyes and Mamajan was hidden under her blue tent. "Now make scary faces," I advised while looking through my camera lens. As the boys started to frown and purse their lips, I was already caught in the game, amused to discover how stereotypes about Taliban abroad had been assimilated in their region of origin.

What surprised me the most was to discover that even here, the local imagination was filled with the twin figures of the Islamic fundamentalist and his female victim. For Massoma it was very clear that her mother could not expose her face in front of the camera if she was to act as the Taleb's wife. Even here, in this destitute suburb of Kabul, deprived of clean water and electricity, it was possible to envision the burka-clad body of the Afghan woman as a visible sign of the West's invisible enemy. In the mud of Dasht-e Bashri, irony was the "art of the weak" (Certeau 1984) and people laughed about and played with this piece of cloth which had become under the Taliban regime the universally recognized symbol of Islamic fundamentalism.

The double irony that is easily detectable in this situation—Massoma's mother being caught in the impromptu situation of having to perform her own oppression in order to support her son's freedom abroad and the anthropologist becoming an accomplice in the masquerade of representation—is very revealing of the ambiguities and inconsistencies of subjectivity that characterize the contemporary world. To quote George Marcus (2001, 211):

> It seems to me that there are practices, anxieties, and ambivalences present in any location that are specifically keyed as a response to the intimate functioning of nonlocal agencies and causes, and for which there are no convincing commonsense understandings. The basic condition that stimulates this widespread predicament of irony is an awareness of existential doubleness, deriving from a sense of being *here*

with major present transformations ongoing that are intimately tied to things happening simultaneously *elsewhere* but without certainty and authoritative representations of what the connections are.

This sense of inescapable "doubleness" that Marcus discusses above is very relevant in accounting for the tensions surrounding women's visibility in contemporary Afghanistan. Indeed, what irony reveals perhaps most evidently is the conflict between the inner and the outer, between private desires and understandings on one hand and public pressures and official transcripts on the other.

The *chadari* in itself does not tell us much about the type of subjectivities, negotiations, and aspirations that exist under the veil. More often than not, women use the *chadari* as a strategic device, as a means to remain anonymous and maintain a sense of safety. The *chadari*, more than a mere status symbol, has become a functional instrument, a sort of "mobile home" (Abu-Lughod 2002) or a "symbolic shelter" (Papanek 1973), the costume worn by women for a public play that has been written by others. And ironically, it is this theatrical dimension of the veil as a form of social makeup that allows women to go to work, go to the bazaar, or, even, as in the case of Massoma's mother, to purposefully perform the role of the "oppressed Afghan woman" in order to reach out to foreign audiences. This is what James Fernandez and Mary Taylor Huber (2001, 6) call "the Hobbesian paradox that men (and women) in their natural condition of life—'solitary, poore, nasty, brutish, and short'—can only gain their freedom by giving up their freedom."

In December 2001 while NATO troops were bombing Afghanistan, *Time* magazine featured a photo spread of Afghan women without veils accompanied by an article claiming that the U.S. victory was the "greatest pageant of mass liberation since the fight for suffrage." The unveiled women in the photograph, exposed to the gaze of Western audiences whose imagination was already filled with images of burka-clad women roaming in ruins, was the ultimate evidence of the fantastic leap forward that the military intervention had initiated in the "mullahs' country." Indeed, after 9/11, the West was bombarded with images of Afghan women covered from head to toe under their blue burkas. The necessity to "lift the veil," to use another headline of *Time* magazine published on December 2, 2001, became a key argument in the U.S. moral grammar of war and in the effort to rally public support for the military intervention. In this new colonial narrative, "Muslim woman can only be one of two things, either uncovered, and therefore liberated, or veiled, and thus still, to some degree, subordinate" (Hirschkind and Mahmood 2002, 352–53).

Ironically, years after the intervention of the coalition forces, as security continued to worsen and Karzai's government, acting on the advice of the United States, its ally, which was eager to find an exit plan, attempted to bring the insurgents/Taliban to the negotiations table, women tended to reveil and use dissimulation instead of exposure as a safer strategy to move about public spaces. In the West, visibility and power have been defined as synonymous terms rather than as historically related positions. This is because, as Brian Silverstein (2008, 119) puts it, "the institutionalization of a distinction between the public and the private is considered central to the functioning of liberal political culture, as is the situating of religion in the private." Social scientists (Rosaldo and Lamphere 1974; Ortner 1996) have tended to analyze gender relations in other societies through the prism of the public/domestic divide and to explain the "universal oppression of women" through women's relegation to the domestic domain and their "invisibility" in the public realm. However, as much as these categories may be useful to describe women's situations in Western societies, they largely misrepresent the position of women living in the Muslim world. In Afghanistan, masculine and feminine spheres of influence are segregated and often complementary,[2] and religion is not separated from other spheres of life. Women's veiling is a religious sign of modesty, the marker of gender segregation, but should not be systematically read as a sign of women's oppression. According to anthropologist Jon Anderson (1982) who observed various situations in which the veil is used among Ghilzai Pashtuns, the veil is less a means to separate men and women than a device that brings them together by regulating the terms by which they are socially present. It is part of a broader pattern of comportment called *haya*, or "extreme politeness," by which persons who could be legitimately married to each other are prevented from direct contact and interaction. Indeed, it can be said that men wear a veil, too, since their interactions with other marriageable women are accompanied by a constellation of behaviors that are equivalent to veiling. For instance, when a man and a woman encounter each other outside the *kor* (household inhabitants), restraint applies equally to both. The man will divert his gaze or act as if the woman was absent. He may additionally cover his face and turn away. He may also cover his mouth and avoid eye contact. This display of disengaging actions is to be understood as a form of respect on the man's part. "Put another way, the veil is part of a pattern of comportment in which both sexes participate with slightly different but overlapping inflections" (Anderson 1982, 402).

The disciplining of women's bodies in Afghanistan like anywhere else in the Muslim world is never total and absolute but rather is constantly challenged, contested, and negotiated. As Emma Tarlo explains in her work on dress and identity in India, the problem of what to wear is not merely mundane but also a social, cultural, and political dilemma. It involves elements of choice and constraint, identification and differentiation (Tarlo 1996, 318). Women are immensely aware of the conditions under which they have to negotiate their entry into the public domain. This knowledge is an embodied knowledge. It is the product of long years of conflict during which women have suffered from officially sanctioned discrimination. Visibility over these past three decades has found new meanings and been associated with danger. Women's veiling practices in the post-Taliban context are to be understood within the broader historical, social, and political context within which women maneuver their lives.

In this chapter, I discuss the different and contradictory meanings attached to women's veiling practices and dissimulation strategies. Through an analysis of women's self-presentation, I underline the complex ways in which women are attempting to become legitimate actors in the public sphere. Paradoxically, it is through the veil that Muslim women make themselves visible, asserting through their covered bodies a set of values that contradict Western notions of modernity according to which withdrawal from religion is the prerequisite to women's emancipation.

Scholars working on gender in Islam have often interpreted the various styles of veiling available in Muslim societies as embodied markers of particular ways of practicing piety or producing pious selves through body discipline (Mahmood 2005) or as an expression of opposition to Western definitions of modernity (Mernissi 1992; Kandiyoti 1991). If all these explanations are valid, my research among women MPs and activists in Afghanistan suggests that the performative and strategic dimensions of veiling are the dominant motives that guide women's political gestures. The women I interviewed and observed during my fieldwork were more invested in expressing pious identities via clothing than in cultivating virtuous selves through body discipline. Veiling and clothing were part of intricate strategies aimed at managing others' impressions in the context of public interactions where the presence of women was broadly considered as "abnormal," as something imposed by the "outside" world. Issues of religion and faith were not the main focus of their attention even though all of these women were undeniably strong believers.

The Legacy of Fear and the Occupation

The short period of relative liberalism that marked the three or four years after the eviction of the Taliban gave opportunities for individuals to experiment with the way they appeared in public. During my first stay in 2003–4, one could see in the streets of Kabul, especially in the city center where stores selling brightly colored clothes imported from neighboring countries had reopened, young men with blue jeans and long hair and girls wearing colorful veils over semilong blouses. These street scenes had become rarer in 2007. An increased level of insecurity as the result of regular suicide attacks, robberies, and kidnappings had initiated a return to physical conformity in public spaces.

The necessity to physically conform is closely related to the increasing level of public violence that women have experienced over the past decades. The Taliban and the mujahideen created a precedent by allowing unrelated men to punish women for infractions perceived to threaten diffuse notions of "honor." Since the invasion, the state has been unable to protect women in their transition from the private to the public sphere. In conflict-affected areas women "continue to face sexual violence, abduction, or forced or underage marriage" (Azarbaijani-Moghaddam 2009, 67). However, the perpetrators remain immune from prosecution since sexual violence is a taboo and the justice system is structurally incapable of enforcing the law (see Chapter 3).[3] "Forms of public violence including deliberate attacks on girl students and women teachers continue today and remain unpunished" (Azarbaijani-Moghaddam 2009, 67).

The explanations I often heard from women wearing *chadari* was that it allowed them some privacy and created a sense of security when the outside world, beyond the walls of the house, was seen as threatening, chaotic, and oppressive. Many times during my journey in Kabul I wished I could wear one too. After a bad experience in a taxi, which could have turned into another story of a kidnapped foreigner if I had not had the life-saving reaction of opening the door to escape from the moving car, I eventually purchased one in a local bazaar. I did not make great use of it because the reduced vision, with the additional impossibility of wearing glasses under the knitted covering made for the eyes, turned what I thought could be a protective piece of equipment into a dangerous experiment for the untrained user that I was. But for many women the *chadari* increased their mobility while guaranteeing their anonymity, a precious asset when conservatism and insecurity were on the rise in Kabul.

It is when I heard Mehria Azizi's story that the association of visibility with danger became clearer to me. Mehria was a camerawoman working for the Afghan Media and Culture Center in Kabul. After the collapse of the Taliban, Mehria and thirteen Afghan women set out to chronicle the lives of women in their country. Collaborating on the documentary film *Afghanistan Unveiled*, marked the first time any of them were able to travel freely inside Afghanistan—in fact, it was the first time any of them had been outside of Kabul. They were the first female journalists to be trained in Afghanistan for more than a decade. They spent a year learning the fundamentals of film production, then set out for the rural provinces of Afghanistan. Several times the filmmakers found themselves in verbal confrontations with Afghan men in the provinces who thought they had no business walking around showing their hands and faces. A few weeks before we met, Mehria's younger brother had been kidnapped and her family had had to give a ransom of U.S.$5,000 to get him back. Another brother had been attacked and had ended up at hospital with a broken nose. Mehria received constant death threats on the phone as well as anonymous letters. She complained to the police on several occasions but her complaints never got registered.

Listening to Mehria's story and to the stories of other female public figures I came across during my fieldwork, I started to get a sense of the price women had to pay for their public visibility. The international community had encouraged their reappearance in the public domain through the funding of NGOs working in the field of gender and government lobbying. However, women who had taken this opportunity and who were willing to participate in public life did not benefit from any protection. This meant that public women had to take immense risks for speaking out or find alternative protective mechanisms in order to reach the public.

As explained in the previous chapters, the foreign occupation of the country and its insistence on the necessity to carry out important and rapid social reforms have created tensions at different levels of Afghan society. This development can be easily compared to the situation of India under British rule when Gandhi called for a return to traditional handspun Indian clothes (*khadi*) as a means to reassert Indian values as morally superior as well as socially, politically, and economically more appropriate to India. As Tarlo explains, Gandhi hoped that *khadi* would work as a "blanket" covering social and religious differentiation within society and hence uniting all Indians against the West (Tarlo 1996, 321). However, conformity was never absolute and individual Indians interpreted the *khadi* rule in subtle ways, imbuing it with notions of loyalty to family, self, caste, religion, and race. Veiling practices among women politicians denote a similar assemblage of meanings, accommodating ethnic and religious allegiances while preserving a sense of autonomy.

The current preoccupation of the Afghan government with controlling women's appearances in public places is to be understood in the light of this external pressure. With the return of conservative elements within the political arena, an area of cultural resistance has emerged around women and the family. In *Women and Gender in Islam* (1992), social historian Leila Ahmed has underlined the relation between colonial encounters and the emergence of specific discourses on the veil in the Muslim world. In Egypt under British rule or in Algeria under French domination, political elites used the veil as a symbol of Muslim women's oppression to justify the colonial enterprise. Veiling, under such circumstances, turned into an act of resistance against the modernizing elite co-opted by the colonial establishment (L. Ahmed 1992, 152).

> The veil came to symbolize in the resistance narrative, not the inferiority of the culture and the need to cast aside its customs in favor of those of the West, but on the contrary, the dignity and the validity of all native customs, and in particular those customs coming under fiercest colonial attack—the customs relating to women—and the need to tenaciously affirm them as means of resistance to Western domination.... Standing in the relation of antithesis to thesis, the resistance narrative thus reversed—but thereby also accepted—the terms set in the first place by the colonizers. (L. Ahmed 1992, 164)

It is certainly possible to draw a parallel between the current situation in Afghanistan and earlier colonial periods during which discourses on women and the veil first started to emerge. After years of total disregard for the Afghan people, the sudden interest of the West in the plight of Afghan women and the focus on the burka confirm that old colonial narratives on the veil have been reactivated in order to justify military occupation. At once urged to take back their "freedom" and unveil by the West and pushed to remain faithful to Afghan "culture" by the new regime, women in occupied Afghanistan have become a "figment in someone's else dream," as Azar Nafisi (2003) beautifully phrases it in her memoir *Reading Lolita in Tehran*. This renewed public attention to women's bodies and the use of "colonial feminism" (L. Ahmed 1992) as an imperialist tool to assert domination has trapped the struggle for women's rights in struggles over culture. Various political developments that have taken place in the years that followed the U.S. invasion confirm this vision.

In order to preserve an illusion of political autonomy and resist Western influence, conservative MPs have submitted various draft laws aimed at preserving patriarchal authority. These draft laws proposed the reinstallation of the religious police, the reopening of the Ministry for the Prevention of Vice and the Promotion of Virtue, and a ban on Western clothes such as jeans, long hair for men, and cosmetics and makeup for women (see Chapter 4). These legal proposals announced a return to homogeneity after a brief period of diversity associated with anarchy and loose morals.

"I spent all those years fighting against Islamic fundamentalism and the compulsory wearing of *chadari* for women and now I advise women to wear it again," complained Hamida,[4] a twenty-four-year-old representative of a southern province at the National Assembly and former university professor. Married by force to a local commander, the young MP became a widow twenty-four days after her marriage. She is now a single mother, well determined to bring change for the women of her province whose sufferings she has "felt in [her] own heart." But Hamida is also aware that in the current political situation the scope of her possibilities is extremely reduced. "I have to be very careful not to upset anyone. If I don't wear *chadari* when I return to my province, commanders and mullahs, the ones who are in power at the local level, will say: 'She is a bad woman. She does not respect Islam. Don't vote for her!' And my people will listen because they are illiterate, poor, and traditional," she explained to me in the parliament conference room, lowering her voice to avoid indiscreet ears.

Visibility, over these past three decades, has found new meanings. In Western societies, the visibility of people brings about public security in urban spaces. Public figures are expected to reveal their private life and expose it to public scrutiny. For Afghan women, public visibility has become equal to insecurity and to being subjected to constant control by others (commanders, the police, religious leaders, family, and neighbors). Even though the moral police have officially disappeared in most cities, the new Islamic republic still expects people to conform to Islamic prescriptions. Several male students at Kabul University mentioned to me being arrested by the police on several occasions and asked for the identity of the female friend accompanying them. They eventually had to bribe the policemen in order to avoid arrest.

This controlling gaze is an apparatus whose effects are similar to the one of Bentham's Panopticon—a huge prison with only a single jailer—that Michel Foucault describes in *Discipline and Punish* (1977). Indeed, the Panopticon is designed to allow an observer to view all prisoners without the prisoners being able to tell whether they are being watched, thereby conveying the sense of an invisible omniscience. Thus the visibility of an individual and his awareness of the existence of authority and the possible presence of a surveillant result in his constant obligation to observe discipline. The efficiency of the system lies in the fact that the individual "assumes responsibility for the constraints of power," making himself "the principle of his own subjection" (Foucault 1977, 202–3). The fear experienced by the prisoner constitutes the central motor of self-discipline. In the case of Afghanistan, fear of punishment has resulted in the production of "docile bodies" that have internalized power hierarchies to the extent that they have become almost natural. The reluctance of women to remove their *chadari* is a good illustration of the long-lasting psychological effects of the Taliban's "technologies of power."

As Afghan sociologist Nasrine Gross explained to me during an interview,[5] the Taliban rule has been particularly traumatic for Afghans because for the first time their faith, a fundamental component of their identity, has been radically questioned. If before the Taliban people rarely interrogated the depth of their own faith, the harsh rules and punishments imposed by the religious students contributed to the spread of a general feeling of guilt regarding religion that made such personal interrogation commonplace. Indeed, under the constant control of the religious police, men and women, especially in the cities, were persistently reminded of their inherent "sinning" nature. The long-term effect of such a trauma is noticeable in people's obsessive urge to justify the way they physically present themselves or to make comments on the ways other people look. Of course, in any society, people are always expressing something with clothing, sending out intentional or unintentional signals about themselves. Clothing is an important visual aspect of performance, part of the expressive equipment identified with the performer. In the case of Afghanistan, as clothing has become the center of political attention, physical displays that do not strictly match standards of Islamic modesty are perceived as potentially threatening to the social order.

From the civil war to the Taliban regime, Afghan women have lived with the same feeling of continual but secret and unverifiable control. Thus, the experience of wearing *chadari* has become in fact the paradoxical experience of some kind of freedom along with an acceptance of enclosure and discipline. To be disciplined and similar to others allowed women to be less subjected to others' sight and consequently to be freer in their movements. This dissimulation and social invisibility in terms of appearance and behavior is constantly shifting according to variables such as place and time and is defined by the status, gender, and age of social actors. To maintain their security and right of presence in social spaces, individuals must obey assorted codes that are particular to each space or vis-à-vis the others. While such codes existed in Afghanistan well before the Taliban, the Taliban regime has refashioned them, forcing individuals to play roles and to adopt new appearances according to their moral system. In the new Islamic republic, even though such rules are no longer officially sanctioned, they remain an unwritten law. As a result, dissimulation through conformism constitutes the dominant strategy to access public spaces.

Women have adopted strategies of dissimulation and invisibility that have become part of a process of social inclusion and negotiation. For instance, women continue to wear the full-covering *chadari* in order to go to work and attend public meetings and demonstrations. In June 2007, for example, hundreds of women organized a collective peace prayer at the sacred Shrine of the Prophet (Kherqa Sharif) in Kandahar, a mosque that is normally barred to women. The mullah even allowed the women to broadcast their prayers from the shrine loudspeaker (AdvocacyNet 2007). A few months later, in January 2008, six hundred women rallied in Kandahar to protest the kidnapping of an American female aid worker (BBC News 2008). This public event was even more surprising in that it took place in one of the most conservative areas of the Pashtun south where women are rarely seen in public spaces. Women's demonstrations of this type were not isolated occurrences. In May 2005, hundreds of widows marched in Kabul in protest against the kidnapping of Clementina Cantoni, an Italian aid worker from CARE International. A river of blue *chadari* suddenly flooded Kabul city center, displaying photographs of Cantoni and carrying banners requesting her immediate release. Under the Taliban regime women protested on several occasions, such as against an edict that closed public baths and the rise of the price of bread.

Protected from external gazes, able to see without being seen, women could occupy the public arena without disrupting social expectations of female modesty. Their "absent presence" under the disciplinary monotony of the *chadari* enabled them to step into spaces traditionally occupied by men.

Women were proud to recount how they distorted the original meaning of the *chadari* during Taliban rule by hiding in their garments books and stationery used in the clandestine schools they ran from their homes. Retelling stories of covert disobedience, defiance, and resistance against the moral police was always a source of excitement and laughter for them. To ridicule the rules imposed by the Taliban was their favorite technique for exorcising fears and anxieties accumulated during this time while regaining a sense of self-worth. Clandestine organizations like the sewing circles of Herat run by Muhammad Ali Rahyab, a professor of literature at Herat University, reached an almost mythic status inside and outside Afghanistan.[6] There, instead of sewing dresses, women studied banned writers such as Shakespeare, Joyce, Nabokov, Tolstoy, Dickens, Balzac, and Dostoevsky, as well as classic Persian literature. One of these underground literary circles gave birth to the renowned Afghan poetess Nadia Anjuman who was only in grade 10 when the Taliban took power in the eastern provincial capital. Her poetry, produced "under the *chadari*," helped her transform into hope the grayness of her secluded life. "Memories of Light Blue,"[7] written in reference to the *chadari*'s most usual color, is one of those attempts at transcending the dullness of the everyday:

You, exiles of the mountains of oblivion
You, diamonds of your names sleeping in quagmire of silence
You, the ones your memories faded, memories of light blue
In the mind of muddy waves of forgotten sea
Where are your clear-flowing thoughts?
Where did your peace-marked silver boat moon craft go?
After this death-giving freeze, the sea calms
The clouds, if they clear heart from bitterness
If daughter of moonlight brings kindness, induces smiles
If the mountain softens heart, grows green and turns fruitful
Will one of your names, above the mountain peaks, become
    the sun?
Sunrise of your memories
Memories of light blue
In the eyes of tired-of-flood-water fish and

Scared-of-rain of darkness
Will it become a sight of hope?

Women who have broken into the political apparatus share this common-sense understanding of the possible physical and social dangers associated with visibility. In the section that follows, I look more precisely at political women's public performances in a space where their presence remains highly contested: the Afghan National Assembly. Indeed, the new constitution ratified in 2004 foresaw a 25 percent quota for women in the parliament, a political move initiated with a view to repairing past injustices. This legislation was passed thanks to the pressure of women's groups and the international community, but *jihadi* leaders who occupied the majority of seats in the National Assembly broadly perceived women's presence at their side as "abnormal" and as a result of exogenous forces, with little or no endogenous legitimacy at all.

Even though adding women in politics can never be a guarantee for gender equality in the broader society, the presence of women in the parliament has undeniably been a positive step. It remains that the women who have joined the legislative apparatus are not only divided along political, class, and ethnic lines but also their room for maneuvring within such a conservative environment is extremely narrow. As a result, many female MPs have had to develop subtle strategies in order to gain political recognition and validation from their male counterparts. This included, among other techniques of body discipline, a constant attention to the way they looked and veiled in public.

Veiled Politics

An observation of clothing and veiling practices among women involved in politics in Afghanistan reveals the central and contested place of Islam in the new Islamic republic. It also highlights the central question of what can and cannot be discussed by women in public. In this respect, the comparison between parliamentary women and female university students is very telling. As I discussed in Chapter 4, female university students struggled to veil as little as possible in order to display a modern yet Muslim persona. In contrast, women MPs often had to veil more strictly if they wanted to gain entry into mainstream politics. Different social positions involved alternative uses of the body.

In general, women sitting in the parliament[8] can be divided into two categories: conservative/nationalist women who defend a formalist approach to the Koran and "progressive" women who support an interpretive approach. While the majority of them belong to the first group and have been co-opted by various mujahideen factions, women from both tendencies agree that Islam provides them with a means to "speak" in public. However, their bodily statements mirror their political inclinations and, to some extent, their different understanding of Islam and the place of women in society.

Indeed, for both men and women, self-presentation is central to conveying meanings regarding political affiliations and as a result clothing reflects a political posture. President Karzai, for instance, played the card of reconciliation between the "old" and the "new" by choosing to wear at once the traditional long-sleeved *chapan*,[9] a karakul hat, and the black suit of Western diplomats. Observing the clothes of the MPs sitting on the benches of the Afghan National Assembly is already revealing of their political inclinations, or at least of the political identities they strive to project to their audience. Long-bearded men in traditional *peran tomban* (large pajamas), turbans, and *pakols* (woolen headgear mostly worn by Tajiks) mix with clean-shaven men in Western suits. On the women's side, the length and colors of chadors are a source of constant comments.

Generally, political women's veiling practices are informed by the geographic location of their respective constituencies. Women MPs originating from rural areas felt more compelled to veil in a more conservative manner than their female colleagues who came from urban areas. "For Shukria Barakzai [MP for Kabul Province], it does not matter if she wears small veils because people who vote for her are educated . . . they come from the city. For me it is different. My people did not go to school. My people are illiterate and conservative. So I have to pay attention to the veils I wear," an MP from Farah explained.[10]

Women who are affiliated with *jihadi* groups tend to dress more traditionally than women who belong to more liberal groups. Their veils are longer and less colorful (black, white, or light beige) and their interpretation of women's rights is based on a belief in the inherently different nature of men and women. Many of them wear *chadari* or long chadors when returning to their province of origin but abandon them as soon as they return to Kabul. Their public performances convey nationalist meanings about the primary role of women as mothers and family caretakers.

For female MPs who affiliate themselves with more liberal groups, choices of veil colors and length are a matter of perpetual arrangement and meticulously weighted decisions. Veils and clothes change according to the audience they face and the context in which they navigate. Their decision to wear *chadari* when traveling to the provinces is mostly influenced by the security situation or the individual dressing practices of their female colleagues. Their performances are more contradictory and less consistent than conservative women and involve constant negotiations and calculations. "If I don't wear *chadari* when I go back to my province and my colleague Bilqhis does, then she appears as the modest one and I appear as the amoral one," an MP from a northern province noted to underline the necessity to embody strict Muslim norms in order to reach out to more "traditional" or rural audiences.[11]

For both "nationalist" and "progressive" women clothing is linked to different conceptions of the place of Islam in politics. For nationalist women, wearing long veils and occasionally *chadari* is partly a means to conform to proper religious and cultural practices. But most important, it is about honoring the work achieved by the mujahideen during the jihad and opposing the hegemonic influence of the West, in particular the United States, in internal affairs. On February 23, 2007, in a public gathering organized by *jihadi* leaders in Kabul National Stadium, Shakila Hashimi, MP of Logar (a province controlled by the Taliban), took the microphone and harangued the crowd, denouncing the blasphemy committed by her fellow MP Malalai Joya who had accused some mujahideen sitting in the parliament of being war criminals (*Islah-e Milli* 2007). The rally had been organized in order to gain public support for a legal proposal preventing the state from independently prosecuting people for war crimes committed during conflicts in recent decades.[12]

That Hashimi was given the opportunity to talk in a conservative assembly of prominent political leaders and military commanders not particularly renowned for their progressive approach to women's issues was in itself very telling. It showed that far from being united, women from different political and ethnic backgrounds tended to engage in identity politics and put forward the specific political agenda of their own ethnic or religious groups while dismissing or ignoring the ones of their own gender.

Vice President Mohammad Karim Khalili, Speaker of the Wolesi Jirga (Lower House) Mohammad Younus Qanooni, former *jihadi* leaders, commanders, and a number of MPs took part in the gathering. Surrounded by heavily armed men and raising an accusative finger to the sky, her speech suddenly reached a climax: "Marg ba Malalay Joya! Marg ba oquk-e bachar!" (Death to Malalai Joya! Death to human rights!), she screamed while receiving an overwhelming round of applause.

The association of Joya with human rights, and therefore with the West, was typical of nationalist discourses. Indeed, Joya was regularly accused by her detractors of being sponsored by Western leftist groups and as a result was declared to be an infidel or a communist and therefore disrespectful of national values. During her campaign in Farah for the legislative elections, Joya's enemies circulated pamphlets on which she appeared bareheaded. The pamphlets called her a "prostitute" sold to the West and attacked her for her lack of modesty: "If Joya removes her veil now, soon she will remove her pants too," commented one of these pamphlets (Mulvad 2006). Joya's fearless interventions in parliamentary sessions unfailingly provoked sexual insults, physical attacks, and death threats. A secularist at heart, Joya regularly appeared unveiled on foreign TV stations and in newspapers, Western journalists being particularly fond of her outspoken and fearless character. The outburst of resentment against the values she defended (women's rights, human rights, and secularism) ironically forced her to constantly wear *chadari* when traveling in the country.

In such a nationalist atmosphere, female MPs having a more progressive agenda for women have to retain as a primary goal the support of their own constituencies while lobbying potentially supportive men within the parliament. If some of them admit to supporting Joya behind closed doors, they pay attention not to be associated too closely with her.[13] The way they look in public is a fundamental issue of concern, many of them preferring not to talk to the media or appear on television at all in order to have free rein to make deals behind the scenes. In the same way, many "liberal" female candidates to the legislative elections conducted their campaign under the *chadari* and gradually removed it once elected. This was for instance the tactic adopted by Fatima Azim (pseudonym), now representative of a northern province in the National Assembly, currently running a small, low profile group of female MPs involved in civic education activities in rural areas.

I gave all my speeches wearing *chadari*. My family is an intellectual family. My father is a university professor and my mother is the director of a kindergarten. It is not common in our family for women to wear *chadari*. When I started my speeches, I just removed a little corner of the veil to be able to speak. If I had not presented myself this way, my people would have thought that I was disrespectful of our traditions. You know, wearing *chadari* is essential in my province. It has become a tradition. Now, since I have been elected at the parliament, my people sometimes see me in the press and they see that I don't wear *chadari* anymore. They are getting used to it. When I return to my province to attend political meetings, I wear long veils instead of *chadari*. For people, it is becoming normal to see political women without it. Slowly, slowly people will change their mind. We should not go too fast.[14]

Younger female MPs who have lived abroad during the war are less eager to compromise and less reluctant to openly support Joya. This is for instance the case of twenty-seven-year-old Sabrina Saqeb, a representative of Kabul Province who returned from her exile in Iran especially to run for the elections. At first glance, the poster she printed for her campaign resembled an advertisement for a Bollywood blockbuster. It showed her smiling face, her hair covered under a bright canary yellow veil over a background of a similar color, an image designed to transmit hope and change to Afghanistan's youth. But the image gave rise to severe criticisms from conservative clerics and political leaders. "'Her posters are driving our youth towards sin,' thundered the Dari language *Cheragh* newspaper," (quoted in Walsh 2005) supported by Rabbani, former president of Afghanistan and former head of the major opposition party, the United National Front before his assassination in 2011. "It is a political weapon against true Islamic voters" (Walsh 2005). Sitting in UNIFEM Resource Centre for Women Parliamentarians, with her lipstick, fluent English, and matching Nike trainers and headscarf, Sabrina Saqeb undeniably brought a touch of glamor to Afghan politics. She recalled: "I got several telephone calls during my campaign. Once, an old man told me: 'What is this color? What is this poster? We are Muslim people! This is an Islamic country!' And I told him: 'What is wrong with Islam? I have my scarf on and if you are talking about the color, this is my favorite colour, I like it. And if you are talking about my smile, it is one of my features. This is not abnormal to smile. I wanted to show what the wish of the young generation in Afghanistan is. You know, young people are tired of darkness.'"[15]

Saqeb's response to her critics was to a great extent the product of her lack of political experience and her secondhand knowledge of the power relations at stake in the political apparatus. She envisioned Islam as a religion that promoted gender equality and granted many freedoms to women. She was inspired by Islamic feminism and its achievements in Iran, Malaysia, and elsewhere. Devoutly Muslim, she called herself a feminist but avoided using this term in the parliament for fear of receiving the same treatment as Joya and losing her already fragile credibility due to her young age and her modern physical appearance.

> Feminism has some negative connotations here. It is understood like: "You want your rights. You want to divorce men." You know, if you are talking about women's rights, the two main things men think about are: women want to be free to wear whatever clothes they like, and then, women want to get divorced. Because of this, men have a negative understanding of women's rights. Men feel threatened. People who are more conservative or more religious, like mullahs and others, they are thinking that the women who are active in the field of women's rights, they come from the West, their ideas come from the West, they want to be free like the women in the West and they want to get divorced.[16]

The political characters represented by Malalai Joya and Sabrina Saqeb, in spite of their differences, present common distinctive features that help us delineate the boundaries of women's political participation and public visibility in contemporary Afghanistan. Both MPs are young and educated and both display a physical appearance that does not conform to traditional standards of Islamic dressing. In addition, both speak fluent English and take their political inspiration from abroad. Joya looks at Western secularism while Saqeb draws her political views from models of Islamic feminism that have emerged within other Muslim countries. However, neither of them benefited from a strong social base of support outside of their limited constituencies: a few Revolutionary Association of the Women of Afghanistan (RAWA)/ Maoist/ secularist supporters for Joya and a few university students for Saqeb.

The reasons behind Joya and Saqeb's political marginality are varied, but undeniably the outward-looking political postures they embody cannot receive a strong echo in the context of the occupation. Of course, neither Joya nor Saqeb's political projects aim to target Islam or Afghan culture, but those laws and customs to be found in society that express androcentric interests, indifference to women, or misogyny. Such a discourse, as seductive as it may be for the urban and educated person's consciousness, has currently no place in the Afghan political landscape. Without nationalist/Islamic veils to ideas of reform related to women's issues, the persuasiveness of Joya and Saqeb's discourses remains absolutely marginal.

So what do we learn from political women's public performances? What do their veiling and clothing practices teach us about the nature of power relations in contemporary Afghanistan? Why are women who have made their ways into the highest political circles still reluctant to completely abandon the *chadari*? What emerges from the ethnographic material I have presented above is that in a context of foreign occupation, where women's bodies have become the symbolic markers of the broader social body, veiling represents the privileged medium of expression of one's nationalist endeavors and resistance against external influences. The veil ensures the cohesion of the collective and provides a sense of national continuity when society is threatened by fragmentation from the presence of an external enemy. By strictly conforming to gendered norms, nationalist women strengthen their integration within their own political groups. Progressive women, that is, women who are more radically inclined to advance women's rights through an interpretive approach to the sharia, cannot simply avoid the nationalist discourse for this would lead, as the case of Joya demonstrates, to their total marginalization. The groups to which they belong are too weak already in the political landscape and cannot afford a radical rejection of nationalist politics. In short, in public settings, women from both tendencies have to adjust their performance to conform to gendered norms of appropriate behaviors in order to maintain their public presence.

The mobilization of religious repertoires in nationalist movements has been observed in Algeria during its revolution when the meanings of the veil as a cultural and social object was transformed as a result of the French colonizers' attempt at eradicating Islam from the public domain. In response to these attacks, many Algerians turned inward, retreating into the traditional Islamic community and family life that remained the only safe havens from which a sense of independence could be preserved. Rick Fantasia and Eric Hirsch (1995, 149) explain that when the colonial elite attempted to expand its control over the private sphere through new laws designed to supposedly "liberate" women, Islam became the "language of refusal," and, as a consequence, traditional gender practices such as the veiling and cloistering of women were reinforced. According to Frantz Fanon (1967, 42), "Every new Algerian woman unveiled announced to the occupier an Algerian society whose systems of defense were in the process of dislocation, open and breached." A public figure like Joya who appeared unveiled on Western television, addressed Western audiences dressed in "un-Islamic" clothes, and advocated for secular democracy was perceived as a threat for the same reasons Fanon underlines in the case of colonized Algeria. Her unveiled body displayed on satellite TV channels became a source of fear because it carried the signs of shattered boundaries and disappearing worlds.

One can argue that the symbolic and social function of the Afghan *chadari* is similar to the sari in rural India. While the sari constrains married women's movements in certain ways, allowing them to perform *laj karvu* (lit. "doing shame') more easily by pulling their veil over their head when in the presence of unrelated strangers, the *chadari* is another public manifestation of women's unavailability and therefore is a garment that maintains women's reputation and that of their families (Tarlo 1996, 164). Clothing therefore embodies the relationships between individuals, families, and groups. Choosing not to wear the *chadari* can be interpreted as a noticeable sign of immodesty. But as the veiling practices of the women I have described here demonstrate, if the veil's aim is to conceal women, it does not deprive them of a means of expression (Sharma 1978, 224).

Mahbouba Seraj, who returned to Afghanistan in 2001, worked with women MPs under a UNIFEM program designed to enhance female representatives' political skills and help them develop alliances among themselves in matters related to women's rights. She explained to me that the greatest difficulties for these women were to gain the support of their male colleagues, since men were the ones who had the real power to initiate change:

> If you want, as a woman, to make it in the political arena, you need three things: First, you need to have a well-known family name. Second, you need to be Pashtun, since the Pashtuns represent the main ethnic group in the country. Finally, you need the support of men. This support, you cannot get it if you're young because respect is gained with age and experience. But the support of men is decisive. This is the reason why it is difficult to build alliances between women. They compete to get men's recognition and they cannot see the advantage of working together yet.[17]

Several other women MPs who mentioned receiving regular misogynist comments when they referred to women's rights in the National Assembly confirmed these dynamics. "Wear a proper veil first, *hamshira* [sister], and then you will be authorized to talk. This is what some of them [men] tell me

sometimes," complained Masooda Babak,[18] founder of a women's organization and MP for Kabul Province in 2007. Even in more liberal circles, prejudices against women are widespread. Women are often accused of hysteria
and are reproached for their lack of rational thinking or their ignorance of
the rules applying to political negotiations.

In these circumstances, displaying a respectful Muslim persona through
proper veiling and clothing amounts to affirming one's patriotic allegiances
and a certain form of recognition for the historical heritage of the jihad. With
a parliament dominated by *jihadi* factions for whom women's rights are certainly not the priority, women are left with little choice but to conform in
order to gain men's recognition. The emotional glue conveyed by nationalist
ideas, despite their systematic reproduction of gender stereotypes, cannot simply be ignored. As Tamar Mayer (2000, 6) puts it, "because the nation was
produced as a heterosexual male construct its 'ego' is intimately connected
to patriarchal hierarchies and norms. These enable men and nation to achieve
superiority over women and a different Other by controlling them. As a result the intersection of nation, gender and sexuality is a discourse about a
moral code, which mobilizes men (and sometimes women) to become its sole
protectors and women its biological and symbolic reproducers." Nationalist/
conservative women and, to some extent, progressive women too are participating in defending the "moral code." Through their dress, women compete
to embody the perfect model of the "pure" and dedicated Muslim mother/
sister. But progressive women's indirect or direct participation in the reinforcement of this discourse allows them to gain credit and support in their
own political groups when women's rights issues are put on the negotiation
table.

In her study of the women's piety movement in Egypt, Saba Mahmood
(2005) distinguishes between veiling practices as embodied production of self,
the purpose of which is to produce or create selfhood, and veiling practices
as signs of collective identity. She argues that while the latter endows some
nationalist or identity-oriented dispositions and rests on a conception of self
as distinct from the outside world, the former are predicated on a sense of
self constructed through norms and conventions. Indeed, embodied practices
are forms of socialization that involve forced and forceful reiterations—what
Bourdieu came to theorize as "habitus"—so that the subject, caught in a set
of "structuring structures," appears as if behaving "naturally." Building on
Bourdieu's concept of "habitus" and Foucault's theory of power and discipline,
Judith Butler (1997a) offers a new reading of the notion of performativity by

applying it to gender. She argues that gender is not a fact or an essence but a set of reiterated acts that produce the effect or appearance of a coherent substance. In short, gender is something that people do rather than an entity or a quality they possess. It is a set of acts, a performance, it works and derives its compulsive force from the fact that people mistake the acts for the essence and in the process come to believe that they are mandatory.

However, the distinction Saba Mahmood makes between embodied and identitarian veiling practices (2005, 118–19) may be erroneous and both forms of subjectivities may coexist among the Afghan political women who are the subject of my study. The ethnographic material I have presented here demonstrates that conceptions of the relationship between the self and the body are not radically opposed. Progressive and nationalist women equally strive to cultivate virtuous selves while expressing pious identities through clothing. All of them (except Malalai Joya who defends secularism) insist that they do not aspire to the freedom enjoyed by Western women. They all view Islam as the basis of gender equality and the family as the core unit within which women can develop and empower themselves.

The concept of performativity developed by Butler is too much centered on the individual to fully grasp the multiplicity of other factors that shape political women's performances. These factors include the space within which the performance occurs, the others involved, and how they might see and interpret what they witness. The theory of "performance" developed by Erving Goffman (1969) seems to integrate these factors in greater depth by relocating the individual in the context in which he or she navigates and in a set of relations. In Goffman's view, the performance is not the mere product of discourses as Butler suggests, but it is an act that is validated through interactions with different audiences. These different interactions constitute the reality of the every day.

Nationalist as well as progressive women navigate in the public sphere and the projection of identities is part of the construction of collectivities. Even those more liberal women who are most concerned with embodying modern Muslim personae are also engaged in performances, while the most nationalist-oriented women are concerned with embodying piety and national autonomy. Their encounters with the public are necessarily performative in the sense of "theatrical" and changing according to audiences and situations. As Goffman argues, there is no essential self (1967, 85): "While it may be true that the individual has a unique self all his own, evidence of this possession is thoroughly a product of joint ceremonial labor, the part expressed through the individual's demeanor being no more significant than the part conveyed by others through their deferential behavior toward him."

Selves performing identities do not need to be conceptualized as autonomous or distinct from the social world. Among women MPs sitting on the benches of the National Assembly, the veil serves both to inculcate piety and to express identity, both intentionally and unintentionally. I qualify the body practices that I have described in this section as "performances" in the sense of Goffman (1956), not because I assume that women's veiling practices are mere cynical or alienated responses to a dominant discourse, but in order to highlight women's acknowledgement of and participation in a moral system in which their bodies are constant centers of attention.

A Room of One's Own

Public spaces are imbued with multiple ideologies that contextually frame the multifaceted subjectivities that actors who navigate within them possess. Scholars have argued that models of the public sphere founded on the modern nation-state create and necessitate individuated subjectivities (Habermas 1989). I have shown that by contrast, in Afghanistan, the public sphere simultaneously sanctions political women's subjectivities as Muslim women, as mothers/wives/daughters, and as dependent upon men. Their capacity to maintain a public position depends on their ability to embody such subjectivities. As has been observed in other postcolonial contexts, women activists in Afghanistan are being rooted in nationalism and the struggle against foreign influence. Therefore, when they articulate demands for rights, they inevitably run the risk of being stigmatized as antinationalist and antireligious.

Women know, when stepping into male dominated domains, the risk they face of getting caught in the middle of an international discursive struggle portrayed as a simple matter of human rights on the one hand and a nationalist discourse that defends with absolute certainty "Afghan culture and traditions" on the other. In order to maneuver in this very narrow corridor, Afghan women have had to create and reinvent new public spaces for themselves. Women entering public spaces are therefore bringing with them expectations of traditional, feminine behaviors. The parameters of women's public behaviors are strictly circumscribed in both covert and overt ways. Women's public presence is justified through the language of women as "carers of the nation." This suggests that women are entering an anomalous space neither purely private nor strictly public but rather a public space restricted by traditional principles of sociability, thereby modifying but not fundamentally disrupting rigid distinctions between public and private, male and female.

Women employed in the ministries and NGOs, as well as women elected to the Afghan National Assembly, are very careful to present themselves as dutiful mothers or daughters. The way these women talk about their "people" is very similar to the way they talk about their children. Dr. Masooda Jalal, for instance, who was the only female candidate for the 2004 presidential elections, used the slogan "Vote for the Mother" for her campaign.[19] Mahbouba Seraj, a woman's rights activist running Koran reading groups for women in rural areas, insists that despite the fact that she has no children, she has motherly feelings for the women with whom she works.[20] She likes to call herself "Mother Afghanistan" (*Modar-e Afghanistan*), and the way she interacts with the women who attend her Koran classes is in many ways similar to a mother taking care of her own children, patting them, kissing them, and encouraging them to learn. In her opinion, women are teachers and have the religious duty to be educated in order to be able to educate their children. For these "visible" women, maintaining a motherly image in the public domain is an effective means to gain recognition and legitimacy.

Ceremonies organized on March 8, 2007, for International Women's Day by the Ministry of Women's Affairs and other women's organizations under the patronage of prominent feminine political figures followed the same discursive lines. In Shar-e-Naw's luxury hotel reception rooms, walls were covered with banners on which one could read the following passages of the Koran: "Women rock the cradle with one hand and carry the earth with the other," "Paradise lies on the feet of mothers," "Thanks to women, men can reach mountaintops." Girl scouts dressed up in military uniforms sang the Afghan national anthem, while radio presenter Rana Nooristani, whose mother is a representative of Nooristan Province at the National Assembly, read poems in which women embodied the beauty of the Afghan landscape: "Women, you're the beauty of the land, the basis of life. You know the secrets of life. God created you. You, modest queen."[21]

Among the various government officials and religious leaders attending the ceremony, one figure in particular attracted my attention: General Khotul Mohamadzai. Wearing a military uniform covered with medals, she was among a small group of military officers present here. In her traditional annual speech, she glorified the sacrifices made by Afghan soldiers to protect the motherland: "My respected mother, I write about your dignity with my blood. As long as I live, I'll always be yours, my mother. At home or in a deserted place, you are a treasure of love for your daughters and sons. You are a patriotic woman. May each drop of our blood be sacrificed for you." At the end of the ceremony, a present was distributed to all the female attendees: a bridal veil and a Koran.

General Mohamadzai's public discourses had not changed since the early eighties when she had been appointed a general by the Communist regime, eager to showcase women in a political apparatus that wanted to present itself as modern and progressive. This is what I would discover when I came to interview her in her modest apartment in Makrorayan a few days later, this time without video cameras to record what she had to say. "I hate politics and I hate war," Mohamadzai confided to me after she had recounted how she lost all her family members during the successive conflicts.[22] Widowed a few years after her wedding, Mohamadzai lived with her only son in a flat decorated with various trophies, prizes, and official photographs. While she turned the yellowed pages of an old photo album, I realized the instrumental role women like Mohamadzai had played in sustaining the democratic pretense of the successive governments, a role Mohamadzai continued to occupy in the new Islamic republic.

As tactical as these performances may well be, they are part of a specifically feminine repertoire that allows women to engage in public without fundamentally challenging the gender order. If the nationalist discourse remains a favorite avenue, it often goes with a religious decorum. Indeed, models of the Islamic government are based on religious figures such as the Prophet Muhammad, his daughter Fatimah, and Khadijah and Aisha, his first and third wives. Women who have entered the political arena have appropriated Fatimah, Khadijah, and Aisha's models in new ways. By adapting and conforming their appearances and their behaviors to these predetermined Islamic sociocultural models, Afghan women have gradually managed to access arenas traditionally reserved for men. Their knowledge of the Koran and their ability to refer to it in different circumstances are powerful tools to commune with the public and sometimes to bring about small changes for women under the veil of compliance and invisibility. For instance, a few businesswomen have emerged in Kabul, most of them supported by U.S.-based organizations. They are running small and medium-sized enterprises specializing in jam making, tailoring, and regional trade. During interviews, these women often mentioned Khadijah, a rich merchant of Mecca who became the prophet's first wife, as the original source of their inspiration.

Being able to refer to the Koran and to demonstrate one's mastery of religious texts was therefore pivotal for women to assert their presence in public arenas. Women's rights activists commonly used this tactic to gain access to women living in remote rural areas and to avoid the suspicion or reluctance of local mullahs. They reclaimed the heritage of Islam as a religion that originally attempted to protect women against the discrimination and violence that marked the pre-Islamic order and promoted women's rights through an Islamic framework. Among the rights they wanted other women to be aware of were the right to inheritance, to *mahr* (the money a woman can claim from her future husband before her marriage and in case of divorce), to *nikah* (a religious marriage contract in which mutual consent should be expressed for the marriage to be valid), to education, to health, and to respect (as a daughter, mother, sister, and wife).

These were, in women's rights activists' opinion, the legitimate rights women could claim in a Muslim society. On her arrival to a village, Mahbouba Seraj would first meet the mullah and the village chief. Greetings were long and elaborate and news from the city and nearby villages was exchanged before the purpose of the visit was eventually revealed. A male colleague who ran discussion groups with local village men and mullahs would always accompany her. Obtaining men's consent and including them in the debates was the precondition of getting access to the women. She would be very careful not to use the jargon of international human rights and would use her royal lineage and her age (she was a *kala safed*, a white head) as the means of entry into the community. She would then gather the women in the house of a well-established local woman (usually a nurse, midwife, or schoolteacher) who already enjoyed some kind of public recognition for her work within her constituency. Discussions would usually start on this note:

MAHBOUBA. Before Islam appeared, what do you think the life of
humans was like?
WOMAN. Before Islam appeared, when a child was born and she was
a girl, they would bury her alive.
MAHBOUBA. Yes, you're right. When a girl was born at that time,
people would bury her alive. People were illiterate and they did
not know about their rights. No woman could get married or

> receive heritage. Society did not treat women well. They threw
> girls in rivers and they buried them alive. Because of this, God
> sent his prophet Muhammad to the people. Fourteen hundred
> years ago, God sent Prophet Muhammad to the people of Saudi
> Arabia. And women started to have rights.

Conversations dealt with issues related to marriage, inheritance, violence, and education. The gatherings usually ended with a meal offered to all the participants as a token of their newly formed friendship. These women's gatherings were quite revolutionary in rural areas where women's spheres of sociability were often reduced to their own family circles with little opportunity for unrelated women to meet and converse. There, in the safe space created by the motherly figure of Mahbouba, women were encouraged to talk freely about their problems and sorrows and find collective solutions for themselves. A new public sphere not predicated upon an assumption of secular liberalism and the attendant separation of public and private, politics and religion, or group and individual provided discursive fields within which Muslim women could contest notions of work, body, honor, and piety. This political repertoire, imbued with collective moral virtues derived from religious wisdom, allowed women to gain a sense of pride and self-worth while contesting the margins of the gender order. Mahbouba said, "A woman gave birth to Prophet Muhammad. It's not possible for a woman to give birth to Prophet Muhammad if she is dirty. I don't understand these ideas according to which women are dirty. Islam says that no woman is dirty. Prophet Muhammad says that the paradise is at the feet of mothers. I want to tell you that Prophet Muhammad says that women should take care of their children so they become good Muslims and they guide other people in society."

The cultivation, embodiment, and display of virtuous selves, copied on famous Islamic female figures, were the common denominator of the women who ran for office in the legislative elections. Many of them ran their campaign from home, receiving visitors in the same manner as a queen holding court, listening to people's demands and problems while using their networks of personal contacts to help them find solutions. It is thanks to the direct or tacit support of their male relatives that such gatherings were made possible. They were proud to say that they did not individually decide to run for the elections but were rather called by their own people to take part in the electoral competition. A common argument they used to justify their participation was that, unlike most male candidates, they had "no blood on their hands,"

Figure 19. Women attending a Koran class in Waras, Hazarajat, 2007. Photo by Julie Billaud.

they did not commit any crimes during the war, and that, as mothers who had suffered the death of their husbands and sons, they were dedicated to establishing peace in their country.

What emerges out of the examination of these feminine public performances is a general sense of deference and respect for rules of conduct, which, from the outside, may be understood as mere reinforcement of gender hierarchies. But by behaving according to society's expectations of appropriate feminine/Muslim comportments, women were able to create for themselves an alternative public space from which they could participate in public affairs. It is their behaviors as women holding a class status or position that expressed compliance, not their other substantive selves dedicated to achieve change for women. For these rules were parts of a necessary cultural "ceremony"— that is, "a highly specified, extended sequence of symbolic action performed by august actors on solemn occasions when religious sentiments are likely to be invoked" (Goffman 1956, 476)—to follow in order to become legitimate in the public arena. Because "the rules of conduct which bind the actor and the recipient together are the bindings of society" (1956, 496), women were careful to create terms of familiarity with the "superordinates." By doing so, they struggled to enlarge the scope of their possibilities for themselves and for other women.

CHAPTER 6

Poetic Jihad: Narratives of Martyrdom, Suicide, and Suffering Among Afghan Women

I inherited from my grandfather
A bottle of deadly poison
I will sacrifice myself.
    —Nadia Anjuman, *Gul-e Dodi* (Flowers of Smoke)

In November 2007 Fatana Gailani, founder of the Afghanistan Women Council and wife of Pir Sayed Gailani, a prominent political and religious figure, organized a conference for the International Day for the Elimination of Violence Against Women in Jalalabad, her native city. Jalalabad is located in Nangahar, a province bordering Pakistan predominantly populated by Pashtuns, which has faced a constant rise of attacks against governmental institutions and NATO troops since the fall of the Taliban regime. Having interviewed her a few days before in her office in Kabul, Gailani had invited me to accompany her on her trip in order to sit in on her program and attend the conference. We were accommodated in the family's *kala* (fortified house) whose palm grove and rose garden, with fortified walls, testified to the family's affluence in spite of the bullet holes in tree trunks that reminded one of the recent wars.

On this occasion, Gailani had invited important political figures to attend the conference held in the reception hall of the old state-run Spinghar Hotel located in the city center next to the governor's office. The women beneficiaries of her microfinance and literacy program had all arrived at once,

veiled with nicely embroidered white chadors, and sat in silence at the back
of the conference room. As a representative of a women's NGO, Gailani had
organized such an event with official motive to raise awareness about everyday forms of violence against women. In reality, the conference rapidly turned
into a personal political campaign during which she tried to rally support
for her candidacy to the next parliamentary election. Various local figures,
including a law professor at the University of Nangahar, the chief of police,
religious leaders, and commanders had been invited to participate and deliver speeches. Besides Fatana Gailani, only one woman, Sheela Babari, the
director of the Department of Women's Affairs, was given the opportunity
to talk. After having denounced "these shameless women who ask for divorce
and abandon their children and husband in the name of democracy," Babari
ended her speech with these words: "My dear brothers and sisters, keep an
eye on your daughters and never let them go out without a leash tightly attached to their necks!" The audience responded with a storm of applause.

A central figure of women's resistance to the Soviet occupation, Gailani
had run a clinic for women as well as girls' schools in the refugee camps in
Pakistan. Having returned to Afghanistan shortly after the fall of the Taliban, she was well aware that women's liberation would not come just with
foreign military intervention but through women's involvement in politics
and greater economic opportunities for the people of Afghanistan. While supporting rural women through microcredit and literacy programs, Gailani also
took the opportunity of this new visibility to forge her political reputation.
She wanted her beneficiaries to know that the loans given by her NGO were
coming from her and not from Karzai's government, which she considered
corrupt and nepotistic. She also understood the importance of gaining the
trust of male politicians. Using their language and their codes, and to a great
extent reproducing their gender stereotypes, were key to obtaining their support.

The speech she delivered on that day in front of a dominantly masculine
audience of local officials and ex-mujahideen made references to jihad and
martyrdom in a manner similar to the speeches one could often hear in higher
political circles. In an emphatic lecture that lasted for almost an hour, Gailani
talked "of her feelings with an open heart," as she phrased it. Raising an accusative hand to the audience in the manner of a preacher, she declared:

> I always tell my colleagues that women's jihad has been to care for the
> orphans, to support the widows, and to clean the tears of the mothers.

[During the jihad] We provided education for hundreds of children and health services for the women. *We* promised on God and on the Koran that *we* would never lie to our people and *we* would never say anything false. This struggle has built our personality. *We* are struggling for the truth. *We* never committed any crime. *Inshallah*, we will succeed because God promised it.

What was striking in Gailani's discourse was the ambiguity of the general message. Who was included in the "we" that she used in the statements "*We* never committed any crime," "*We* are struggling for the truth"? Was she referring to the mujahideen or to the women who struggled on their side, caring for the orphans and the widows? While reasserting women's primary roles as caretakers during the jihad, Gailani seemed at the same time to stress women's respectability and purity at a moment when massive killings of innocent people were taking place. This speech, together with the one given by the director of the Department of Women's Affairs, delivered in the context of a celebration for the International Day for the Elimination of Violence Against Women, was ambivalent on many levels. While standard nationalist tropes regarding the role of women in society were mobilized, this rhetoric was used as an entry point for expressing women's concerns.

Notions of jihad, self-sacrifice, and martyrdom had a lot of appeal in a political environment where military commanders had reached the status of national heroes after the eviction of the Taliban. Indeed, when the new National Assembly was elected in 2005, a majority of former *jihadi* leaders who had been evicted by the Taliban returned to power. Their main source of self-legitimization stood in the fact that they had once conducted jihad against the Soviet occupiers and later on against the Taliban and, as such, a great number of their followers had been martyred to protect the nation. In spite of the downfall of the fundamentalist Islamist regime of the Taliban and its replacement by a supposedly "democratic" Islamic republic, narratives of martyrdom and jihad remained central arguments to assert political authority.

In Afghan nationalism, as in Indian nationalism (Chatterjee 1993, chapter 6), women came to be viewed as guardians of tradition. As Gloria Goodwin Raheja and Ann Grodzins Gold observed, "Gandhi further essentialized 'tradition' and female sexuality through his appeals, in the nationalist cause, to the 'female' virtues of sacrifice, purity, humility, and silent suffering that could be deployed in the service of the independence movement" (1994, 6). Similar patterns of nationalism have been studied by anthropologist Audrey

Shalinsky (1993) who documented how the various *jihadi* parties in Pakistan distributed audiocassettes both in the camps under their control and in Afghanistan, which promoted, through lyric tales and stories inspired from the life of the Prophet Muhammad, appropriate behaviors for women in time of jihad. These stories linked together religion, courage, honor, and territory, drawing parallels between women's duty to sacrifice themselves for their kin as well as men's duty to sacrifice themselves for the nation. As a consequence, the jihad against the Soviets was endowed with a moral dimension, which women had the responsibility to maintain through appropriate behavior and (re)production of future soldiers and *umma* (community of believers in Islam) members (Shalinsky 1993, 674). The feminine model promoted in nationalist discourses was one of the silent and enduring mother. Female poets themselves made a great use of this imagery. In a poem entitled "Assamayi Mountain,"[1] Afghan poetess Laila Sarahat Rushani praises patience and courage, values that are metaphorically associated with the stillness of the Afghan mountains but also with the rootedness of women as central pillars of tradition:

Oh Assamayi Mountain
In your stony breaths
Is the spirit of a thousand silent sparks.
Oh stone, oh patience
Your height is faith's resolve—
History's sublime poem
Oh mountain
The myth of sacred pride is
Inscribed
In your conscious mind
The endless pain of this city is
Engraved in your cold stony vein for so long
Oh stone, oh patience[2]
Oh silent witness of crimes.
What wound was swelling
In your inner-stone's bleeding heart
That suddenly sundered your heart?
Oh stone, oh patience![3]

The concept of *jihad* today refers to actual fighting against "infidels." In the West, *jihad* is generally translated as "holy war." However, the word in itself has several meanings and also refers to exerting oneself for some praise-worthy aim (Olesen 1996, 11). The term *jihad* therefore encompasses a greater fight, that is, a believer's inner struggle against the *nafs* (the lower or passion-ate soul filled with unrepressed desires), which aims at purifying the spiri-tual heart. It is through this discursive exercise that Muslims can witness a higher truth and "establish evidence for a transcendent discourse that is per-suasive to an audience susceptible to that discourse" (Calhoun 2004, 332). While all Muslim men and women are exhorted to rid themselves from un-ruly emotions through prayers, knowledge seeking, and self-discipline, jihad that involves actual combat has traditionally been reserved for men.

As a source of political credibility, notions of jihad and martyrdom reas-serted the masculine nature of the state as defined in the new Islamic repub-lic. I was, however, surprised to realize that such rhetoric was widely used by female politicians too, claiming their participation in the national liberation movement and the suffering they endured during the war as evidence for their political credibility. But women's references to "martyrdom" did not encom-pass exactly the same meanings as men's. Playing with the polysemy of the concept, women's jihad and martyrdom could be understood as a symbolic reinterpretation of a national mythology in which women's bodies already played a central and ambiguous role.

Indeed, the national history of Afghanistan does not lack female fighters who did not hesitate to sacrifice themselves to defend the sanctity of the na-tional territory. At the heart of it appears the character of Malalai who led an Afghan battalion against English invaders during the second Anglo-Afghan war in Maiwand. The legend says that there came a point in the battle when the Afghan army, despite its superior numbers, started to lose morale and the tide seemed to be turning in favor of the British. Seeing this, Malalai, the daughter of a shepherd who lived next to the battlefield, took off her veil and shouted out:

Young love! If you do not fall in the battle of Maiwand,
By God, someone is saving you as a symbol of shame! (Ewing 2005)

Using her veil as a banner, she encouraged the soldiers to find a new re-solve and to redouble their efforts until she was herself struck down and died. The killing of Malalai was considered as *namardi* (cowardly, lit., "unmanly") and the offense outraged the Afghan army. Malalai's death "spurred on her countrymen and soon the British lines gave way, broke, and turned, leading to a disastrous retreat back to Kandahar and the biggest defeat for the Anglo-Indian army in the Second Afghan War" (Ewing 2005).

But Malalai is not an isolated figure in the Afghan national mythology. She belongs to a long-standing tradition of female warriors who committed suicidal acts of bravery to defend the motherland. Indeed, as in the epic tales of medieval times, Afghan history is full of powerful female fighters. Tales of warriors, horses, and fortresses feature young women such as Shah Bori, described as a girl with a taste for male clothing and horse riding. She is said to have liked living the life of a warrior, refusing for a long time to get married. She has also been said to have died fighting the troops of King Babur in the sixteenth century. Nazauna is another female warrior figure who, legend has it, single-handedly protected the Zabol fortress with her sword in the eighteenth century. In 1980, another heroic example by the name of Naheed appears in Afghan national history (Majrouh 2003). She led the first demonstration of schoolgirls and female university students on the streets of Kabul, openly denouncing the Red Army's occupation of the country. She was martyred while trying to fire a captured Soviet machine gun. Alongside her, hundreds of other innocent young Afghan girls were brutally murdered.

These feminine martyrs have passed through the history of the country, giving their names to modern state institutions such as Malalai High School, the first high school for girls opened by Queen Soraya and sponsored by the French government in the 1930s as part of King Amanullah's modernization program. Malalai High School has trained the first generation of active women in Afghanistan, following the education model of Jules Ferry schools in France and remains to this day the most renowned educational institution for girls (Gross 1998). More recent prominent feminine figures such as Malalai Joya, the MP evicted from the parliament in 2007, or Malalai Kakar, the first policewoman of Kandahar shot dead by the Taliban in 2008, have inherited their names from Malalai of Maiwand. They share in common with their ancestor deep patriotic sentiments together with a sense of self-sacrifice.

Reflecting on the meaning of these terrible tales, I came to wonder which cultural and social patterns had produced such a long lineage of exceptional women martyrs. Did these characters play the same roles as other national icons one could find elsewhere? Were they part of a man-made story in which women fighters were at once heroines and victims, instrumentalized to foster nationalistic feelings? Like the character of Antigone in the Greek mythology, Malalai, Naheed, Nazauna, and Shah Bori assumed a fundamentally ambiguous position, simultaneously challenging and reproducing the expectations of their gender all at once. On the one hand, their deaths embodied the suffering of the nation occupied by foreign invaders; on the other hand, their sacrifice triggered nationalistic feelings around the necessity to protect the motherland. It is because they performed stereotypical masculine roles in the national story that they reached the status of heroines. Their jihad was meant to be a masculine battle, not a feminine one.

The ambiguity and marginality of feminine acts of bravado is appealing because it challenges the honor system by underlining men's incapacity to protect women as bearers of the nation. Stories of female warriors reposition women on the front line of the jihad against the enemies of Islam, making them the pioneers of the national battle while underlining the fragility of gender relations as framed by the honor ideology. It is because men fail to perform their role as protectors that women are martyred. The killing of women by the "infidels" (*kafer*) is *namardi*, unmanly, but the men who made the sacrifice of women possible by failing to protect them are also to be shamed for failing to prevent their deaths.

Women who enter political spheres are perceived as threatening for these same reasons. Politics in Afghanistan, as in many other countries, is perceived as a dangerous masculine game that may involve violent death. In the turbulent political history of the country, shifts in power have often been achieved through bloody coups with political leaders either killed (President Daud in 1978, Prime Minister Taraki in 1979, President Najibullah in 1996 Commandant Ahmad Shah Masood in 2001) or forced into exile (King Amanullah in 1929, King Zahir Shah in 1973). In politics, as in *buzkachi* games (Afghanistan's national sport comprising a sort of local polo played with a headless calf weighing about 150 pounds), masculinity is constructed through a man's capacity to take risks and put his life in danger for serving the nation while protecting its womenfolk.

Women assuming the same roles and accepting the responsibility to take the same levels of risk through their mere presence in political arenas are challenging conceptions of the "public" as a space reserved for hegemonic masculine values. Their presence in the public provokes an ambivalence of feelings in the same way as Malalai of Maiwand on the battlefield. Women who accept their symbolic martyrdom by challenging the gender order do so with the view of opening doors for future generations of women. The notion of "sacrifice" is indeed a frequent leitmotif in their public speeches. What is put forward is a form of sacrifice made for future generations, a sacrifice that does not involve blood, confirming their innocence and purity and their traditional role as mothers.

Joya, who survived several assassination attempts since her participation in the Constitutional Loya Jirga in 2002, made it clear that death threats would not make her renounce her struggle for justice and women's rights. She said, "Never again will I whisper in the shadows of intimidation. I am but a symbol of my people's struggle and a servant to their cause. And if I were to be killed for what I believe in, then let my blood be the beacon for emancipation and my words a revolutionary paradigm for generations to come." (World Pulse Magazine, 2005). Using the same lyrical tone in an interview with BBC News conducted in 2006, she stated, "They will kill me but they will not kill my voice, because it will be the voice of all Afghan women. You can cut the flower, but you cannot stop the coming of spring" (Coghlan 2006). A leitmotif in Joya's interviews was that she was less afraid of death than of her country's return to religious fundamentalism and war. Abandoned by the political elite in power and therefore evicted from the parliament for her denunciation of war criminals, Joya embodied a romantic persona fashioned by notions of self-sacrifice and martyrdom of a different nature than the ones used by mainstream parties. Like other women's rights activists seeking political recognition, the image of women as pure and with "no blood on their hands" almost assumed a religious dimension.

"As women, we don't have power, guns or money. We have endured a lot of misery but our hands are not stained with the blood of others. We have to open a breach and make our voice heard. No matter if we fall before we reach the end of the road," explained Hawa Alam Nooristani, a female MP from Nooristan Province who had been shot in the legs while visiting a village during her campaign for the parliamentary elections. Like many other Afghan women, she bore the scars of the ongoing conflict on her body, but these scars were an embodied proof of her determination, of her capacity to endure and continue the struggle for women. Hitching up the hem of her dress, Nooristani made me look at the soft spots of skin which had been pierced by the bullets: "See? We will never forget!" she said, pointing at the scars as if the damaged flesh brought an undeniable element of truth to her words. "We will never forget!" she insisted, making me witness her wounded body on which was written a truth that could not be acknowledged otherwise.

The discourse of dedication, struggle, and sacrifice is an entrenched aspect of women's political identity. Their struggles and their connection to the martyrdom of other heroic women of Afghan national mythology illustrate another aspect of mirroring conventional forms of resistance and political struggle for nation building. The courage and strength on which they construct their subjectivity is connected to their willingness to face death in the service of the nation. However, this readiness is intersected with a commitment to nonviolence that reconfigures nationalist politics in new feminine terms, whereby the quietist dimension of jihad is reemphasized. By mobilizing this affective repertoire, women anchor their performance in a culturally meaningful universe of shared values. It is because women call to mind powerful cultural symbols deeply anchored in the collective imagination of Afghans that their discourse is endowed with a persuasive and transformational potential. These practices also reveal the simultaneously improvisational, flexible, unstable, contradictory, and yet strategic deployment of martyrdom in Islamic discourses.

In the section that follows, I want to push the concept of "feminine martyrdom" further by looking at the more dramatic gesture of suicide. Based on material collected in the National Women's dormitory in Kabul, I explore young women's narratives of self-sacrifice as well as two case studies of failed suicide attempts by female students. While only two instances of suicide attempts occurred during my stay in the dormitory, these events had a specific cultural and political resonance that illustrates well some of the contradictions and tensions cutting across contemporary Afghan society, especially in the sensitive arena of gender relations. While deciphering the social imaginaries and the moral universe in which such dramatic acts were realized, I underline the rebellious and communicative dimensions of young Afghan women's suicide and its anchorage in the subversive imaginary universe of women's poetic expression. I locate these "suicidal performances" in the wider cultural and political context of post-Taliban Afghanistan and I highlight the power of emotional performances for young women to voice their discontent and to gain public validation. I suggest analyzing suicide as an expressive feminine form, a subversive repetition of a culturally intelligible means of expression.

Poetic Resistance

In 2007, women's self-immolation became a growing issue of concern among NGOs and journalists in Afghanistan (Motlagh 2007; Tang 2007). In the press, the phenomenon was mostly explained through a mixture of psychological, social, and economic factors. The "liberation" had created expectations among women that had remained unmet "experts" said, describing women who had set themselves on fire as the "*shahid* of the traditional world" (Mann 2006). Since the eviction of the Taliban, more women had become aware of their rights and, unable to enjoy them fully, some had chosen to put an end to a meaningless life rather than endure continuous oppression. Community pressure on women had increased due to poor economic conditions.

Maybe because of its spectacular dimension, suicide through self-immolation attracted more media attention than other forms of suicide, like poisoning. The use of kerosene, a common product found in kitchens to light cooking fires, was the weapon of choice for these generally young women, most of whom lived in the rural areas of the country. When women did not immediately succumb to their wounds and were brought to health facilities, families usually tried to cover up these self-inflicted acts behind stories of domestic accidents. Some Afghan friends commented that women's self-immolation had always existed even though it had never been part of "Afghan culture" since Islam forbade suicide. Like most social phenomena they considered shameful or taboo (like drug addiction, divorce, or lack of modesty), women's self-immolation was seen as a foreign practice Afghans had brought to the country on their return from exile, something that was entirely alien to local social practices.

Not fully satisfied with these explanations, I started to discuss the issue with the women I had met in the course of my fieldwork. Orzala Ashraf Nemat, an Afghan women's rights activist, running an underground shelter for women victims of violence in Kabul, commented on the issue in these terms: "I don't see such women as victims. To me, victims are those who accept to suffer. But if they try to show to their inside and outside worlds that they don't accept repression, they are not victims anymore. In most of the cases, I see it as *a way of protest*."[4] The link between feminine forms of protest and female suicide became more obvious when confronted with ethnographic material collected among female students boarding in the National Women's Dormitory on Kabul University campus. Female suicide, it seemed, mobilized a number of well-known cultural ideas about women's inherent emotional fragility and irrationality but it also communicated "something else" to their inside/outside world, that is, to their families and the wider community. The highly visible and public dimensions of the act ambiguously worked both as a reminder of the potential danger of women's "uncontrollable nature" and as a means for women to communicate their discontent by creating public scandals revealing secrets supposed to be kept within the family (*rosusi*).

Self-harm was part of this "poisonous knowledge" (Das 2000) women had acquired during years of war marked by displacement and hardship. This embodied experience of violence had deeply transformed and shaped their subjectivity, forcing them to develop coping strategies in order to make their lives meaningful again. By processing violence within local structures of feelings, women had tended to root their subjectivity within the social order and create continuity instead of resisting the norms responsible for their subjugation. In her work on women victims of violence during the partition of India, Veena Das (1996) urges us to consider women's ability to survive the ongoing presence of pain not so much as a dramatic transgression and defiance but in terms of the "doing of little things" that does not have the sense of "passive submission but of an active engagement" (1996, 11–12). The experience of pain, as she explains it, does not fully translate itself into passive suffering but rather reveals ways of inhabiting the world that must be explored through an analysis of the language in which pain resides.

Das's work on violence is relevant to explain the transgressive dimension of women's self-harm in contemporary Afghanistan as it sheds light on the extremely ambiguous nature of an act that inscribes itself in the continuity of shared cultural meanings while marginally challenging gendered norms. Indeed, while women's self-immolation started to make the headlines, the issue of rape gradually became publicized with families coming to Kabul in search for justice for their dishonored daughters. We saw on television and in newspaper reports mothers threatening to commit collective suicide if criminals were not prosecuted (Nagpal 2009). In the National Women's Dormitory, girls shared with a mixture of excitement, admiration, and disapproval the melodramatic stories of female suicide. These stories portrayed women who had resorted to such an extreme act either as deeply convinced of their due right to make certain demands pertaining to their lives and therefore as courageous and desperate justice seekers or, more simply, as victims of patriarchal oppression. But in both cases, it was always with great sensationalism that stories dealing with probably one of the greatest social taboos were recounted. Suicide certainly had a romantic appeal among girls who spent a great part of their everyday lives reading poetry and classic Persian literature in which such stories abounded.

But if the truthfulness of these tales exchanged in the intimacy of dormitory girls' bedrooms could probably be questioned, it nevertheless seemed to me that the vivacity with which girls talked about female suicide was not the mere product of excitement provoked by discussions about illicit or socially repressed acts. Suicide talked to them in a much deeper and meaningful way. It echoed themes that had a specific cultural resonance and that Afghan poet Sayd Bahodine Majrouh highlighted in *Songs of War and Love* (2003). In the introduction of this collection of *landays*[5] (lit., "short ones") exchanged between Pashtun women refugees in Pakistan, Majrouh argues that women's poetry challenges society in a similar way to female suicide. "In her innermost self," he writes, "the Pashtun woman is indignant and skeptical, feeding her rebellion. From this deep-seated and hidden protest that grows more resistant with every passing day, she comes out with only two forms of evidence in the end—her *suicide* and her *song*" (emphasis added). It is Majrouh's conviction that Afghan women's poetry, like their suicides, challenges the society by glorifying "three themes associated with blood" (xvi)—love, honor, and death. "By eliminating herself in such an accursed way," he goes on, "a woman thus tragically proclaims her hatred of the community's law" (xv). Indeed, Afghan custom (*rawaj*) considers suicide a cowardly act and men will rarely resort to it. This is because men are expected to be in full control of their *nafs* (inner self) and are responsible for controlling women's unruly temper. As a result, men who "lose control" of themselves are automatically stigmatized as *namardi* (unmanly), *dewana* (crazy), while women are more sympathetically labeled as *mariz* (sick). As Majrouh mentions, women's choice of the means to end their lives emphasizes the iconoclastic meaning of the sacrifice: women will either resort to self-immolation or poison, not bullets or ropes, which are the tools used by men to wage wars or to tie up cattle or pull heavy loads.

Among the rare Afghan female poets with whom dormitory girls were familiar, two names were consistently cited with great enthusiasm: tenth-century poet Rabia Balkhi from the northern city of Balkh and contemporary poet Nadia Anjuman from the western city of Herat. Interestingly, these two poets, in spite of the distance that separates them in time, had each reached the status of national legends because of their tragic fate. A legend said that in the tenth century Rabia Balkhi wrote her last love poems with her own blood. Born in the court of the Samanids where many Persian poets held residence, Rabia fell in love with Baktash, the Turkish slave of her brother Haares. Mad with rage at the discovery of his sister's secret liaison, Haares killed Baktash. It is said that Rabia retreated into the house's *hamam* (bath), cut her veins, and wrote these last words on the bath walls: "When you see things hideous, fancy them straight away / Eat poison, but taste sugar sweet." Rabia's story and her poetry literally had this "taste of blood" (xvi) to which Majrouh refers.

The great Persian epics such as *Shahnameh* (Book of Kings), written in the tenth century by poet Abolqasem Ferdoosi, impregnated the dormitory girls' dreamy imaginations in powerful ways. These stories of honor, courage, and impossible love ended, as for Majnun Layla[6] and for Rabia and Baktash, in the death of the two protagonists. "I will tell you a story to show you that love can destroy mountains," Maryam, a dormitory girl, said once. And she spoke, while other girls sat in circle around her and attentively listened:

My grandfather, on my mother's side, was a dictator. He had seven wives [*she laughed*]. My aunt was a nurse in Iran. At that time, my entire family had moved to Iran. It was during the Iran-Iraq war. One day, a young soldier arrived at the hospital where my aunt was working. He was wounded and my aunt took care of him. This man was very handsome. He was Iranian. He fell in love with my aunt at first sight. He wanted to marry her. My aunt fell in love as well. The man went to my grandfather to ask for my aunt's hand. My grandfather, who was a real dictator, always refused. My seven uncles refused as well. So there was only one solution left for my aunt. One day, she cut her veins. When my grandfather discovered my aunt on the verge of death, he got totally panicked. He understood he could not fight against such a strong love. He finally accepted to give her to this man. Since then, my aunt is still living in Iran and is married to this man, with whom she had four children. So you see, if your love is very strong, no one can destroy it.

Stories like these were told and retold in the dormitory. They fueled the girls' imaginations with ideals of courage, love, and self-sacrifice. They frequently referred, always with a touch of admiration, to the heroic Afghan women who had chosen death to defend greater ideals like the national heroine Malalai of Maiwand. Women's self-harm belonged to the romantic and chivalrous universe of women's protest, assuming almost a legal dimension, bringing veracity to their claims. But if love of the nation was encouraged, romantic love was generally regarded with at least distrust or, at most, disrespect. Only the dramatic gesture of self-harm could bring the element of legality that initially lacked in such a claim.

Nadia Anjuman's story can be placed in the continuation of this lineage of self-sacrificing women. Nadia wrote clandestinely during the Taliban rule in one of the famous "sewing circles"[7] of Herat run by Afghan poet and professor Muhammad Ali Rahyab. She died under mysterious circumstances in 2005—probably killed by her husband although suicide was the official explanation—after the publication of her first collection of poems under the title of *Gul-e Dodi* (Flowers of Smoke). Thousands of people, among them government officials, Herati poets, and students, attended her funeral.

Nadia Anjuman's poems—one of which I quote in this chapter's epigraph—communicate grief, sorrow, and sadness, which combined together convey strong impressions of despondency and suffering. Her poetry denounced political oppression under the Taliban, but it also made more general commentaries on the restrictions imposed upon women as a result of the honor system.

The girls in the dormitory, some of whom had written poetry during their years of exile or when locked in their homes during the Taliban regime, sincerely admired the two poets. A number of girls living in the dormitory told me that during their years of exile in Pakistan or in Iran, writing poetry became a means to deal with their worries and anxieties. In an article published in the Dari-language women's magazine *Sadaf* (Pearl), an Afghan girl recalls how writing poetry helped her keep hope when the outside world was no longer accessible: "Slowly, I found out that controlling words would help me find a voice, and so I found the poet inside of me. For five years I patiently tolerated the clouds that had come into my life because I believed in the saying: 'patience is difficult but has its rewards.' . . . After some time, the clouds vanished and the light of hope started to shine again. Bathed in light, I ran to my white world" (Najwa 2006)[8]. Nadia Anjuman's story of struggle against a marriage arranged by her family against her will spoke to them in a similar way as the one of Rabia Balkhi. In many instances they felt the same anxiety as the poet regarding their future marriages, the restrictions it would possibly impose on their lives, and the pressure their families would press upon them to conform to norms of feminine modesty, endurance, and containment. They could relate to her desire to express her dissatisfaction.

Girls, grown up with hurting soul
And wounded bodies
Happiness has escaped their faces
Hearts, old and cracked[9]

The exact reasons for Nadia Anjuman's death remain obscure. Did she swallow some poison to put an end to an unhappy marriage, staging her death as she had already announced it in her writings? Did she succumb to the beatings of her jealous husband? These questions will remain partially unanswered. But if Anjuman is gone, her poetry will remain, all the more so in that her death brought a heroic and romantic aura to her literary production. Her poems are fine examples of her arresting style and fearless examination of self and society. They describe her sentiments but they are perceived by others as personal statements about interpersonal relationships, and it is this public denunciation, even though hidden under layers of ambiguous meanings, that made her songs so potentially threatening.

Poetry, as an aesthetic and spiritual domain of life, is about beliefs and values and therefore about politics (Abu-Lughod 1986). In countries like Afghanistan where two-thirds of the population is illiterate, oral poetry has been traditionally used as a channel for commenting on society and politics. Poetic composition and performances structure social relations and provide individuals with a form of political expression and persuasion. Poetry is a discourse of defiance, an expressive tool used by those in a position of subordination to comment on and challenge social hierarchies. Studying the poetry of women is particularly interesting since the ambiguous messages that are channeled through their literary work allow them to express covert forms of dissent.

The correlation between emotions, affects, and poetic expressive forms seems to me central for an understanding of suicide and self-harm that takes into account the cultural makeup of women's subjectivities. Indeed, poetry in Afghanistan is an important form of cultural expression. A person's ability to quote famous Persian poets or to make references to folktales is generally regarded with high respect. In villages where women are often illiterate and perceived as ignorant, it is common for them to use Afghan proverbs or short pieces of poetry to comment on public affairs. Their capacity to utilize this form of popular knowledge provides them with the credibility and the legitimacy that they often lack when it comes to participating in community decisions.

Poetry both reflects and shapes gendered "structures of feelings," providing social interactions with a specific aesthetics that follows the "texture of collective experience" (Filmer 2003). While placing private subjective feelings within a common universe of shared meanings, poetry opens room for oppositional cultural practices. The tension that exists between the privacy of feelings and the publicity of linguistic utterance enables the imaginary exploration of possible alternatives to the existing order of social and cultural relations. "Literature's significance is in providing an analytical and exploratory environment in which structures of feeling can discover how to articulate their emergence" (Filmer 2003, 216). The social and cultural dimensions of Afghan women's suicide highlight the communicative potential of emotional performances in mediating women's protests. While inscribing itself in a poetic tradition in which women's dissent can be legitimately expressed, women's suicide calls upon popular knowledge about gender roles and highlights women's central responsibility in both preserving and challenging the honor code.

Emotional Performance

In the last months of my fieldwork, I personally became the witness of two suicide attempts by two sisters who were students at the University of Kabul and to whom I was quite close. Besides the fact that these acts, like any other acts carried out due to despair, were the outcome of deep feelings of alienation, I also believe that they illustrate well the rebellious dimension of female social performances that Majrouh mentions. My aim here is not to diminish the real pain Khadija and Fawzia (pseudonyms) actually felt when they decided, one after the other, to swallow a cocktail of cheap tablets purchased in the bazaar. I am deeply convinced that the two of them were profoundly unhappy about their situation and that they could not think of any other way to relieve the pressure they felt weighing upon them. However, I also think there is something else to be read in these stories, something that has to do with the ways in which women in subordinate positions find the means to channel demands that cannot be expressed otherwise. These types of "performances" are, I believe, indicative of the subaltern positions (as Hazara, as women, and as "returnees") that the two sisters occupied since physically performing an act is often the result of a failure of performativity in speech—that is, a failure to trigger action through speech acts (Spivak 1988). Neither Khadija nor Fawzia really intended to end their lives but what they achieved through this collective gesture was quite powerful—not only did they get the last word in a family dispute that had lasted for months, but they also managed, momentarily, to reverse some of the power dynamics in which their relations to male family members were entangled.

Let me recount the story. The younger sister, Khadija, was a singer, a musician, and a student in musicology at the University of Kabul. She had developed a talent and a taste for music while in exile with her family in Iran during the civil war. There, Khadija, together with her mother and sister, wove carpets to complement the sporadic earnings of their father and brothers. While weaving, they listened to the radio and Khadija sang along. Once, Khadija showed me a picture of herself all dressed up in a black outfit with a panther print headscarf. She stood in a middle of a boys' band in which all the boys wore leather jackets, crossing their arms on their chest in a nonchalant parody of virility. The picture had been taken during her time in high school at Esfahan when some friends had recruited her as the singer of their underground rock band. At the time, her parents did not see any objections to this extracurricular activity as long as she did well at school and helped with the weaving. Once back in Afghanistan, however, the situation of the family changed dramatically. The family house had been destroyed during the fighting and the father struggled to find a job. The family eventually ended up renting a small room in a collective house in a poor suburb of Kabul, deprived of electricity and running water. The girls managed to enroll in the university after successfully passing their entrance exams. Both Khadija and Fawzia found part-time jobs to support the family, but their income, even added to that of their father, barely covered the household expenditures. In such a situation, and in the larger Afghan economic context of the time, being a female singer and musician was much less acceptable than in Iran.

The intensity of public debates around art and entertainment in the Muslim world denotes broader popular concerns about the "common good" and the "good Muslim." Being a devout Muslim and a performer, particularly for women, is generally perceived as a contradiction (Van Nieuwkerk 2008). This perception is reinforced in the case of Afghanistan because the military occupation, largely associated with a form of moral pollution, has strengthened a new form of cultural nationalism that calls for the moralization of the public sphere along "Islamic" lines. Musicians have always suffered from social stigma in Afghanistan, and female ones even more so (Doubleday 2006). A sign of this general contempt for the world of musicians can be found in the name of the district of Kabul where musicians have traditionally lived: Kharabat. *Kharab* in Dari has many meanings—something damaged, like a house hit by a rocket, a car that won't start, something or someone bad or naughty; *abat* means a place where people live. Consequently *kharabat* means a place where naughty people live. When the Taliban took over Kabul in 1996, their primary objective was to reestablish order and bring back morality in the capital city that had been perceived since the Soviet occupation as the center of sin and corruption. One of the first edicts they promulgated banned music, even at wedding ceremonies. As a result, most Afghan musicians lost their means of subsistence and fled abroad. The ones who stayed buried their instruments to avoid repression. After the downfall of the regime, music reasserted itself in the streets of the capital with tape and CD shops reopening in Shar-e-Naw, their front windows showcasing colorful albums of the most popular Afghan singers as well as foreign pop stars. Despite this rebirth, the stigma associated with musicians remained strong, especially for women singers.

Khadija was not ready to give up her passion and she continued taking music lessons and performing at official ceremonies without letting her parents know. Unfortunately the news of her activities spread like wildfire throughout her neighborhood, and her father Ahmed, alerted by Khadija's younger brother, eventually found some music scores in her bag. A huge argument ensued during which Ahmed destroyed her music scores and threatened to keep her locked in the house, a punishment he could not afford since Khadija was contributing to the household income by working in a marketing agency while engaged in her studies.

A few days later, I received a phone call from her sister Fawzia. Khadija had swallowed a cocktail of tablets and was at the hospital. I jumped into a taxi and found Fawzia, Khadija, their cousin (also a singer), and their father Ahmed in a narrow, dirty, and dark hospital room, an IV drip suspended above Khadija's bed and inserted into her forearm. She was safe now, but weakened and she could hardly walk. We hired another taxi and drove back to the family house in Dasht-e Bashri. In the car the father, who had been speechless for quite a while, started to talk again and each of his sentences was punctuated by Khadija's groans, her fingers clutched tightly into her sister's and cousin's hand. "Dard darom! Dard darom!" (It hurts! It hurts!), she sobbed, while pointing at her heart.

The argument continued at home, but this time Ahmed had lowered his voice, leaving space free for Fawzia, Khadija, and their mother to burst into loud sobbing and screams, a collective demonstration of pain that I had never witnessed before, except at funerals, when women rally together to mourn the dead, weeping one after another while recounting aloud biographic elements of the departed's life. Unable to engage in a discussion with the women of the house, Ahmed desperately turned to me: "We are Muslims, you understand, Julie? We are Muslims and Afghans and Khadija is behaving in a non-Muslim way. Singing is not for respectable women. Everyone talks . . . you see [*pointing at the next-door neighbors*], everyone talks . . . it is a shame . . . it dishonors the whole family." Khadija, suddenly recovering her lucidity, responded: "I am a Muslim too. I wear *hijab*. I pray. I read the Koran. I am educated. I work hard for the whole family. The Koran does not say that singing is bad. Singing brings peace in people's hearts! Only ignorant people talk badly about singers." Before Ahmed had the opportunity to open his mouth, she rolled her eyes, got off the ground to catch her breath and mimicked a dramatic fainting fit that kept him voiceless and petrified as if the performance of pain had brought an indisputable element of truth to his daughter's speech. This scene repeated itself several times, Khadija and Fawzia taking turns to defend their views in front of a father who seemed totally overwhelmed by the situation.

Just five days after this episode, I received a phone call from Fawzia, who alerted me in a voice I could hardly recognize on the phone that she had swallowed tablets like her sister: "They have to understand, Julie, that we are not bad girls or bad Muslims. If they cannot get this, then there is no point for me to live either." I knew that, for a while, Fawzia had been pressured by her father to find a job other than the one she already had as a gym teacher at Bagh-e Zanana, a job he found inappropriate for a woman to hold. He also complained about the way she dressed, which was not modest enough for his liking. Fawzia wore blue jeans and sneakers, and small colorful veils like most of the young professionals who attended courses at the University of Kabul. But Fawzia's father had never been to the university. He was a day laborer struggling to make ends meet and to provide for his five children. His situation made him particularly sensitive to gossip from relatives and neighbors and, as it became more and more difficult to find jobs in Kabul, he consequently became more and more tense about the family reputation.

Fawzia, Khadija's eldest sister, was a martial arts champion and one of the few female members of the Afghan Olympic team. She had taken part in an international competition in Sri Lanka shortly after the fall of the Taliban. If under family pressure she had eventually given up this title, she continued to practice once a week in a small gym club located on the outskirts of Kabul with a private coach without her parents' knowledge. Like her sister, Fawzia led a double life, but the public visibility she had gained over time, attracting the recently reborn press that now flourished thanks to foreign sponsors in the capital city, made it difficult for her to cover up her secrets. Rumors ran wild that with the liberation of Afghanistan, women and girls in particular were being left without control, using the pretext of democracy to engage in "un-Islamic" activities. Sports and music undoubtedly belonged to this category.

It is interesting to note that Fawzia harmed herself just a few days after her sister as if she had wanted to validate the rightfulness of her claim. Of the two sisters, Khadija was the most daring and vocal. As the elder sister, Fawzia felt more compelled to preserve "family values." It was not rare to hear her complain about Khadija's "bad behavior." In the meantime, Fawzia tended to use dissimulation instead of visibility more consistently as a safer strategy to preserve family honor while continuing her activities. She strove to remain unnoticed, practicing martial arts in an underground club to avoid being the target of gossips. She taught martial arts to girls only in Bargh-e Zanana (Women's Garden) in Kabul, a park exclusively reserved to women. Conversely, Khadija was more "transparent" and open about her activities, mingling with both boys and girls on the university campus. She did not hesitate to sing in public at official ceremonies. But this time, the father had gone too far: Fawzia felt that all her efforts for reconciling her family's expectations with her own interpretations of Islam, honor, and modernity did not achieve any positive result. "We are good Muslim girls, Julie. We are educated. They need to understand," she kept on repeating during the taxi ride back to the dormitory. Too much ashamed to bring her daughter back home where the neighbors could have witnessed the scandal for the second time, Ahmed had decided that his daughter was well enough to return directly from the hospital to her dormitory room.

I do not think that Khadija and Fawzia sincerely wanted to put an end to their lives. Both of them were passionate about music and sports and they had many university friends who supported them. They were also very upset about their family not approving of their choices, and it was not rare for me to be used as an intermediary when there was a disagreement between them and their parents. "Women are the honor of a house," the mother told me once. "If women misbehave, then the whole family's reputation is damaged." And indeed, in a house without furniture, electricity, and running water, reputation was all that was left to preserve. It felt uncomfortable taking the girls' side when I could also empathize with their parents' worries. It is easier to be liberal-minded when there is always bread on the table. But I was also full of admiration for Khadija and Fawzia's commitment to pursue careers in fields that were not particularly favorable to women and in which they obviously had talent.

The contradictions in which the two sisters were caught, at once encouraged to become educated women while expected to remain faithful to a rather strict version of the code of honor, were to a large extent the result of the multiple displacements their family had endured. In Iran where they had grown up, the notion of "community" had taken up a different meaning and had remained limited to the extended family. In Kabul, the family's social disembeddedness was seen with suspicion by relatives who had remained in the country during the war. Fawzia and Khadija's family was regularly accused of having failed to preserve "traditional Afghan values" during its exile in Iran and this was reflected in the ways in which the two daughters had chosen to enroll in activities considered inappropriate for women. With economic hardship it had become more complicated for their father to counter these accusations and stand up for his daughters' right to make these kinds of untraditional life choices.

Without attempting to diminish the veracity of the pain produced by the real dilemma in which they were caught, I understand Khadija and Fawzia's gestures not as purely desperate acts carried out because of profound feelings of hopelessness. I also see in this reiterated performance an attempt at finding the means to claim "the last word" (Seremetakis 1991) in a dispute in which their voices had been silenced. The public scandal that the girls provoked opened room for making their claims audible, but it did not totally reverse the gender dynamics in which their lives where entangled in the long run. After these events, the negotiations between the father and the daughters continued through other means.

I use the word "performance" here to describe an action that is transformed through culture into a conventionally understandable symbolic product and to underline the communicative nature of female suicide. According to Richard Bauman (1984, 11), "Performance as a mode of spoken verbal communication consists of the assumption of responsibility to an audience for a display of communicative competence. This competence rests on knowledge and ability to speak in socially appropriate ways. Performance involves on the part of the performer an assumption of accountability to an audience for the way in which communication is carried out, above and beyond its referential content." Building on Erving Goffman's (1967) concept of "interactive ritual" and on Bakhtinian notions of "intertextuality" and "dialogism," Bauman defines "performance" as a process through which a discourse that bears traditional authority is "decontextualized" and "recontextualized" in order to manage the impressions of an audience. Bauman argues that "decontextualization" and "recontextualization" carry the potential of deconstructing dominant ideologies because re-citation potentially disrupts original meanings and iterability triggers new forms of representation and knowledge (2004, 10). I see Khadija and Fawzia's suicide attempts as performances in the sense given by Bauman and Goffman here. Both sisters had an intrinsic knowledge of their audience's expectations and the ways in which they could be managed.

The data I use in this case study reveal that the public display of self-harm and emotions is related to women's identity as defined in the honor code. The concept of "performance" helps us to understand how cultural expectations of women's weakness, uncontrollability, and emotionality can be used by women themselves (even though oftentimes unconsciously) in order to renegotiate the gender order. Women's suicide brings shame to men whose first responsibility is to ensure the well-being and respectability of their family. Therefore women's suicide, by making public men's failure, works as a means to contest and challenge gender hierarchies.

The intensity of the episodes I witnessed in the hospital and in the family house made me realize the subversive potential of female suicide. Khadija and Fawzia's performances followed the same communicative patterns. The tears, the specific expression of women's pain and suffering (men do not cry), brought some validity to their claims. Through this performance, girls were not in the position of listeners anymore but opened an expressive space for themselves to voice their demands. While reproducing the stereotype of feminine hysteria, tears and fainting fits asserted the seriousness of their respective demands. In the same way Rabia Balkhi cut her veins to demonstrate her eternal love for Baktash, Fawzia and Khadija swallowed poison to demonstrate the seriousness and sincerity of their aspirations. Their acts served as a kind of displacement to the hostilities. It also allowed them to make their claims audible in a context where their demands were perceived as pure provocation.

Similar feminine strategies have been observed in other honor-based societies where women's communication patterns follow a comparable repertoire. For instance, Nadia Seremetakis (1991, 5) shows how death rituals in Inner Mani (Greece) represent a performative arena where pain figures prominently as an orchestrating and prescriptive communicative paradigm. During these rituals, women's expressions of pain through lamentations and screams allow them to obtain some form of collective validation. Women's capacity to receive such a validation is due to the almost legal value that pain assumes in the Inner Mani ethical code (Seremetakis 1991, 105). "To 'witness,' 'to suffer for,' and 'to come out as representative for'[10] are narrative devices in laments that fuse jural notions of reciprocity and truth claiming with the emotional nuances of pain" (1991, 102).

I believe that Afghan women's public expressions of pain and suffering have a similar function. In her ethnography of Pashtun women in Afghanistan and in Pakistan, Benedicte Grima (1992) points out that in the tribal code of honor, *gham* (worry, sorrow, grief, sadness, hardship) is expected in women. To express *gham* is to do *pashto*, that is, to participate in a moral system in which the preservation of honor is paramount. She states therefore that "[Pashtun] women earn respect and reputation by the amount of hardship and suffering they endure" (1992, 13). However, young unmarried girls are not expected to participate in the *gham* rituals organized by women at moments of life crisis (deaths, illnesses, accidents). Young girls are seen as ignorant and inexperienced until marriage familiarizes them with the *gham* of mature womanhood. She continues: "the precedence given to pain and suffering over joy, and the ritual and narrative around each *gham*, also shapes the memory and perception of women's lives" (1992, 142). "Life stories are told as an attestation of being moral [Pashtun] women" (1992, 13). In such a moral framework, *gham* can be understood as the key to women's social success as well as a means for women to create a temporary sense of autonomy and to develop their own singular voice.

As young unmarried girls, Fawzia and Khadija's performances could not be acknowledged as social expressions of *gham*. However, their violation of *purdah* (women's modesty) through the scandal provoked by their respective suicide attempts and afterward through their screams and tears brought some validity to their grievances. In a culture that values an individual's capacity to suppress and deny the inner self (*nafs*), such behaviors amounted to a loss of control resulting from extreme distress. Their father and brothers' silence in front of these intense emotional displays reveals not only their concern for their daughters/sisters' well-being but also, more generally, men's fundamental fear of women's behaviors. The threatening element of women's emotional expression rests on the fact that a man's honor is assessed through his capacity to remain in control of the gendered order of the family and the community. The only option left for Ahmed, Fawzia and Khadija's father, was to give up a part of his authority and allow both of them to continue their occupations.

A few weeks before writing this manuscript, I received an e-mail from a girl in the dormitory with a link to a video posted on YouTube. "You will recognize this person," she wrote at the end of her e-mail. As the music started to play on my computer speakers, I saw Khadija's round face appearing on the screen. She had been selected to participate in *Afghan Star*, the Afghan equivalent of *American Idol* and the most popular television show in the country. Not only had she made it to the finals, but she also appeared in a traditional Afghan dress singing on stage, the only girl left out of eight participants. Dressed as she was, in the embroidered dress covered with silver jewelry that Afghan women always wear with great pride for official ceremonies and important events, Khadija reiterated a statement she had made earlier to her male relatives: there was nothing in Islam or in Afghan culture and tradition that prevented women from becoming singers.

In spite of my embarrassment regarding such television programs, especially in countries still at war like Afghanistan, I could not help feeling overwhelmed with both joy and anxiety at the sight of Khadija smiling and singing in front of the camera. My worried excitement was not the result of a specific resonance that such public visibility might have had for a European woman like me—live TV shows have never been my cup of tea. But the moving image of Khadija on the computer screen when she was now so far away from my world made me realize the depth of her determination. It also made me wonder whether Khadija's willpower was only the result of her personality and life trajectory or the outcome of broader global/external forces that shaped youngsters' aspirations while encouraging the development of new feminine subjectivities—autonomous, rebellious, self-driven.

In the newly reborn Western-sponsored national press and in international news, it was not rare to see young women like Fawzia and Khadija making the headlines. These feminine figures were gradually becoming the new role models of the younger generations yearning for leisure, romance, and Western pop music rightly deserved after long years of war and destruction. At the same time such stories fed Western imaginations with necessary stories of liberation and women's emancipation in sharp contrast with the images of "Middle Age darkness" personified by the Taliban that were spread by Western media prior to the military intervention. But the attraction of Afghan youngsters for "modern" lifestyles, encouraged by an anarchic opening of the country to liberalism and the market economy while many regions remained at war, was a major source of social tensions, especially for older generations and rural inhabitants who understood the phenomenon as a new form of acculturation. I wondered what would happen to girls like Fawzia and Khadija who had initiated such a reinterpretation of "old values," as they called them, once the already fragile safety nets provided by NGOs and international constituencies completely disappeared from their country.

In order to fully comprehend the instrumental agency of women caught in the multilayered relations of power, it is necessary to move away from liberal models of subjectivity. Fawzia and Khadija, far from initiating a clear break with traditional systems of values, strove to preserve continuity while opening room for interpretation. I see their performance as occupying the exact fragile space of "resistance" as defined by Michel de Certeau's concept of "everyday forms of opposition" (1984). Their poisoning was an attempt at recombining the rules that already existed in their culture in a way that was influenced, but not wholly determined, by those rules. Their "tactics"—"the art of the weak" to quote Certeau again—far from being guided by pure self-determination, were primarily informed by the instinctive and embodied knowledge of their own positionality. As Mary Keller explains, "a significant element of women's power is related to their *placeness*" (2005, 111–12). By using a culturally intelligible expressive form, these young women, as agents involved in a project of self-legitimation, tried to make the best out of their *place*.

A Feminine Expressive Form

Acceptance, suffering, and patience are the main qualities Afghan women are expected to have. Women in general are expected to "sacrifice" themselves for their families, not to defend a just cause or a personal conviction. However, the narratives that I have analyzed above demonstrate that women are particularly resourceful in obscuring their performances and in manipulating the different meanings of the honor rhetoric. The tension created between discourses that are confirming certain notions of womanhood (as emotionally fragile and sexually threatening and so on) and acts of covert reinterpretation that challenge these notions underlines the extremely narrow room for maneuvering that women have to exercise agency. But far from being futile gestures, these ambiguous social practices also highlight how women's engagement with the honor code brings nuances and changes to traditional gender discourses.

The fundamentally ambiguous nature of women's modes of expression demonstrates the difficulty of renegotiating gender norms in the "postwar/

reconstruction" era. Emotional performances such as those of Khadija and Fawzia or of political women invoking "martyrdom" highlight the centrality of emotional repertoires in mediating women's public visibility. These practices also show that as subalterns women are not simply deprived of the ability to influence the social order by pushing the boundaries of the private.

The confining limits of representations of femininity within the honor ideology, which has been reinforced as a result of foreign military occupation, produce the experience of silencing for women. In order to break that silence, women are left with little choice but to veil their protest with complex expressive forms. In the meantime these invisible tactics, which disturb mainstream discourses of womanhood without fundamentally modifying their cultural roots, are crucial adaptations that compel one to acknowledge the extraordinary resourcefulness and agency of women in maneuvering the honor system and the nationalist ideology that it sustains.

The Carnival Continues

I last visited Afghanistan in 2007. As I write, I am in London and I unexpectedly got back in touch with Khadija, the Hazara singer whose story I recount in Chapter 6. Through a common friend called Misha, who studied at the School of Oriental and African Studies and spent some time studying Hazaragi music in Afghanistan a while back, I learned that Khadija was now in London. Misha gave me her phone number and we reunited for a dinner at my house. Khadija has not changed, even though she may have lost some of the roundness of her cheeks. She now speaks perfect English. But she is still the young, enthusiastic, passionate, and curious woman I met in Kabul. How extraordinary it is to find her in London now!

After her appearance on *Afghan Star*, she told me that her life turned into a daily nightmare, to the point that even her parents' house was not safe anymore. Shortly after the show was over, two of her uncles who worked on construction sites in Dubai set out to reestablish the family's honor and purchased plane tickets to Kabul. They had barely landed in Dasht-e Bashri and yet they were ready to wash away the insult by paying a surprise visit to Khadija. Fortunately, Khadija's father was home on that day and he tried to stop them while Khadija managed to escape through the window and find a hiding spot in the neighborhood's *nanbâi* (bakery). A few days after this event, Khadija and her sister, Fawzia—who could not stay in the dormitory either as other students had started to gossip and harass her—moved to a small flat in another neighborhood of Kabul. They stayed there until they had saved enough money to try their luck in India. The waiting period seemed to last forever for Khadija, who could not set foot outside of her house without the fear of insult or even attack. Her parents, split between their love for their daughter and their resentment for the shame she had brought to the family, asked her not to visit them anymore. Her stay in New Delhi did not bring the

Figure 20. A wall in Kabul displays the posters of candidates for the 2009
presidential elections. Photo by Karim Amin.

relief she had expected either. "India is like Afghanistan and then when you
are Afghan, everyone knows you there, too! There was no escape!" Struggling to make ends meet, and with very meager savings, the two sisters had
no other choice but to return to Kabul. There, Fawzia ended up marrying an
old school friend. She is now the mother of a little daughter named Athena
and lives with her husband and in-laws, arguing from time to time with her
mother-in-law as well as enjoying moments of happiness like most other
Afghan women do. "If she had come with me, she would have been a very
different woman. Now, she is just like any other woman there: gossiping and
raising her kid," Khadija confessed with a touch of regret in her voice.

For Khadija, however, marriage was not an option. "It became virtually
impossible for me to live in Kabul," she said. The videos of her performances
traveled across the world to reach Afghan communities exiled in the West
and rewired since 2001 to whatever happens in Kabul. One day she received
an offer that would finally make her escape possible: she was invited by the
Afghan diaspora community in Copenhagen to perform at a concert they had
organized especially for her. She packed her luggage and as she stepped on
the airplane that would bring her to Europe, she knew this was her last good-

bye to Kabul. After her concert in Copenhagen, she traveled to Paris, where she found her brother, who had lived there for seven years as an illegal immigrant. Appalled by the precarious situation under which he lived, she decided not to stay and rented a fake passport to cross the English Channel.

As we sat around the table in my London kitchen, totally amazed by her courage and determination and by her capacity to mobilize the connections she needed to find her way on a new continent, Khadija's burst into laughter. "On my new passport, I was Japanese! So I spent a day roaming around Gare du Nord, trying to prepare myself to cross the border and rehearsing the two Japanese words I knew." She did not make it very far though: As she presented her passport to the customs agent prior to boarding the Eurostar, she was put on the side for police investigation. Sticking to her story line of being a Japanese tourist en route to England, Khadija made a scandal: "If I miss this train, you will have to reimburse my ticket!" And she laughed at the memory of this act she attempted to play out until the very end, polishing her nails while waiting for the Japanese translator to arrive. When he did, of course, the lie could not hold any longer. She spent the night in detention and was released the day after with an order to leave the territory within the next twenty-four hours.

It took her a few extra weeks to find another passport. But she finally made it to London. It did not take her long to obtain refugee status there with the story she had to tell. Like most immigrants eager to establish themselves in their host country, Khadija learned English in no time. She is now accommodated in a women's refuge and enrolled in an art school. With her hipster appearance, she already looks like a trendy young Londoner. Apart from Fawzia who married her school friend and their mother who is still in Kabul, the entire family is now scattered all around the planet: the father, Ahmed, returned to Iran to find work. The second eldest brother is there too, but he is not doing very well: Khadija says he has a problem with drugs and does not send news very often. Farad, the youngest brother, obtained a scholarship to study in the United States. At the moment when he was due to return to Kabul, he crossed the Canadian border and sought asylum there. He is currently living with a host family and attends high school at Saint Catharine's in Ontario. The eldest brother, Farid, obtained his papers just after Khadija: apparently, Khadija's case helped him speed up the process with the French authorities.

Thinking of the amazing story of Khadija, I can't help but admire the resourcefulness she deployed to make her way to a place where she could be the woman she wanted to be. I also realize that her story, like the one of the young education activist Malala Yousafzai from Pakistan who was shot by a Taleb in 2012 while returning home from school, follows a script that Western governments, in a well-known trope of the "white man's burden," are very much eager to hear. That the French immigration authorities could not consider Khadija's brother who also faced hardship a credible "victim" as an Afghan man is very revealing of the way in which the "woman question" in Afghanistan has been framed to serve a specific aim in a continuing war story. Indeed, what could please a European government more in a political climate that has become tougher on immigration with every passing day than to give an indefinite right to remain to a young Afghan woman who, regardless of danger, struggled to find a voice?

*   *   *

Feminists around the world know well enough that positive changes in gender relations cannot be achieved in the course of a day and that each step forward should never be considered as definite. In the case of Afghanistan, such transformations are not likely to occur as long as a sense of national autonomy is not guaranteed. Progressive gender policies can only develop when sovereignty is ensured; that is, when a more straightforward and less unequal relationship to the West can develop. The practices I have described here have to be understood in the light of these broader geopolitical dynamics that have been partly responsible for the colonization of Afghan women's lives over the past decades.

Postcolonial feminist legal scholars such as Ratna Kapur (2004) and Nivedita Menon (2004) have highlighted the contradictions that emerge in the legal field when globalization and liberalism collude to redefine the subject "woman" in Third World postcolonial countries. Menon demonstrates that by following the logic of constitutionalism in its transition toward independence and the building of a modern state, India has inherited from its colonial past a definition of women as autonomous individuals entitled to rights. The shortcomings of these legal developments—that is, the lack of connection between the imagined woman of the liberal legal/radical feminist agenda and the ordinary woman whose life is entangled in intricate social relations that are part of a distinctive ethos—are, I think, worth recalling if we want to go beyond the normative framework that accompanies most "democracy building" efforts (Menon 2004, 209). The analysis and empirical material I presented in this study demonstrate that women are not deprived of imagination when it comes to negotiating the norms that regiment their lives. However, the choreography of these "tactics" occupies a specific moral universe that does not follow the path of a public "coming out" as is the case in more organized forms of social movements in the West or in countries that do not have to bear the burden of imperial domination.

I share with Kapur (2004) the view that we need to be cautious when gender essentialism informs legal interventions in the global South. She writes: "By not remaining sufficiently attentive to cultural and historical specificities, gender essentialism constructed through a VAW [violence against women] discourse has prompted state actors, non-state actors and donors to embrace universalising strategies in responding to human rights violations against women. It has further obscured differences between women located in very different power relationships" (2004, 106). The challenge that Kapur leaves us with is "to think of ways in which to express . . . [our] politics without subjugating other subjectivities through claims to the idea of a 'true self' or a singular truth." This, she argues, would lead "to a reformulation of the notions of agency and choice . . . [where agency] is neither situated exclusively in the individual nor denied because of some overarching oppression. It is situated in the structures of social relationships, the location of the subject, and the shape-shifting of culture" (Kapur 2004, 135).

This critical approach to "agency" is important to keep in mind when analyzing the ideology that guides contemporary state-building projects. As the case of Afghanistan demonstrates, the current struggle over women's rights has caught women in a state of tension between their demands for gender equality within their community and their dependence upon and support for the community as a site for resistance to foreign occupation. The imposition of a universalist framework to establish gender equality has not only hampered Afghan women's capacity to speak for themselves but it has also derailed the conditions of possibility for constructing legal norms differently. This study has shown how legal metanarratives inspired by Western liberal tradition have been used to create modern state institutions that bolster the myth of reconstruction in the West while leaving Afghans with the task of either reproducing "the project of positive unoriginality" (Chakrabarty 1992, 17 citing Morris 1990) or redefining "culture" in fixed and essentialized terms.

However, a closer look at women's body work and performances can help us move away from monolithic representations of nationalism as the absolute political evil and sense the regenerative potential of anticolonial struggles.

According to Partha Chatterjee (1993), "anticolonial nationalism" is not, like Anderson (1991) suggests, merely a modular form of an original nationalism stemming from the European experience. Rather, "the most powerful as well as the most creative results of the nationalist imagination in Asia and Africa are posited not on an identity but rather on a *difference* with the 'modular' forms of the national society propagated by the modern West" (Chatterjee 1993, 5). Chatterjee argues that "anticolonial nationalism" creates its own sphere of sovereignty by distinguishing between the material (the domain of the "outside": science, technology, and statecraft where the West has maintained its superiority) and the spiritual (the domain of the "inside" that bears the essential marks of "cultural identity"). It is in the domain of the "spiritual" that anticolonial nationalism asserts its sovereignty territory.

As much as women are key actors in the preservation of the "traditions" that form the essential marks of identity, their carnivalesque reappropriation of nationalist discourses allows them to fashion a modern national culture that is nevertheless not Western. My analysis of university girls' complex body work in Chapter 4 highlights that while aspiring to embody modern (that is, urban, working-class, and educated) feminine selves, young urban educated women are also concerned with maintaining relationships and preserving the ideal of the "good Muslim" girl. Their symbolic rebellion, through cosmetics and fashion, had little in common with Western feminist movements that strive to break free from patriarchy, religion, and the commodification of their bodies. In their quest for a balance between a modern feminine identity and a Muslim one, these girls experimented—sometimes painfully and sometimes playfully—with the boundaries of the gender system while remaining true to what they understood was part of their culture and religion.

By contrast, because of greater public visibility, women who were more directly involved in politics were more compelled to wear "nationalist veils" in order to achieve legitimacy. This did not mean, however, that their hands were totally tied to nationalist politics. My analysis of veiling practices among women's rights activists and MPs in Chapter 5 shows that these women are both strategic and pragmatic when it comes to managing their audience's impressions in public. Their embodied knowledge of gender norms and social expectations allows them to navigate in different circles and carve out new spaces for negotiations. Their public visibility under the veil is not totally tactical either since all of them are devout Muslims who understand veiling as an Islamic prescription. But contrary to Saba Mahmood's analysis (2005) of women's veiling in the context of the Islamic revival in Egypt, I do not think

Afghan women's body work can solely be explained as an attempt at producing pious selves through body discipline. Although religion informs their actions in a meaningful way, religion is definitely not their only source of guidance.

Afghan women's knowledge does not merely reside in cerebral machinations; it comes alive in practice, that is, in performance. Their resistance is therefore embedded within women's expressive traditions and takes different forms in different contexts and circumstances. These embodied forms of understanding and connecting with the world are what makes them able to cope with the various struggles in which their lives are entangled. The lesson that Western feminists could learn from Afghan women is that if one wants to change the world for the better, one must not just be able to imagine it but also know how to perform it differently.

CHRONOLOGY

1838–42	British forces invade, install King Shah Shujah. He is assassinated in 1842. British and Indian troops are massacred during retreat from Kabul.
1878–80	Second Anglo-Afghan War. A treaty gives Britain control of Afghan foreign affairs.
1919	Emir Amanullah Khan declares independence from British influence.
1926–29	Amanullah tries to introduce social reforms, which stirs civil unrest. He flees.
1933	Zahir Shah becomes king and Afghanistan remains a monarchy for the next four decades.
1953	General Mohammad Daud becomes prime minister. Turns to Soviet Union for economic and military assistance. Introduces social reforms such as the abolition of *purdah* (practice of secluding women from public view).
1963	Mohammad Daud forced to resign as prime minister.
1964	Constitutional monarchy introduced, leading to political polarization and power struggles.
1973	Mohammad Daud seizes power in a coup and declares a republic. Tries to play off Soviet Union against Western powers.
1978	General Daud is overthrown and killed in a pro-Soviet coup. The People's Democratic Party comes to power but is paralyzed by violent infighting and faces opposition by U.S.-backed mujahideen groups.

Soviet Intervention

December 1979   Soviet army invades and props up Communist government.

1980   Babrak Karmal installed as ruler, backed by Soviet troops. Opposition intensifies with various mujahideen groups fighting against Soviet forces. United States, Pakistan, China, Iran, and Saudi Arabia supply money and arms to the mujahideen.

1985   Mujahideen come together in Pakistan to form alliance against Soviet forces. Half of Afghan population now estimated to be displaced by war, with many fleeing to neighboring Iran or Pakistan.

1986   United States begins supplying mujahideen with Stinger missiles, enabling them to shoot down Soviet helicopter gunships. Babrak Karmal replaced by Najibullah as head of Soviet-backed regime.

1988   Afghanistan, the Soviet Union, the United States, and Pakistan sign peace accords, and Soviet Union begins pulling out troops.

Red Army Quits

1989   Last Soviet troops leave but civil war follows as mujahideen push to overthrow Najibullah.

1992   Najibullah's government toppled but a devastating civil war continues.

1996   Taliban seize control of Kabul and introduce hard-line version of Islam, banning women from work and introducing Islamic punishments that include stoning to death and amputations.

1997   Taliban recognized as legitimate rulers by Pakistan and Saudi Arabia. They now control about two-thirds of the country.

1998   The United States launches missile strikes at suspected bases of militant Osama bin Laden, accused of bombing U.S. embassies in Africa.

1999	UN imposes an air embargo and financial sanctions to force Afghanistan to hand over Osama bin Laden for trial.
September 2001	Ahmad Shah Masood, leader of the main opposition to the Taliban, the Northern Alliance, is assassinated.

U.S.-Led Invasion

October 2001	U.S.-led bombing of Afghanistan begins following the September 11 attacks on the United States. Anti-Taliban Northern Alliance forces enter Kabul shortly afterward.
December 2001	Afghan groups agree to deal in Bonn, Germany, for interim government. Hamid Karzai is sworn in as head of an interim power-sharing government.
January 2002	Deployment of first contingent of foreign peacekeepers, the NATO-led International Security Assistance Force (ISAF), marking the start of a protracted fight against the Taliban.
April 2002	Former king Zahir Shah returns but makes no claim to the throne; dies in 2007.
June 2002	Loya Jirga, the grand council, elects Hamid Karzai as interim head of state. Karzai picks members of his administration who serve until 2004.
August 2003	NATO takes control of security in Kabul, its first-ever operational commitment outside Europe.

Elections

January 2004	Loya Jirga adopts new constitution, which provides for a strong presidency.
October–November 2004	Presidential elections; Hamid Karzai is declared winner.
September 2005	Afghans vote in first parliamentary elections in more than thirty years.

December 2005	Parliament opens with warlords and strongmen in most of the seats.

October 2006　NATO assumes responsibility for security across the whole of Afghanistan, taking command in the east from a U.S.-led coalition force.

August 2007　Opium production soars to a record high, according to UN reports.

June 2008　President Karzai warns that Afghanistan will send troops into Pakistan to fight militants if Islamabad fails to take action against them.

July 2008　Suicide bomb attack on Indian embassy in Kabul kills more than fifty.

September 2008　U.S. President George W. Bush sends an extra 4,500 U.S. troops to Afghanistan, in a move he described as a "quiet surge."

February 2009　NATO countries pledge to increase military and other commitments in Afghanistan after the United States announces dispatch of 17,000 extra troops.

New U.S. Approach

March 2009　U.S. President Barack Obama unveils new strategy for Afghanistan and Pakistan. An extra 4,000 U.S. personnel will train and bolster the Afghan army and police along with providing support for civilian development.

August 2009　Presidential and provincial elections are marred by widespread Taliban attacks, sporadic turnout, and claims of serious fraud.

October 2009　Karzai declared winner of August presidential election after second-place opponent Abdullah Abdullah pulls out before the second round.

December 2009　U.S. President Obama decides to boost U.S. troop numbers in Afghanistan by 30,000, bringing the total to 100,000. He states that the United States will begin withdrawing its forces by 2011.

July 2010	Whistle-blowing website WikiLeaks publishes thousands of classified U.S. military documents relating to Afghanistan.

General David Petraeus Takes Command of U.S., ISAF Forces

August 2010	Dutch troops quit.
September 2010	Parliamentary polls marred by Taliban violence, widespread fraud, and a long delay in announcing results.
November 2010	At the summit in Lisbon, NATO reaches an agreement to hand control of security to Afghan forces by end of 2014.
July 2011	President's half brother and Kandahar governor Ahmad Wali Karzai is killed in Taliban campaign against prominent figures.
September 2011	Ex-president Burhanuddin Rabbani, a go-between in talks with the Taliban, is assassinated.
November 2011	President Karzai wins the endorsement of tribal elders to negotiate a ten-year military partnership with the United States at a *loya jirga* traditional assembly. The proposed pact will see U.S. troops remain after 2014 when other foreign troops are due to leave the country.
December 2011	At least fifty-eight people are killed in twin attacks at a Shia shrine in Kabul and a Shia mosque in Mazar-i-Sharif. Pakistan and the Taliban boycott the scheduled Bonn Conference on Afghanistan; Pakistan refuses to attend after a NATO air strike kills Pakistani soldiers on the Afghan border.
January 2012	Taliban agree to open office in Dubai as a move toward peace talks with the United States and the Afghan government.

NATO Withdrawal Plan

May 2012	NATO summit endorses the plan to withdraw foreign combat troops by the end of 2014.

July 2012	Tokyo donor conference pledges $16 billion in civilian aid to Afghanistan up to 2016 with the United States, Japan, Germany, and the United Kingdom supplying the bulk of funds. Afghanistan agrees to new conditions to counter corruption.
September 2012	United States hands over Bagram high-security jail to the Afghan government, although it retains control over some foreign prisoners until March 2013. The United States also suspends training new police recruits in order to carry out checks on possible ties to the Taliban following a series of attacks on foreign troops by alleged police and Afghan soldiers.
March 2013	Two former Kabul Bank chiefs, Sherkhan Farnood and Khalilullah Ferozi, are jailed for the multimillion-dollar fraud that led to the near collapse of the bank and the entire Afghan banking system in 2010.
June 2013	Afghan army takes command of all military and security operations from NATO forces. President Karzai suspends security talks with the United States after Washington announces it plans to hold direct talks with the Taliban. Afghanistan insists on conducting the talks with the Taliban in Qatar itself.
November 2013	Consultative loya jirga assembly of elders backs President Karzai's proposed security agreement to provide U.S. military with bases after NATO troops formally withdraw in 2014. President Karzai delays signing the deal.
January 2014	Taliban suicide squad hits a restaurant in Kabul's diplomatic quarter, the worst attack on foreign civilians since 2001.
February 2014	Start of presidential election campaign, which is marked by a rise in attacks by the Taliban.

April 2014	Presidential election inconclusive, goes on to second round between Abdullah Abdullah and Ashraf Ghani.
June 2014	Second round of presidential election, with more than fifty reported killed in various incidents during voting.

NOTES

Introduction

1. His main argument is that three somewhat incompatible cultural principles that form the building blocks of Afghan identity, namely Islam, honor, and *rule* (state governance), continue to cohabit and increasingly compete against each other as the nation-state attempts to impose itself as the only legitimate political entity.

2. In spite of its outward desire to make Afghanistan enter the concert of "modern" nations by unifying the country around values promoted by Marxist ideology, Olivier Roy (1986) explains that tribal tensions within the party itself were responsible for its split into two factions: Parcham and Khalq.

Chapter 1. Queen Soraya's Portrait

1. Farida Mahwash remains the only female singer in Afghanistan to have received the title of "Ustad." This title was awarded by the Ministry of Information and Culture. This was a controversial step as this honorific title is normally reserved for men. The 1960s and 1970s were the golden age of music, the heyday of Radio Afghanistan and Kabul as a cultural center. Farida Mahwash is remembered as the greatest woman singer of the time. She came from a very respectable Kabul family; her mother taught the Koran. Farida Mawash started work at the radio station as a typist. Her wonderful voice and exceptional musical abilities were discovered by the director of music at Radio Afghanistan, where her career as a radio singer was launched.

2. Detachments for the defense of the revolution were created shortly after the Saur Revolution. As resistance against the Soviet occupation grew all over the country, in cities as well as in rural areas, the government recruited "volunteers," who were given weapons in order to fight against the "enemies of the Revolution perpetrating acts of sabotage." They took part in guarding industrial enterprises, public buildings, and maintaining order (Baryalai, Spantghar, and Grib 1984, 187).

Chapter 2. National Women's Machinery

1. The World Bank website lists the national poverty rate as 35.8 percent in 2011. http://data.worldbank.org/country/afghanistan.

2. As of 2014, the World Health Organization (WHO) website lists the life expectancy for men as fifty-eight, for women, sixty-one, and the mortality rate for children before five as 9 percent (WHO, 2014, "Countries: Afghanistan" http://www.who.int /countries/afg.en).

3. According to UNICEF, "It is believed that 760 children were killed or maimed during the first half of 2013. There were reports of attacks against schools and health facilities, abductions, denials of humanitarian access, sexual violence and recruitment. The number of attacks on children increased by 30 per cent during 2013" (UNICEF annual report 2013—Afghanistan).

4. This scene was recorded during a "gender-empowerment training" program conducted at the Ministry of Women's Affairs in March 2007. I was introduced to the trainer, Sonila Danaj (pseudonym), through my friend Haroon, an Afghan medical doctor working part-time as a civil servant for the Ministry of Health and part-time as a freelance translator for various organizations. I attended this training program as a participant-observer. The discussions reported here were recorded with a tape recorder. I recorded participants' reactions in my journal.

5. The Constitution of the Islamic Republic of Afghanistan stipulates in Article 138 that "a provincial council is to be formed" in each of country's thirty-four provinces that should "take part in securing the developmental targets of the state and improving its affairs in a way stated by law" and give "advice on important issues falling within the domain" of each province.

6. Extract from Sonila Danaj's blog. The comments she makes here do not refer to the training described in this section but to another training she had conducted earlier with a group of representatives from other provinces. Last accessed on April 29. 2008 http://www.journeytowardpeace.blogspot.com.

7. Nancy Dupree (1984) mentions that after the Red Army invaded the country, popular support for reforms sharply diminished and dissidence started to emerge under covert forms even within governmental offices. "Women in government offices began slowdowns, particularly in the Ministry of Education's literacy program. Books and papers were purposely delayed, misdirected, lost, and damaged. More than the usual time was spent in the office gossiping, knitting, and thumbing through magazines. False attendance reports were submitted" (334). This account echoes some of the personal communications I collected while conducting fieldwork in the MoWA in 2007.

8. Personal communication, June 16, 2007.

9. Personal communication with Afghan sociologist Nasrine Gross, May 16, 2007.

10. Personal communication with Masooda Jalal, former minister of women's affairs, November 2007.

11. "*Culture* and systems of governance (including the formal, traditional, and customary systems) have severely curtailed the human rights and livelihood options open to rural Afghan women and girls" (USAID 2004, 45); "priorities and interests must be reconciled with a view to ensuring that the *culture of impunity* is tackled" (ICG 2008,

ii); "this *culture of impunity* has to stop" (DiManno 2008, quoting President Hamid Karzai; emphasis added).

12. The Afghan Compact and the Afghan National Development Strategy, presented during the London conference held in January 2006, both contain provisions supporting the integration of the Afghan economy into the global free market economy. For more details, see http://www.ands.gov.af/.

13. Cullather demonstrates how a development project in the Helmand Valley, which started in the 1950s under Zahir Shah thanks to U.S. funding, mobilized collective imaginaries of progress based on Western experiences of development. "Exporting an American model of progress required continual redefinition of the sources of American greatness and renewed efforts to plant its unique characteristics in foreign landscapes. . . . The Helmand project symbolized the transformation of the nation, representing the legitimacy of the monarchy, the expansion of state power, and the fulfillment of the Pashtun destiny" (2002b, 5–6).

Chapter 3. Public and Private Faces of Gender (In)Justice

Note to epigraph: From *Poetry of the Taliban*, poems compiled from the Taliban website and elsewhere, by Alex Strick van Linschoten and Felix Kuehn (London: Hurst, 2012).

1. In an interview with a *New York Times* reporter, Interior Minister Ahmed Ali Jalali commented, "The spirit of this constitution will provide an opportunity for the country *to move on the path of democracy*" (Carlotta Gall, "New Afghan Constitution Juggles Koran and Democracy," *New York Times*, October 19, 2003; emphasis added).

2. Personal communication, February 4, 2007.

3. Shuras are councils of elders responsible for delivering justice and taking political decisions.

4. Personal communication with Mustafa Kazemi, October 25, 2007.

5. Cornelia Schneider mentions that the consensus over a strong presidential system was reached "because of the efforts of the UN's special envoy and the U.S. ambassador to Afghanistan who held closed-door negotiations with rival delegates on January 3, 2004" (2005, 199).

6. According to CorpWatch, DynCorp is "the world's premier rent-a-cop business." DynCorp "runs the security show in Afghanistan, Iraq, and the U.S.-Mexico border. They also run the coca crop-dusting business in Colombia." See http://www.corpwatch .org/article.php?list=type&type=18.

DynCorp mercenaries have been accused of various human rights abuses in their different countries of operation, notably in Bosnia, where DynCorp police trainers would have been involved in scandals related to trafficking of women, weapons, and passports. In Afghanistan, DynCorp is the principal contractor in charge of the police training program.

7. Personal communication, September 6, 2007.

8. These data were collected on August 1, 2007, during my visits with the JSSP women's rights adviser (here called Brenda to preserve anonymity) to the Family Response Units located in Kabul. All the details were recorded in my field diary.

9. She is interviewed in the BBC documentary *Beneath the Veil* by journalist Saira Shah, Channel 4, June 2001 (Shah 2001).

10. Personal communication, September 23, 2007.

11. Personal communication, September 19, 2007.

12. Personal communication, August 18, 2007.

Chapter 4. Moral Panics, Indian Soaps, and Cosmetics

1. Among private publications in Afghanistan, *Arman-e-Milli* is one of the most popular with a circulation of 4,200. Launched just after the fall of the Taliban, *Arman-e-Milli* is widely seen as the mouthpiece of Jamiat-e Islami, the political party associated with the Northern Alliance (Commandant Masood's party). The articles quoted in this chapter were translated in English with the help of my friend Lutfia Atay.

2. In 2009, two years after the end of my fieldwork, the Men's National Dormitory was finally renovated with USAID's financial support.

3. I use the word "abject" to follow discussions initiated by Yael Navaro-Yashin (2003; 2009), Jonathan Friedman (2003), and Julia Kristeva (1982).

4. The creation of women's dormitories on university campuses in Afghanistan has been one of the most visible measures undertaken by the international community to promote women's access to higher education after the fall of the Taliban regime. Altogether, four women's dormitories have been built in regional universities. At the time of my fieldwork, the girls' dormitory in Kabul was half empty and I received reports that the ones built in Jalalabad and Kandahar were used by male students since no female students had turned up. It is interesting to note that the creation of "boarding schools" inspired by the British educational model was also central to modernization efforts in rural Iran in the late 1930s. Zohreh Sullivan provides a powerful account of how girls living in these institutions were bound to their bunk beds with their chador to prevent them from falling down at night (1998, 224).

5. Personal communication with the director of the National Women's Dormitory, February 17, 2007.

6. *Cheragh* is a non-English daily newspaper whose stance is generally critical of the government. *Cheragh* used to be financed by Burhanuddin Rabbani, the president of Afghanistan before Karzai and head of Jamiat-i Islami-ye Afghanistan. The articles extracted from this publication were translated with the support of my friend Lutfia Atay,

7. Personal communciation with Ramzia, student boarding at the National Women's Dormitory, February 13, 2007.

8. Personal communication, May 21, 2007.

9. The Hazaras speak Farsi and are mostly Shiite Muslims (primarily Twelver Shiites, some Ismaili Shiites), yet there are also some Sunni Muslim Hazaras. They settled in Afghanistan at least as far back as the thirteenth century. Hazaras have always lived on the edge of economic survival. As a result of Pashtun expansionism in the late eighteenth and early nineteenth centuries, which was fueled by Sunni prejudices against the Shiites (thus attracting the help of the mostly Sunni Tajiks and Uzbeks), the Hazaras were driven to the barren dry mountains of central Afghanistan (the Hazarajat), where they live today separated into nine regionally distinct enclaves. Suffering from continuous racism and discrimination, Hazaras usually represent the lowest and poorest segments of Afghan society (Bacon 1951).

10. Personal communication with a civil servant at the Ministry of Women's Affairs, February 9, 2007.

11. Personal communication, October 4, 2007.

12. During our conversation, Habiba and Farida showed me some pictures of their lives in Tehran. They recounted with great nostalgia the picnics they had in Tehran's parks with their family and friends on Fridays, the comfort of the apartment they shared with relatives, and the friendships they developed with Iranians. They remembered Iran as a place where they could mix more easily with boys and girls alike, even though they had to beware of the moral police. Their descriptions of Tehran youth echoed those of Kaveh Basmenji in his book *Tehran Blues: How Iranian Youth Rebelled Against Iran's Founding Fathers* (2005).

Chapter 5. Strategic Decoration

1. Repression by the Taliban of the Hazara ethnic group, which is predominantly Muslim, was particularly severe. Although the conflict between the Hazaras and the Taliban was political and military as well as religious and it is not possible to state with certainty that the Taliban engaged in its campaign against the Shia solely because of their religious beliefs, the religious affiliation of the Hazaras apparently was a significant factor leading to their repression. The Taliban have been accused of committing mass killings of the Hazaras, particularly in the north. It has been claimed that the Taliban massacred thousands of civilians and prisoners during and after the capture of Mazar-i-Sharif in August 1998; this massacre reportedly was aimed at ethnic Hazaras. In September 1998, approximately five hundred persons were killed as the Taliban gained control of the city of Bamiyan. The Hazaras regained control in April 1999 following prolonged guerrilla-style warfare; however, the Taliban recaptured Bamiyan in May 1999 and reportedly killed a number of Shia residents (Minority Rights Group International 2008).

2. This complementarity is not based on notions of gender equality, even though equity is the guiding value behind these arrangements. For further analysis of the sexual division of labor in Afghan rural communities, see Lindisfarne-Tapper 1991, 100–131.

3. Because sexual violence is a crime that diminishes the honor of a woman and her family, victims have often been reluctant to report it to the authorities. However, in recent years some reports have underlined a behavioral shift with families (probably encouraged by the media and human rights organizations) beginning to go public and threatening to commit mass suicide if the perpetrators were not brought to justice (IRIN-News 2008; Nagpal 2009; Muahid 2008).

4. Personal communication, October 3, 2007. To preserve her anonymity, the name of this MP and her province of origin have been changed.

5. Personal communication, May 25, 2007.

6. See Christina Lamb's *Sewing Circles of Herat: A Personal Voyage Through Afghanistan* (2002).

7. Poem translated by David Tayari, http://www.thehypertexts.com/, accessed in January 2009. Note from the translator: "light blue" means "great hopes" in Persian.

8. The National Assembly consists of two houses: the lower house, Wolesi Jirga (House of the People), and the upper house, Meshrano Jirga (House of the Elders). The Wolesi Jirga is mainly composed of Pashtuns (118 seats), Tajiks/Aimaqs (53 seats), Hazaras/Shias (41 seats), and Uzbeks (20 seats). For further details on the ethnic and political composition of the Afghan parliament, see Wilder 2005.

9. *Chapan* is a long coat worn over clothes, typically during the cold winter months. Usually worn by men, these coats are adorned with intricate threading and come in a variety of colors and patterns.

10. Personal communication, October 3, 2007.

11. Personal communication, April 6, 2007.

12. The lower house of parliament, the Wolesi Jirga, approved the bill after President Hamid Karzai revised an initial bill that had been approved by both chambers of parliament, giving amnesty to all Afghans involved in war crimes during the last three decades of fighting.

13. Some women's rights activists also disagreed with Joya's insistence on secularism as a means to enhance women's rights. They perceived her approach as disconnected with the political reality and political sensitivities of the country. In their view, gender equality was embedded in Islam. Joya's desire to disconnect politics from religion was, in their opinion, a dangerous path to advance the cause of women.

14. Personal communication with MP from northern Afghanistan, June 30, 2007.

15. Personal communication, August 29, 2007.

16. Ibid.

17. Personal communication with Mahbouba Seraj, women's rights activist, October 7, 2007.

18. Personal communication with Masooda Babak, MP from Kabul, September 16, 2007.

19. Personal communication with the former minister of women's affairs Masooda Jalal, November 22, 2007.

20. Personal communication with Mahbouba Seraj, September 28, 2007.

21. Observations conducted during International Women's Day, March 8, 2007.

22. Personal communication with General Khotul Mohammadzai, April 8, 2007.

Chapter 6. Poetic Jihad

1. The Assamayi Mountain is located south of Kabul. In 1991, a part of the mountain cracked.

2. In Persian mythology, Singue Sabour is a magic stone to which one can confide one's sorrows. Like a sponge, the stone absorbs words and secrets until it cracks. After the explosion of the stone, the one who has confided to the stone is forever relieved from his or her sadness. This poem written by Rushani uses a similar metaphor.

3. This poem was translated into English by Sharif Fayez, the first appointed minister of higher education after the fall of the Taliban. He holds an M.A. in English literature from the University of Northern Colorado and a Ph.D. in American literature and Oriental studies from the University of Arizona. Fayez taught English literature at the University of Kabul in the 1970s and at the University of Mashad in Iran during the Soviet occupation. He is the founder of the American University of Afghanistan. http://www.ariaye.com/english/poem2.html.

4. Personal communication, September 26, 2007.

5. A *landay* is a brief piece of oral poetry consisting of two verse lines of nine and thirteen syllables respectively. Majrouh, who collected and edited the *landays*, was assassinated while in exile in Pakistan in 1988. *Songs of War and Love* (2003) is the English translation, originally called *Suicide and Song* in Pashto. The volume was also translated into French (1988).

6. The story of Majnun Layla is based on the real story of a young man called Qays ibn al-Mulawwah from the northern Arabian Peninsula in the Umayyad era during the seventh century. Upon seeing Layla, Qays fell passionately in love with her. He became mad when her father prevented him from marrying her. For that reason he came to be called Majnun Layla, which means "Driven mad by Layla" (Shafaq 1952).

7. During the five years of the Taliban rule in Herat city, poets and writers organized a fierce resistance—not with weapons, but with books and poetry. A network of clandestine literary circles, officially called "sewing circles" to avoid attracting the authorities' attention, flourished all throughout the city (Lamb 2002). There, young women, faces and bodies hidden by their Taliban-enforced uniform of sky-blue *chadari* and flat shoes, would come several times a week to read and comment on "illicit" literature. In their handbags, concealed under scissors, cottons, sequins, and pieces of fabric, were notebooks and pens. On the program were classic Persian writers and poets as well as foreign authors such as Dostoyevsky, Brecht, and Shakespeare. Their teachers would also encourage them to develop their own literary

creativity by initiating them into writing poetry, right under the nose of the religious police.

8. *Sadaf* is a Dari-language women's magazine. This article was translated with the help of my friend Lutfia Atay.

9. From Nadia Aujuman's *Ghazal* (a form of lyric poem) "Soundless Cries" translated by Abdul S. Shayek, http://www.persianmirror.com/community/writers/MSN/2006/AfghanPoets.cfm.

10. The mourners occupy these three functions in death rituals among Inner Mani people.

BIBLIOGRAPHY

Abu-Lughod, Lila. 1986. *Veiled Sentiments: Honor and Poetry in a Bedouin Society.* Berkeley: University of California Press.

———, ed. 1998. *Remaking Women: Feminism and Modernity in the Middle East.* Princeton, N.J.: Princeton University Press.

———. 2002. "Do Muslim Women Really Need Saving? Anthropological Reflections on Cultural Relativism and Its Others." *American Anthropologist* 104 (3): 783–90.

AdvocacyNet. 2007. "Afghan Women Demand a Halt to Intimidation and Murder." News bulletin, June 22. http://news.gather.com/viewArticle.action?articleId= 281474977040181.

Afghan Ministry of Justice. 2005. *Justice for All: A Comprehensive Needs Analysis for Justice in Afghanistan.* Kabul: Islamic Republic of Afghanistan, Ministry of Justice.

Ahmed, Faiz. 2007. "Afghanistan's Reconstruction, Five Years Later: Narratives of Progress, Marginalized Realities, and the Politics of Law in a Transitional Islamic Republic." *Gonzaga Journal of International Law* 10 (3): 269–314. http://www.gonzagajil.org.

Ahmed, Leila. 1992. *Women and Gender in Islam.* New Haven, Conn.: Yale University Press.

Ahmed-Ghosh, Huma. 2003a. "A History of Women in Afghanistan: Lessons Learnt for the Future; or, Yesterdays and Tomorrow: Women in Afghanistan." *Journal of International Women's Studies* 4 (3): 1–14.

———. 2003b. "Writing the Nation on the Beauty Queen's Body: Implications for a 'Hindu' Nation." *Meridians* 4 (1): 205–27.

Anderson, Jon. 1982. "Social Structure and the Veil: Comportment and the Composition of Interaction in Afghanistan." *Anthropos* 77 (4): 397–420.

An-Na'im, Abdullahi Ahmed, ed. 1995. *Human Rights in Cross-Cultural Perspectives: A Quest for Consensus.* Philadelphia: University of Pennsylvania Press.

Ansari, Tamin. 2001. "Leaping to Conclusions." *Salon,* December 17. http://www.salon.com/2001/12/17/role_of_women/.

Appadurai, Arjun. 1996. *Modernity at Large: Cultural Dimensions of Globalization.* Minneapolis: University of Minnesota Press.

———. 2004. "The Capacity to Aspire: Culture and Terms of Recognition." In *Culture and Public Action*, ed. Vijayendra Rao and Michael Walton, 59–84. Stanford, Calif.: Stanford University Press.

Apthorpe, Raymond. 2012. "Effective Aid: The Poetics of Some Aid Workers' Angles on How Humanitairan Aid 'Works.'" *Third World Quarterly* 33 (8): 1545–59.

Aretxaga, Begona. 1997. *Shattering Silence: Women, Nationalism, and Political Subjectivity in Northern Ireland*. Princeton, N.J.: Princeton University Press.

———. 2003. "Maddening States." *Annual Review of Anthropology* 32 (January 1): 393–410.

Arman-e-Milli. 2007. "Zanan az democracy soy istefada mikunand" ("Women Misuse Democracy"). May 3.

Asad, Talal. 1991. "Afterword: From the History of Colonial Anthropology to the Anthropology of Western Hegemony." In *Colonial Situations: Essays on the Contextualization of Ethnographic Knowledge*, ed. George Stocking Jr., 314–24. Madison: University of Wisconsin Press.

Azarbaijani-Moghaddam, Sippi. 2006. *Women's Groups in Afghan Civil Society: Women and Men Working Towards Equitable Participation in Civil Society Organizations*. Kabul: Counterpart International.

———. 2009. "The Arrested Development of Afghan Women." In *The Future of Afghanistan*, ed. J. Alexander Thier, 63–72. Washington, D.C.: U.S. Institute of Peace.

Bacon, Elizabeth E. 1951. "The Inquiry into the History of the Hazara Mongols of Afghanistan." *Southwestern Journal of Anthropology* 7 (3): 230–47.

Bakhtin, Mikhail. 1984a. *Problems of Dostoevsky's Poetics*. Ed. and trans. Caryl Emerson. Minneapolis: University of Minnesota Press.

———. 1984b. *Rabelais and His World*. Trans. Hélène Iswolsky. Bloomington: University of Indiana Press.

Balogun, Oluwakemi M. 2012. "Cultural and Cosmopolitan Idealized Femininity and Embodied Nationalism in Nigerian Beauty Pageants." *Gender & Society* 26 (3): 357–81. doi:10.1177/0891243212438958.

Barfield, Thomas. 2008. "Culture and Custom in Nation-Building: Law in Afghanistan." *Maine Law Review* 60 (2): 347–73.

———. 2010. *Afghanistan: A Cultural and Political History*. Princeton, N.J.: Princeton University Press.

Barker, Kim. 2008. "Afghanistan Seeks to Clean up Soaps on TV." *Chicago Tribune*, May 21.

Barker, Michael J. 2008. "Democracy or Polyarchy? U.S.-Funded Media Developments in Afghanistan and Iraq Post 9/11." *Media, Culture & Society* 30 (1): 109–30.

Barry, Michael. 2002. *Le royaume de l'insolence: L'Afghanistan, 1504–2001*. Paris: Flammarion.

Baryalai, Makhmud, Abdullo Spantghar, and Vladimir Grib, eds. 1984. *Afghanistan: The Revolution Continues*. Moscow: Planeta.

Basmenji, Kaveh. 2005. *Tehran Blues: How Iranian Youth Rebelled Against Iran's Founding Fathers.* London: Saqi.

Bauman, Richard. 1984. *Verbal Art as Performance.* Prospect Heights, Ill.: Waveland Press.

———. 2004. *A World of Others' Words: Cross-Cultural Perspectives on Intertextuality.* Malden, Mass.: Blackwell.

Benjamin, Walter. 1986. "Critique of Violence." In Reflections: Essays, Aphorisms, Autobiographical Writings, trans. Edmund Jephcott, ed. Peter Demetz, 277–300. New York: Schocken Books.

———. 1969. "Theses on the Philosophy of History." In *Illuminations,* ed. Hannah Arendt. New York: Schocken, 1969.

BBC News. 2006. "Afghans Get a Taste of the Catwalk." BBC News, July 9.

———. 2008. "Afghan Women Stage Rare Protest." BBC News, January 30.

Bhabha, Homi K. 1994. *The Location of Culture.* London: Routledge.

Boltanski, Luc. 2008. "Institutions et critique sociale: Une approche pragmatique de la domination." *Tracés,* hors série 8, "Présent et futurs de la critique," 17–43.

Bourdieu, Pierre. 1984. *Distinction: A Social Critique of the Judgment of Taste.* Cambridge, Mass.: Harvard University Press.

Bush, Laura. 2001. "Laura Bush Delivers Radio Address." *CNN/Transcripts,* November 17. http://transcripts.cnn.com/TRANSCRIPTS/0111/17/smn.23.html.

Butler, Judith. 1990. *Gender Trouble.* New York: Routledge.

———. 1997a. *Excitable Speech: A Politics of the Performative.* London: Routledge.

———. 1997b. *The Psychic Life of Power: Theories in Subjection.* Stanford, Calif.: Stanford University Press.

Calhoun, Lindsay R. 2004. "Islamic Martyrdom in the Postcolonial Condition." *Text and Performance Quarterly* 24 (3–4): 327–47. doi:10.1080/1046293042000312797.

Castillejo-Cuéllar, Alejandro. 2005. "Unraveling Silence: Violence, Memory and the Limits of Anthropology's Craft." *Dialectical Anthropology* 29 (2): 159–80. doi:10.2307/29790734.

Centlivres, Pierre, and Micheline Centlivres-Demont. 2007. *Revoir Kaboul: Chemins d'été, chemins d'hiver entre l'Oxus et l'Indus.* Carouge-Geneva: Zoé.

Centlivres-Demont, Micheline. 1994. "Afghan Women in Peace, War, and Exile." In *The Politics of Social Transformation in Afghanistan, Iran, and Pakistan,* ed. Myron Weiner and Ali Banuazizi, 333–65. Syracuse, N.Y.: Syracuse University Press.

Certeau, Michel de. 1984. *The Practice of Everyday Life.* Trans. Steven Rendall. Berkeley: University of California Press.

Chakrabarty, Dipesh. 1992. "Postcoloniality and the Artifice of History: Who Speaks for 'Indian' Pasts?" *Representations* 37 (Winter): 1–26.

Chatterjee, Partha. 1993. *The Nation and Its Fragments: Colonial and Postcolonial Histories.* Princeton, N.J.: Princeton University Press.

Cheragh. 2007a. "Being Unveiled Is Not the Meaning of Democracy." September 4.

———. 2007b. "Dokhtar-e Afghan Film Is the Lowest Example of Western Debauchery." September 23.

———. 2007c. "Strange Cultural Invasion with Officials as Watchers." July 30.

Chinkin, Christine. 2003. *Peace Agreements as a Means for Promoting Gender Equality and Ensuring Participation of Women*. United Nations Division for the Advancement of Women. http://www.un.org/womenwatch/daw/egm/peace2003/reports /BPChinkin.PDF

CIA. 2008. "The 2008 World Factbook." https://www.cia.gov/library/publications/the -world-factbook/geos/af.html.

Clarke, Kamari Maxine, and Mark Goodale, eds. 2010. *Mirrors of Justice: Law and Power in the Post–Cold War Era*. Cambridge: Cambridge University Press.

Coburn, Noah, and John Dempsey. 2010. *Informal Dispute Resolution in Afghanistan*. USIP (U.S. Institute of Peace) Special Report. Washington, D.C.: United States Institute of Peace.

Coghlan, Tom. 2006. "Afghan MP Says She Will Not Be Silenced." BBC News, January 27.

Cohen, Stanley. 2002. *Folk Devils and Moral Panics: The Creation of the Mods and Rockers*. 3rd ed. London: Routledge.

Comaroff, Jean. 1985. *Body of Power, Spirit of Resistance: The Culture and History of a South African People*. Chicago: University of Chicago Press.

Comaroff, Jean, and John L. Comaroff, eds. 2006. *Law and Disorder in the Postcolony*. Chicago: University of Chicago Press.

Comaroff, John L. 2001. "Colonialism, Culture, and the Law: A Foreword." *Law & Social Inquiry* 26 (2): 305–14. doi:10.1111/j.1747-4469.2001.tb00180.x.

Comaroff, Joshua. 2007. "Terror and Territory: Guantanamo and the Space of Contradiction." *Public Culture* 19 (2): 381–404.

Cooley, Alexander, and James Ron. 2002. "The NGO Scramble: Organizational Insecurity and the Political Economy of Transnational Action." *International Security* 27 (1): 5–39.

Cowan, Jane K. 1990. *Dance and the Body Politic in Northern Greece*. Princeton, N.J.: Princeton University Press.

———. 2007. "The Supervised State." *Identities: Global Studies in Culture and Power* 14 (5): 545–78.

Cowan, Jane K., Marie-Bénédicte Dembour, and Richard Wilson, eds. 2001. *Culture and Rights: Anthropological Perspectives*. Cambridge: Cambridge University Press.

Crewe, Emma, and Elizabeth Harrison. 1998. *Whose Development? An Ethnography of Aid*. London: Zed Books.

Cullather, Nick. 2002a. "Damming Afghanistan: Modernization in a Buffer State." *Journal of American History* 89 (2): 512–37.

———. 2002b. "From New Deal to New Frontier in Afghanistan: Modernization in a Buffer State." Working Paper no. 6, Project on the Cold War as Global Conflict, International Center for Advanced Studies, New York University, New York.

————. 2010. *The Hungry World: America's Cold War Battle Against Poverty in Asia.* Cambridge, Mass.: Harvard University Press.

Das, Veena. 1988. "Femininity and the Orientation to the Body." In *Socialisation, Education and Women: Explorations in Gender Identity,* ed. K. Chanana, 193–207. New Delhi: Orient Longman.

————. 1996. *Critical Events: An Anthropological Perspective on Contemporary India.* Oxford: Oxford University Press.

————. 1998. "Wittgenstein and Anthropology." *Annual Review of Anthropology* 27: 171–95.

————. 2000. "The Act of Witnessing: Violence, Poisonous Knowledge, and Subjectivity." In *Violence and Subjectivity,* ed. Veena Das, Arthur Kleinman, Mamphela Ramphele, and Pamela Reynolds, 205–25. Berkeley: University of California Press.

————. 2007. *Life and Words: Violence and the Descent into the Ordinary.* Berkeley: University of California Press.

————. 2010. "Engaging the Life of the Other: Love and Everyday Life." In *Ordinary Ethics: Anthropology, Language, and Action,* ed. Michael Lambeck, 376–99. New York: Fordham University Press.

Das, Veena, and Deborah Poole. 2004. *Anthropology in the Margins of the State.* Santa Fe, N. Mex.: School of American Research Press.

Daulatzai, Anila. 2006. "Acknowledging Afghanistan: Notes and Queries on an Occupation." *Cultural Dynamics* 18 (3): 293–311.

————. 2008. "The Discursive Occupation of Afghanistan." *British Journal of Middle Eastern Studies* 35 (3): 419–35. doi:10.1080/13530190802532953.

De Lauri, Antonio. 2010. "Legal Reconstruction in Afghanistan: Rule of Law, Injustice, and Judicial Mediation." *Jura Gentium* 7 (1): 7–32. http://www.juragentium .org/topics/wlgo/en/delauri.htm.

————. 2012a. *Afghanistan: Ricostruzione, ingiustizia, diritti umani.* Milan: Mondadori Università.

————. 2012b. "Inaccessible Normative Pluralism and Human Rights in Afghanistan." FMSH Working Paper no. 21. Fondation Maison des sciences de l'homme, Paris. http://halshs.archives-ouvertes.fr/docs/00/73/40/35/PDF/FMSH-WP-2012_DeLauri .pdf.

————. 2013. "Entre loi et coutumes: L'interconnexion normative dans les cours de justice de Kaboul." *Diogène* nos. 239–40 (July–October 2012): 66–85

DiManno, Rosie. 2008. "Kabul's Big, Bad Warlord." *Toronto Star,* May 13.

Dorronsoro, Gilles. 2005. *Revolution Unending: Afghanistan, 1979 to the Present.* New York: Columbia University Press.

Doubleday, Veronica. 2006. *Three Women of Herat: A Memoir of Life, Love and Friendship in Afghanistan.* London: Tauris Parke.

Dupree, Louis. 1973. *Afghanistan.* Princeton, N.J.: Princeton University Press.

Dupree, Nancy Hatch. 1984. "Revolutionary Rhetoric and Afghan Women." In *Revolutions and Rebellions in Afghanistan: Anthropological Perspectives,* ed. M. Nazif

Shahrani and R. L. Canfield, 306–40. Berkeley, Calif.: Institute of International Studies, University of California.

———. 1986. *The Women of Afghanistan*. Stockholm: Swedish Committee for Afghanistan.

———. 2001. "Afghan Women Under the Taliban." In *Fundamentalism Reborn? Afghanistan and the Taliban*, ed. William Maley, 145–66. London: Hurst.

Edwards, David. 1994. "Afghanistan, Ethnography, and the New World Order." *Cultural Anthropology* 9 (3): 345–60.

———. 1996. *Heroes of the Age: Moral Fault Lines on the Afghan Frontier*. Berkeley: University of California Press.

Emadi, Hafizullah. 2002. *Repression, Resistance, and Women in Afghanistan*. London: Praeger.

———. 1991. "State, Modernization and the Women's Movement in Afghanistan". *Review of Radical Political Economics* 23 (3–4): 224–43.

Englund, Harri. 2006. *Prisoners of Freedom: Human Rights and the African Poor*. Berkeley: University of California Press.

Ewing, Garen. 2005. "Malalai: Afghan Heroine of Maiwand." http://www.garenewing .co.uk/angloafghanwar/biography/malalai.php.

Fanon, Frantz. 1967. *A Dying Colonialism*. New York: Grove Press.

Fantasia, Rick, and Eric L. Hirsch. 1995. "Culture in Rebellion: The Appropriation and Transformation of the Veil in the Algerian Revolution." In *Social Movements and Culture*, ed. Hank Johnston and Bert Klandermans, 144–59. Minneapolis: University of Minnesota Press.

Farmer, Ben. 2011. "Afghanistan's Women Languishing in Prisons 10 Years After Fall of Taliban." *Telegraph.co.uk*, December 4.

Ferguson, James, and Akhil Gupta. 2002. "Spatializing States: Toward an Ethnography of Neoliberal Governmentality." *American Ethnologist* 29 (4): 981–1002. doi:10.1525/ae.2002.29.4.981.

Fernandez, James W., and Mary Taylor Huber. 2001. "Introduction: The Anthropology of Irony." In *Irony in Action: Anthropology, Practice, and the Moral Imagination*, ed. James W. Fernandez and Mary Taylor Huber, 1–37. Chicago: University of Chicago Press.

Filmer, Paul. 2003. "Structures of Feeling and Socio-Cultural Formations: The Significance of Literature and Experience to Raymond Williams's Sociology of Culture." *British Journal of Sociology* 54 (2): 199–219. doi:10.1080/0007131032000080203.

Foucault, Michel. 1977. *Discipline and Punish: The Birth of the Prison*. New York: Pantheon Books.

Friedman, Jonathan, ed. 2003. *Globalization, the State, and Violence*. Boston: AltaMira Press.

Gardner, Katy, and David Lewis. 1996. *Anthropology, Development and the Post Modern Challenge*. London: Pluto Press.

Gluckman, Max. 1963. *Order and Rebellion in Tribal Africa: Collected Essays with an Autobiographical Introduction.* London: Routledge.

Goffman, Erving. 1956. "The Nature of Deference and Demeanor." *American Anthropologist* 58 (3): 473–502.

———. 1967. *Interaction Ritual: Essays in Face-to-Face Behavior.* Garden City, N.Y.: Doubleday.

———. 1968. *Asylums: Essays on the Social Situation of Mental Patients and Other Inmates.* Harmondsworth: Penguin.

———. 1969. *The Presentation of Self in Everyday Life.* London: Allen Lane.

Göle, Nilüfer. 1996. *The Forbidden Modern: Civilization and Veiling.* Ann Arbor: University of Michigan Press.

———. 2002. "Islam in Public: New Visibilities and New Imaginaries." *Public Culture* 14 (1): 173–93.

Green, Linda. 1994. "Fear as a Way of Life." *Cultural Anthropology* 9 (2): 227–56.

Gregorian, Vartan. 1967. "Mahmud Tarzi and Saraj-ol-Akhbar: Ideology of Nationalism and 'Modernization' in Afghanistan." *Middle East Journal* 21 (3): 345–68.

Grima, Benedicte. 1992. *The Performance of Emotion Among Paxtun Women: "The Misfortunes Which Have Befallen Me."* Oxford: Oxford University Press.

Gross, Nasrine Abou-Bakre. 1998. *Qassarikh-e Malalay: Khaterat-e Leessa-ye Dokhtoran-e Afghanistan; (In Dari, Memories of the First Girls' High School in Afghanistan.* Falls Church, Va.: Kabultec.

Habermas, Jurgen. 1989. *The Structural Transformation of the Public Sphere.* Cambridge, Mass.: MIT Press.

Hansen, Karen Tranberg. 2004. "The World in Dress: Anthropological Perspectives on Clothing, Fashion, and Culture." *Annual Review of Anthropology* 33 (1): 369–92. doi:10.2307/25064858.

Hart, Vivien, and Helen Irving. 2005. "Gender Equity in Constitution-Making." Sussex Research Online oai:sro.sussex.ac.uk:21778.

Hasrat-Nazimi, Waslat. 2011. "'King of the Women'—An Unlikely Afghan." Deutsche Welle, October 13. http://www.dw.de/king-of-the-women-an-unlikely-afghan/a-15457529

Heath, Jennifer, and Ashraf Zahedi. 2011. *Land of the Unconquerable: The Lives of Contemporary Afghan Women.* Berkeley: University of California Press.

Herman, Ken. 2005. "Laura Bush Praises Progress Made by Afghan Women." Cox News Service, May 30.

Herzfeld, Michael. 2005. *Cultural Intimacy: Social Poetics in the Nation-State.* 2nd ed. New York: Routledge.

Hirschkind, Charles, and Saba Mahmood. 2002. "Feminism, the Taliban, and Politics of Counter-Insurgency." *Anthropological Quarterly* 75 (2): 339–54.

Hoffman, D. 2003. "Frontline Anthropology: Research in a Time of War." *Anthropology Today* 19 (3): 9–12.ICG (International Crisis Group). 2008. *Afghanistan: The*

Need for International Resolve. Brussels: International Crisis Group. http://www
.crisisgroup.org/home/index.cfm?id=5285.

IRIN-News. 2008. "Sharp Rise in Reported Cases of Violence Against Women." http://
www.irinnews.org/Report.aspx?ReportId=77156.

Isby, David. 2011. *Afghanistan: Graveyard of Empires*. New York: Pegasus Books.

Islah-e Milli. 2007. "Why Did Shakila Hashemi Apologise?" March 3. http://www.af
ghanwire.com/article.php?id=4454.

Kafka, Ben. 2012. *The Demon of Writing: Powers and Failures of Paperwork*. New York:
Zone Books.

Kakar, Palwasha. 2003. "Tribal Law of Pashtumwali and Women's Legislative Authority." Afghan Legal History Project, Harvard Law School. http://www.law.harvard
.edu/programs/ilsp/research/alhp.php.

Kandiyoti, Deniz, ed.. 1991. *Women, Islam and the State*. Basingstoke: Macmillan.

———. 2005. *The Politics of Gender and Reconstruction in Afghanistan (Occasional Paper 4)*. Kabul: United Nations Research Institute for Social Development.

Kapur, Ratna. 2004. *Erotic Justice: Law and the New Politics of Postcolonialism*. London: Routledge.

Keller, Mary. 2005. *The Hammer and the Flute: Women, Power, and Spirit Possession*.
Baltimore: Johns Hopkins University Press.

Kennedy, David. 2004. *The Dark Side of Virtues: Reassessing International Humanitarianism*. Princeton, N.J.: Princeton University Press.

Khodr, Zeina. 2008. "Afghanistan Debates Indian Soap Operas." *Al Jazeera English*.
http://uk.youtube.com/watch?v=FBcXLYZKInA.

Killid. 2007. "Media Is Development: Afghanistan Media and Civil Society Forum."
In *Media Is Development*. Kabul Intercontinental Hotel. http://ipsnews.net/afghan
istan/MedaiReport.PDF. Accessed XX

Kristeva, Julia. 1982. *Powers of Horror: An Essay on Abjection*. New York: Columbia
University Press.

Lamb, Christina. 2002. *The Sewing Circles of Herat: A Personal Voyage Through Afghanistan*. New York: HarperCollins.

Lefebvre, Henri. 2004. *Rhythmanalysis: Space, Time and Everyday Life*. Trans. Stuart
Elden and Gerald Moore. London: Continuum.

Lewis, David, and David Mosse. 2006. *Development Brokers and Translators: The Ethnography of Aid and Agencies*. Bloomfield, Conn.: Kumarian Press.

Lindisfarne-Tapper, Nancy. 1991. *Bartered Brides: Politics, Gender and Marriage in an
Afghan Tribal Society*. Cambridge: Cambridge University Press.

Mackenzie, Richard. 2001. "The United States and the Taliban." In *Fundamentalism
Reborn? Afghanistan and the Taliban*, ed. William Maley, 90–103. London: Hurst.

Mahmood, Saba. 2001. "Feminist Theory, Embodiment, and the Docile Agent: Some
Reflections on the Egyptian Islamic Revival." *Cultural Anthropology* 16 (2): 202–36.

———. 2005. *Politics of Piety: The Islamic Revival and the Feminist Subject*. Princeton,
N.J.: Princeton University Press.

Majrooh, Parvin Ali. 1989. "Afghan Women Between Marxism and Islamic Fundamentalism." *Central Asian Survey* 8 (3): 87–98.

Majrouh, Sayd Bahodine. 2003. *Songs of Love and War: Afghan Women's Poetry.* New York: Other Press.

Makhlouf, C. 1979. *Changing Veils: Women and "Modernization" in North Yemen.* London: Croom Helm.

Mankekar, Purnima. 1998. "Entangled Spaces of Modernity: The Viewing Family, the Consuming Nation and Television in India." *Visual Anthropology* 14 (2): 32–45.

Mann, Carol. 2006. "Les shahidé du monde traditionnel: Le suicide des jeunes filles afghanes." *Recueil Alexandries,* Collections Esquisses, February. http://www.reseau
-terra.eu/article439.html.

———. 2010. *Femmes afghanes en guerre.* Paris: Éditions du Croquant.

Marcus, George. 1995. "Ethnography in/of the World System: The Emergence of Multi-Sited Ethnography." *Annual Review of Anthropology* 24:95–117.

———. 2001. "The Predicament of Irony and the Paranoid Style in Fin-de-Siècle Rationality." In *Irony in Action: Anthropology, Practice, and the Moral Imagination,* ed. James W. Fernandez and Mary Taylor Huber, 209–23. Chicago: University of Chicago Press.

Marsden, Magnus. 2005. *Living Islam: Muslim Religious Experience in Pakistan's North-West Frontier.* Cambridge: Cambridge University Press.

Mattei, Ugo, and Laura Nader. 2008. *Plunder: When the Rule of Law Is Illegal.* Chichester: John Wiley & Sons.

Mayer, Tamar. 2000. "Gender Ironies of Nationalism: Setting the Stage." In *Gender Ironies of Nationalism: Sexing the Nation,* ed. Tamar Mayer, 1–24. London: Routledge.

McLarney, Ellen. 2009. "The Burqa in Vogue: Fashioning Afghanistan." *Journal of Middle East Women's Studies* 5 (1): 1–20.

Meneley, Anne. 2007. "Fashions and Fundamentalisms in Fin-de-Siècle Yemen: Chador Barbie and Islamic Socks." *Cultural Anthropology* 22 (2): 214–43.

Menon, Nivedita. 2004. *Recovering Subversion: Feminist Politics Beyond the Law.* Urbana: Permanent Black/University of Illinois Press.

Mernissi, Fatima. 1992. *The Veil and the Male Elite: A Feminist Interpretation of Women's Rights in Islam.* London: Perseus.

Merry, Sally Engle. 2005. *Human Rights and Gender Violence: Translating International Law into Local Justice.* Chicago: University of Chicago Press.

Minority Rights Group International. 2008. *World Directory of Minorities and Indigenous Peoples—Afghanistan: Hazaras.* http://www.refworld.org/docid/49749d693d.html.

Mitchell, Timothy. 1991. "The Limits of the State: Beyond Statist Approaches and Their Critics." *American Political Science Review* 85 (1): 77. doi: 10.2307/1962879.

Moghadam, Valentine. 1994. "Building Human Resources and Women's Capabilities in Afghanistan: A Retrospect and Prospects." *World Development* 22 (6): 859–76.

———. 2002. "Patriarchy, the Taleban, and the Politics of Public Space in Afghanistan." *Women's Studies International Forum* 25 (1): 19–31.

———. 2004. "A Tale of Two Countries: State, Society and Gender Politics in Iran and Afghanistan." *Muslim World* 94 (4): 449–68.

Monsutti, Alessandro. 2005. *War and Migration: Social Networks and Economic Strategies of the Hazaras of Afghanistan.* London: Routledge.

———. 2012. "Fuzzy Sovereignty: Rural Reconstruction in Afghanistan, Between Democracy Promotion and Power Games." *Comparative Studies in Society and History* 54 (3): 563–91. doi: 10.1017/S0010417512000230.

Moors, Annelies. 2003. "Islam and Fashion in the Streets of San'a." *Etnofoor* 16 (2): 41–56.

Morris, Rosalind C. 2006. "The Mute and the Unspeakable: Political Subjectivity, Violent Crime, and the 'Sexual Thing' in a South African Mining Community." In *Law and Disorder in the Postcolony*, ed. Jean Comaroff and John L. Comaroff, 57–101. Chicago: University of Chicago Press.

Mosse, David. 2004. "Is Good Policy Unimplementable? Reflections on the Ethnography of Aid Policy and Practice." *Development and Change* 35 (4): 639–71.

Motlagh, Jon. 2007. "Self-immolation Tragically Frequent Among Afghan Women." *World Politics Review*, June 22. http://www.worldpoliticsreview.com/article.aspx ?id=873.

Muahid, Ahmad Khalid. 2008. "UNFPA: About 25% Women in Afghanistan Face Sexual Violence," *RAWA News*, December 25. http://www.rawa.org/temp/runews/2008 /12/25/about-25-women-in-the-country-face-sexual-violence.html.

Mulvad, Eva. 2006 *Enemies of Happiness.* [*Vores lykkes fjender*]. Documentary, 59 min. Bastard Film (prod. co.), Copenhagen. Color, DVD, Farsi, Pasthu, Subtitled.

Nader, Laura. 2010. "The Words We Use: Justice, Human Rights, and the Sense of Injustice." In *Mirrors of Justice: Law and Power in the Post-Cold War Era*, ed. Kamari Maxine Clarke and Mark Goodale, 316–32. Cambridge: Cambridge University Press.

Nafisi, Azar. 2003. *Reading Lolita in Tehran: A Memoir in Books.* New York: Random House.

Nagpal, Neeraj. 2009. "More Young Girls Face Rape in Afghanistan." *Merinews.com*, October 3. http://www.merinews.com/catFull.jsp?articleID=15751686.

Najibullah, Farangis. 2008. "Afghanistan: Popular TV Channel Attacked as 'Immoral' and 'Un-islamic.'" *EurasiaNet.org*, January 4. http://www.eurasianet.org/depart ments/insight/articles/pp040108.shtml.

Najwa, Zuhra. 2006. "I Want to Become a Leader." *Sadaf*, January 8.

Navaro-Yashin, Yael. 2002. *Faces of the State: Secularism and Public Life in Turkey.* Princeton, N.J.: Princeton University Press.

———. 2003. "'Life Is Dead Here': Sensing the Political in 'No Man's Land.'" *Anthropological Theory* 3 (1): 107–25. doi: 10.1177/1463499603003001174.

———. 2009. "Affective Spaces, Melancholic Objects: Ruination and the Production of Anthropological Knowledge." *Journal of the Royal Anthropological Institute* 15 (1): 1–18.

Nordland, Rod. 2013. "Foreign Projects Give Afghans Fashion, Skate Park and Now 10,000 Balloons." *New York Times*, May 25.

Nordstrom, Carolyn. 2004. *Shadows of War: Violence, Power, and International Profiteering in the Twenty-First Century.* Berkeley: University of California Press.

Nordstrom, Carolyn, and Antonius C. G. Robben, eds. 1995. *Fieldwork Under Fire: Contemporary Studies of Violence and Survival.* Berkeley: University of California.

North, Andrew. 2004. "Herat in the Shadow of Khan." BBC News, September 16.

Olesen, Asta. 1996. *Islam and Politics in Afghanistan.* Surrey: Curzon Press.

Olivier de Sardan, Jean-Pierre. 2005. *Anthropology and Development: Understanding Contemporary Social Change.* London: Zed Books.

Ortner, Sherry B. 1996. "So, *Is* Female to Male as Nature Is to Culture?" In *Making Gender: The Politics and Erotics of Culture,* 173–80. Boston: Beacon Press.

Oza, Rupal. 2001. "Showcasing India: Gender, Geography, and Globalization." *Signs* 26 (4): 1067–95.

Papanek, Hanna. 1973. "Purdah: Separate Worlds and Symbolic Shelter." *Comparative Studies in History and Societies* 15 (3): 289–325.

Pejcinova, Ana. 2006. "Post-modernizing Afghanistan." *CEU Political Science Journal* 1 (5): 34–55.

Peterson, V. Spike. 1994. "Gendered Nationalism." *Peace Review: Special Issue on Nationalism and Ethnic Conflict* 6 (1): 77–84.

Pile, Steve, and Michael Keith, eds. 1997. *Geographies of Resistance.* London: Routledge.

Popenoe, R. 2004. *Feeding Desire: Fatness, Beauty and Sexuality Among a Saharan People.* London: Routledge.

Raheja, Gloria Goodwin, and Ann Grodzins Gold. 1994. *Listen to the Heron's Words: Reimagining Gender and Kinship in North India.* Berkeley: University of California Press.

Rashid, Ahmed. 1999. "The Taliban: Exporting Extremism." *Foreign Affairs* 78(6): 22–35.

———. 2002. *Taliban: Islam, Oil and the New Great Game in Central Asia.* London: I. B. Tauris.

Richmond, Oliver. 2006. "The Problem of Peace: Understanding the 'Liberal Peace.'" *Conflict, Security & Development* 6 (3): 291–314.

Rieker, Martina, and Kamran Asdar Ali, eds. 2008. *Gendering Urban Space in the Middle East, South Asia, and Africa.* New York: Palgrave Macmillan.

Riles, Annelise. 2004. *The Network Inside Out.* Ann Arbor: University of Michigan Press.

Rosaldo, Michelle Zimbalist, and Louise Lamphere, eds. 1974. *Women, Culture and Society.* Stanford, Calif.: Stanford University Press.

Rostami-Povey, Elaheh. 2007. *Afghan Women: Identity and Invasion.* London: Zed Books.

Roy, Olivier. 1985. *L'Afghanistan: Islam et modernité politique.* Paris: Seuil.

———. 1986. "Le double code afghan: Marxisme et tribalisme." *Revue française de science politique* 36 (6): 846–63.

Rubin, Barnett R. 2006. "Peace Building and State-Building in Afghanistan: Construct-
    ing Sovereignty for Whose Security?" *Third World Quarterly* 27 (1): 175–85.
    doi:10.1080/01436590500370038.
Said, Edward W. 1979. *Orientalism*. New York: Vintage Books.
Salahuddin, Sayed. 2006. "Indian Soap Opera Transfixes Afghanistan." Reuters, May
    16.   http://www.redorbit.com/news/entertainment/506822/indian_soap_opera
    _transfixes_afghanistan/index.html.
Sandikci, Özlem, and Güliz Ger. 2005. "Aesthetics, Ethics and Politics of the Turkish
    Headscarf." In *Clothing as Material Culture*, ed. Susanne Küchler and Daniel Miller,
    61–82. London: Berg.
Sanford, Victoria. 2003. *Buried Secrets: Truth and Human Rights in Guatemala*. New
    York: Palgrave Macmillan.
Scheper-Hughes, Nancy. 1992. *Death Without Weeping: The Violence of Everyday Life
    in Brazil*. Berkeley: University of California Press.
Schneider, Cornelia. 2005. "Striking a Balance in Post-Conflict Constitution-Making:
    Lessons from Afghanistan for the International Community." *Peace, Conflict and
    Development: An Interdisciplinary Journal* 7 (July): 174–216.
Scott, David. 1995. "Colonial Governmentality." *Social Text* 43 (Autumn): 191–220.
Scott, James. 1985. *Weapons of the Weak: Everyday Forms of Peasant Resistance*. New
    Haven, Conn.: Yale University Press.
———. 1990. *Domination and the Arts of Resistance: Hidden Transcripts*. New Haven,
    Conn.: Yale University Press.
Seremetakis, C. Nadia. 1991. *The Last Word: Women, Death, and Divination in Inner
    Mani*. Chicago: University of Chicago Press.
Shafaq, S. R. 1952. "Patriotic Poetry in Modern Iran." *Middle East Journal* 6 (4): 417–28.
Shah, Saira. 2001. *Beneath the Veil*. Documentary, created and reported by Saira Shah;
    directed and produced by Cassian Harrison. Originally aired on Britain's Chan-
    nel 4, June 26, 2001; cablecast on CNN, August 26, 2001.
Shalinsky, Audrey C. 1993. "Women's Roles in the Afghanistan Jihad." *International
    Journal of Middle East Studies* 25 (4): 661–75.
Shanin, Teodor. 1997. "The Idea of Progress." In *The Post-Development Reader*, ed.
    Majid Rahnema and Victoria Bawtree, 65–72. London: Zed Books.
Sharma, Ursula M. 1978. "Women and Their Affines: The Veil as a Symbol of Separa-
    tion." *Man* 13 (2): 218–33.
Shissler, A. Holly. 2004. "Beauty Is Nothing to Be Ashamed Of: Beauty Contests As
    Tools of Women's Liberation in Early Republican Turkey." *Comparative Studies of
    South Asia, Africa and the Middle East* 24 (1): 107–22. http://muse.jhu.edu/journals
    /comparative_studies_of_south_asia_africa_and_the_middle_east/v024/24
    .1shissler.html.
Silverstein, Brian. 2008. "Disciplines of Presence in Modern Turkey: Discourse, Com-
    panionship and the Mass Mediation of Islamic Practice." *Cultural Anthropology*
    23 (1): 118–53.

Smith, Deborah J., and Jay Lamey. 2009. *A Holistic Justice System for Afghanistan.* AREU Policy Note. Kabul: Afghanistan Research and Evaluation Unit.

Spivak, Gayatri. 1988. "Can the Subaltern Speak?" In *Marxism and the Interpretation of Culture,* ed. Cary Nelson and Lawrence Grossbert, 271–313. London: Macmillan.

Stewart, Kathleen. 1988. "Nostalgia—A Polemic." *Cultural Anthropology* 3 (3): 227–41.

Stirrat, R. L. 2000. "Cultures of Consultancy." *Critique of Anthropology* 20 (1): 31–46.

Strick van Linschoten, Alex, and Felix Kuehn. 2012. *Poetry of the Taliban.* New York: Columbia University Press.

Suhrke, Astri. 2007. "Reconstruction as Modernisation: The 'Post-Conflict' Project in Afghanistan." *Third World Quarterly* 28 (7): 1291–308.

Suhrke, Astri, and Kaja Borchgrevink. 2009. "Negotiating Justice Sector Reform in Afghanistan." *Crime, Law and Social Change* 51 (2): 211–30.

Sullivan, Zohreh T. 1998. "Eluding the Feminist, Overthrowing the Modern? Transformations in Twentieth-Century Iran." In *Remaking Women: Feminism and Modernity in the Middle East,* ed. Lila Abu-Lughod, 215–42. Princeton, N.J.: Princeton University Press.

Talpade-Mohanty, Chandra. 2003. *Feminism Without Borders: Decolonizing Theory, Practicing Solidarity.* Durham, N.C.: Duke University Press.

Tang, Alisa. 2007. "Self-immolation by Afghan Women Rising." *Washington Post,* March 15.

Tapper, Nancy. 1984. "Causes and Consequences of the Abolition of Brideprice." In *Revolutions and Rebellions in Afghanistan: Anthropological Perspectives,* ed. M. Nazif Shahrani and R. L. Canfield, 291–304. Berkeley: Institute of International Studies, University of California.

Tarlo, Emma. 1991. "The Problem of What to Wear: The Politics of Khadi in Late Colonial India." *South Asia Research* 11 (2): 134–57. doi:10.1177/026272809101100202.

———. 1996. *Clothing Matters: Dress and Identity in India.* Chicago: University of Chicago Press.

Taussig, Michael. 1992a. "The Magic of the State." *Public Culture* 5 (1): 63–66. doi:10.1215/08992363-5-1-63.

———. 1992b. *The Nervous System.* New York: Routledge.

———. 2003. *Law in a Lawless Land: Diary of Limpieza in Columbia.* Chicago: University of Chicago Press.

Turner, Victor. 1967. *The Forest of Symbols: Aspects of Ndembu Ritual.* Ithaca, N.Y.: Cornell University Press.

UNICEF. 2008. "Funding Appeals and Humanitarian Action Updates." http://www.unicef.org/infobycountry/afghanistan_31224.html.

USAID (U.S. Agency for International Development). 2004. *Human Security and Livelihoods of Rural Afghans, 2002–2003.* Medford, Mass.: Feinstein International Famine Center, Youth and Community Program, Tufts University. http://www.cmi.no/pdf/?file=/afghanistan/doc/Mazurana2.pdf

———. 2005. *Afghanistan Rule of Law Project: Field Study of Informal and Customary Justice in Afghanistan and Recommendations on Improving Access to Justice and Relations Between Formals Courts and Informal Bodies.* Washington, D.C.: Prepared by Management Systems International. http://www.usip.org/sites/default/files/file/usaid_afghanistan.pdf

van Nieuwkerk, Karin. 2008. "'Repentant' Artists in Egypt: Debating Gender, Performing Arts and Religion." *Contemporary Islam* 2 (3): 191–210. doi:10.1007/s11562-008-0061-z.

Walsh, Declan. 2005. "Young and Female—A Brave New Face of Afghan Politics." *Guardian* (London), September 17.

Wardak, Ali, Daud Saba, and Halima Kazem. 2007. *Bridging Modernity and Tradition: The Rule of Law and the Search for Justice.* Afghanistan Human Development Report 2007. Governance and Social Development Resource Center. http://www.gsdrc.org/go/display&type=Document&id=3137

Warner, Michael. 2002. *Publics and Counterpublics.* New York: Zone Books.

Waylen, Georgina. 2006. "Constitutional Engineering: What Opportunities for the Enhancement of Gender Rights?" *Third World Quarterly* 27 (7): 1209–21. doi:10.1080/01436590600933305.

Wilder, Andrew. 2005. *A House Divided? Analysing the 2005 Afghan Elections.* Kabul: Afghanistan Research and Evaluation Unit.

Wilson, Richard A. 2001. *The Politics of Truth and Reconciliation in South Africa: Legitimizing the Post-Apartheid State.* Cambridge: Cambridge University Press.

Wimpelmann, Torunn. 2013. "Nexuses of Knowledge and Power in Afghanistan: The Rise and Fall of the Informal Justice Assemblage." *Central Asian Survey* 32 (3): 406–22.

Yegenoglu, Meyda. 1998. *Colonial Fantasies: Towards a Feminist Reading of Orientalism.* Cambridge: Cambridge University Press.

Yuval-Davis, Nira. 1997. *Gender and Nation.* London: Sage.

Zulfacar, Maliha. 2006. "The Pendulum of Gender Politics in Afghanistan." *Central Asian Survey* 25 (1): 27–59.

INDEX

ACKNOWLEDGMENTS

I wish to express my warm and sincere thanks to my colleagues and friends Anthony Castriota, Jane Cowan, Antonio De Lauri, Nilüfer Göle, Miia Halme-Tuomisaari, Tobias Kelly, Alessandro Monsutti, Vicki-Marie Petrick, and Sylvain Piron for their meticulous readings, constructive criticisms and good advice throughout the course of the writing of this book. Thank you for your invaluable help and constant source of inspiration.

I would like to thank my family for their understanding, help, and encouragement when it was most required. Thanks for your unconditional trust, love, and being so supportive during this research journey. This work would not have been possible without the reassurance that you shared with me the belief that it was worth the effort.

I am grateful to all my Afghan friends and research participants. I would like to thank particularly Lutfia Attay and Hossai Roshani for opening the doors of fieldwork and letting me in to discover Afghan women's worlds. Thank you to Mustafa Babak for being such an elegant and generous *mahram* and trustworthy friend. I will always remember our regular cruising through Kabul to the rhythm of your favorite tunes: these memories form the "soundtrack" of this book. I am eternally indebted to Mahbouba Seraj for offering to take me with her on her long journeys to Hazarajat and Nangahar when I started to suffer from research fatigue. My debt to the women MPs at the Afghan National Assembly, the members of the Afghan Women's Network, Afghan women's rights activists, as well as the female students at the University of Kabul is, of course, immense. Thank you to the dormitory girls living in room 42 for making me feel at home when I was so far away from it.

Finally, I would like to thank my husband, Ahmad Yunus. Thank you for giving me the confidence to believe that I had something valuable to say, for walking me through the thoughts and ideas that now constitute the main arguments of this book, and for accepting the numerous weekends and evenings I spent in front of my computer. For your love and patience, I will remain eternally grateful.